"I love this book!"

Praise for *The Community Economic Development Handb*

"Rich with street-smart guidance from a man who has helped scores of neighborhoods, the *Community Economic Development Handbook* is truly a recipe for rebirth. It is a highly practical, useful guide that inspires a can-do attitude and fills a void in the field. A must for anyone interested in seeing cities thrive."

> PAUL S. GROGAN, President, Boston Foundation and author of *Comeback Cities: A Blueprint for Urban Neighborhood Revival,* Boston, MA

"It's a gem—an exceptionally clear, creative, and practical introductory resource. *Community Economic Development Handbook* links the tools and 'pivot points' that community organizations can directly affect to the larger forces of government action and regional markets. It's not only a much-needed guide for community groups just getting started, but a useful tool for government, social investors, and others who want to expand their work and strengthen neighborhoods through entrepreneurial action."

> XAVIER DE SOUZA BRIGGS, Ph.D., Assistant Professor of Public Policy, John F. Kennedy School of Government, Harvard University, and former Deputy Assistant Secretary, U.S. Department of Housing and Urban Development, Cambridge, MA

"Mihailo Temali has produced a valuable guide for anyone interested in community-based development and neighborhood building. Full of practical advice drawn from decades of experience at the neighborhood level, the *Community Economic Development Handbook* is a resource for grassroots activists from coast to coast."

> MONSIGNOR WILLIAM J. LINDER, Founder, New Community Corporation, Newark, NJ

"I love this book! T'   ..terested in community   ..rd members and staff membe   ..ups, funders, city officials, bankers, p   .. anyone else interested in how to turn around   ..ning neighborhood. It is the only book I've ever seen which lays out the steps of four proven and powerful strategies for revitalizing inner-city neighborhoods. It is a great resource for those in the business already and those getting into the business of community economic development."

> RONALD GRZYWINSKI, Chairman, Shorebank Corporation, Chicago, IL

"What makes Mihailo Temali's *Community Economic Development Handbook* so special and unique is that it provides a practitioner's step-by-step approach to an extremely complex and difficult subject while never losing sight of the visionary's goal of building and renewing healthy communities. I believe this book can provide excellent guidance to community economic development professionals on a very broad range of subjects and at almost any stage of their work. This is a comprehensive tool that the field has needed for a long time."

> MICHAEL RUBINGER, President & CEO, Local Initiatives Support Corporation, New York, NY

"Mihailo Temali's years of community development experience led to this highly useful book, which I would recommend for any community economic development practitioner. The content pulls from his own experience and from many interviews of widely respected leaders in the field. The result is an effective, well-written, and interesting tool."

> ELLEN LAZAR, Executive Director, Neighborhood Reinvestment Corporation, Washington, DC

"Don't just read it; do it!"

"The *Community Economic Development Handbook* provides guidance for both mature and novice practitioners. The handbook is a dramatic new addition to the field. It provides practical tools to embrace the complexity of being the leader of a nonprofit community economic development organization in the world today: how to improve the management of your organization and how to understand the intricate programs and policies in workforce, microbusiness, and commercial development. A valuable tool for practitioners to use on a regular basis to improve the operation of their organization and enhance their capacity to serve their mission and the residents of their communities."

> ROY O. PRIEST, President and CEO, National Congress for Community Economic Development (NCCED), Washington, DC

"Community economic development is about connecting the dots between people, land, and money. This handbook will prove to be pivotal for developing your local assets to improve your local economy. Don't just read it; do it!"

> TED WYSOCKI, President & CEO Local Economic & Employment Development (LEED) Council, Chicago, IL

"Mihailo Temali's strategic step-by-step approach gives organizations and people concrete, hands-on examples of how to turn around a neighborhood economically. His profound experience in neighborhood development organizations is reflected in both the text and the detailed worksheets that get you right to work."

> PETER PALESCH, Senior Advisor, Urban and Municipal Development, GTZ-German Technical Cooperation, Santiago, Chile

"It is a highly practical, grounded primer which also does a great job providing the spirit and philosophical underpinnings of community economic development in the process."

> PAUL FATE, Director of Community Development, Wilder Center for Communities and former Senior Director, Twin Cities office of Local Initiatives Support Corporation, St. Paul, MN

"As a nationally acclaimed leader in community economic development, author Mihailo Temali understands asset-based community building. His work is modestly titled a 'handbook' but it offers much more than the how-to of development. He underscores the importance of social capital and the need for respectful and regular engagement with the diverse population of a community as a means of tapping the resilience and creativity of ordinary people. He shows how to organize and collaborate in detailed ways and how to make that civic engagement dynamic and sustainable over time. Policy makers, local elected officials, neighborhood activists, and lenders interested in bondable loans and continuing business growth—all will gain from learning the lessons of Mihailo Temali's book. In the Twin Cities, we have enjoyed the benefits of Temali's work: a profusion of micro-entreprises, reborn neighborhoods, and the pride of ownership in immigrant communities. Now, with this book, cities across the country will gain the tools needed to build strategies for community economic development."

> GEORGE LATIMER, Professor, Urban Studies, Macalester College, and Mayor, St. Paul, MN 1976-90

"An excellent how-to guide for communities and individuals who are working to make their part of the world a better place. The *Handbook* will assist them in improving their community well-being through economic activity. It is easy to use, the language is clear, and the examples are real."

> KARL STAUBER, Ph.D., President and CEO, Northwest Area Foundation, St. Paul, MN

"Finally, the burgeoning field of community economic development has a guide that any community organization can pick up and use to walk through the rewarding but complex process of revitalizing neighborhoods and building community wealth. This manual offers clear, practical advice built on approaches that blend best practices of economic development and community organizing, and that emphasize participatory process, partnerships, and a focus on results."

> MILLARD "MITTY" OWENS, Ford Foundation, Asset Building & Community Development Division, New York, NY

The Community Economic Development Handbook

Strategies and Tools to Revitalize Your Neighborhood

by Mihailo Temali

FIELDSTONE
ALLIANCE

**SAINT PAUL
MINNESOTA**

Published with the support of The David and Lucile Packard Foundation

FIELDSTONE ALLIANCE

An imprint of Turner Publishing Company

200 4th Avenue North, Suite 950

Nashville, TN 37219

Phone: (615)255-2665   Fax: (615)255-5081

445 Park Avenue, 9th Floor

New York, NY 10022

Phone: (646)291-8961   Fax: (646)291-8962

www.turnerpublishing.com

www.fieldstonealliance.com

Copyright © 2012 by Fieldstone Alliance

Fieldstone Alliance is committed to strengthening the performance of the nonprofit sector. Through the synergy of its consulting, training, publishing, and research and demonstration projects, Fieldstone Alliance provides solutions to issues facing the
nonprofit sector. Fieldstone Alliance was formerly a department
of the Amherst H. Wilder Foundation. If you would like more
information about Fieldstone Alliance and our services, please
contact us at 651-556-4500 or www.FieldstoneAlliance.org.

We hope you find this book helpful! For more information about
other Fieldstone Alliance publications, please see the back of this
book or contact:

Edited by Vincent Hyman, Doug Toft, and Judith Peacock
Designed by Kirsten Nielsen
Cover designed by Rebecca Andrews

Manufactured in the United States of America

Library of Congress Cataloging-in-Publication Data
Temali, Mihailo.
    The community economic development handbook : strategies
and tools to revitalize your neighborhood / by Mihailo Temali.
    p. cm.
    Includes bibliographical references and index.
    ISBN 0-940069-36-9 (pbk.)
    1. Community development—United States—Handbooks,
manuals, etc. 2. Economic development—Handbooks, manuals,
etc. 3. Community organization—United States—Handbooks,
manuals, etc. I. Amherst H. Wilder Foundation. II. Title.
HN90.C6 T433 2002
307.1'4—dc   212002008881

Dedication

This book is dedicated to the many thousands of people across the United States who work tirelessly to revitalize their own inner-city neighborhood. Their energy, knowledge, and commitment are making great things happen in every city of our country.

This book is also dedicated to the memory of the greatest neighborhood organizer I ever met, Gale Cincotta. From coast to coast, those of us in community development will never forget her leadership, her victories, and her inspiration.

Acknowledgments

I would like to thank my wife, Laura, for putting up with me while I wrote this book, and the staff and boards of Western Initiatives for Neighborhood Development (WIND) and the Neighborhood Development Center (NDC) for holding down the fort and assisting scores of inner-city businesses and community groups while I pecked away. I also thank Bryan Barry for suggesting the book in the first place and Doug Toft, Vince Hyman, and Judith Peacock for their patient editing work.

More broadly, I would like to thank Bill Sands and Western State Bank for giving WIND and NDC a supportive platform on which to take hold and grow, as well as the funders who have supported our work so generously. The work of WIND and NDC is the hands-on source for much of this book. Many thanks to my first mentor in community development, Calvin Bradford. I would also like to thank Denny Prchal, Al Emory, Mara O'Neill, Beverley Hawkins, Patty Tototzintle, Joe Errigo, Ronald A. Smith, Dawn Goldschmitz, Ann Briseño, Dan Bartholomay, Paul Fate, John Flory, Dave Gagne, Ronald Wesley Pauline, Wafiq Fannoun, Mike Anderson, and Stacy Millet for many years of wonderful collaboration in community economic development. The lessons I have learned from them and with them make up the heart of this book. A special acknowledgment to the three best organizers I ever worked with—Sharon Voyda, Juan Linares, and Sal Miranda.

I would like to give special thanks to Alan Okagaki, Mitty Owens, and Ted Wysocki for the extra time and insight they gave to reviewing this book. I would also like to thank the following people who gave an early and honest reading of my book and whose suggestions made it much better:

Dan Bartholomay	Rolf Middleton	Chuck Ravine
James Capraro	Curt Milburn	Marty Schirber
Elizabeth Dunning	Kari Neathery	Helen Shor
Dave Gagne	Mara O'Neill	Karl Stauber
John P. Kretzmann	Peter Palesch	Matt Wexler

Finally, a big thanks to my parents, Josip and Agnete Temali, for teaching me by example that there is no higher calling in life than a deep involvement in your own community.

About the Author

MIHAILO (MIKE) TEMALI has nearly twenty years of experience in the field of community-based economic development. He is founder and executive director of the Neighborhood Development Center (NDC) in St. Paul, Minnesota. As executive director, Mike is responsible for program development, fundraising, staffing, and overall management. Since 1993, NDC has provided business-plan training for over 1,600 low-income, inner-city residents, of whom over 300 are currently in business. NDC has made more than 200 loans to these entrepreneurs, and operates an extensive program of ongoing business support, including developing and operating four business incubators.

In addition to serving as NDC's executive director, Mike is founder and president of Western Initiatives for Neighborhood Development (WIND), a community development subsidiary of Western State Bank in St. Paul. WIND has worked with numerous community-based organizations to build their capacity to succeed at economic development. This work ranges from organizational development to small business loan programs and real estate development to commercial district revitalization. WIND and NDC are located on the Internet at www.windndc.org.

Before working with NDC and WIND, Mike was executive director of North End Area Revitalization, Inc. (NEAR). There he raised $3.1 million for programs that led to 130 commercial rehabilitation and expansion projects along Rice Street in St. Paul.

In 2000, Mike served on the Governor's Minority Business Workgroup and the Entrepreneur Academy, founded by Minnesota governor Jesse Ventura. As a Bush Leadership Fellow, he spent extensive time working with economic development organizations in Santiago, Chile, and Boston.

Mike lives in St. Paul, Minnesota, with his wife, Laura, and their two children. He welcomes e-mail contact at mihailo@windndc.org.

Contents

Chapter 1

Community Economic Development—An Overview

Imagine two neighborhoods. The first one has a weak local economy. Storefronts are boarded up. Litter swirls around on the sidewalk. Unemployed people hang out in front of these buildings, unable to get a job. Residents do most of their shopping somewhere else, where they feel safe and have lots of shopping options. Most work outside of the neighborhood since there are few jobs close to home. The houses in the neighborhood are poorly maintained, and, like the storefronts, many of them are boarded up. Nothing ever seems to get better, so people are gloomy about their future.

The second neighborhood has a strong local economy. Businesses fill the commercial buildings. Storefronts are well maintained, with full-sized windows and new signs and awnings. Shoppers and workers come and go, and most people have a decent job. Houses in the surrounding streets seem well maintained. Litter, weeds, and junk in vacant lots are gone. A few new commercial buildings fit in well with the older structures. Progress occurs regularly.

Now, imagine that these two neighborhoods are actually the *same* neighborhood, five or ten years apart in time. The run-down neighborhood represents the "before" picture; the revitalized neighborhood represents the "after" picture.

Beyond the fresher and livelier appearance, what is different in the second picture?

Chapter 1 at a Glance

Chapter 1 introduces some building blocks that will be the foundation for your new effort to improve your local economy. In this chapter, you will learn about

- Two primary goals of most community economic development: to increase the income of families, and to rebuild the community as a whole
- The vehicle for all these efforts: a community-based economic development organization
- Four economic pivot points: commercial district revitalization, microbusiness development, workforce development, and businesses that grow good neighborhood jobs
- A four-step community economic development process

Based on the experiences of community groups across the United States that have actually participated in such a transformation, the answer very often relates to the condition of four key parts of any neighborhood economy. These four *pivot points* can make an enormous difference in the lives of community residents and businesses:

- The condition of the neighborhood's commercial district
- The ability of local entrepreneurs to start and maintain small businesses
- The ability of local residents to find and keep good jobs
- The ability of neighborhood businesses to create good jobs for community residents

These are the economic forces that many well-run community groups change successfully as they strive to improve where they live and work. This book will teach you how to change them in your community.

This vision—creating economic opportunity, reversing negative perceptions, and stimulating purchases and investments—is the vision embraced by most groups doing community economic development in the United States. Some of these communities are African American, some are Latino, some are European American, some are Asian American, and some are Native American. Some are populated by thousands of recent immigrants. More and more, these communities are a dynamic mixture of two or more of these groups.

Their vision is the same—economic progress for their neighborhood. This vision is achieved through activities that focus on increasing the income and assets of local residents; through building the community up as a whole; and through continual, visible changes that make the community a better place to live.

One important note: *Community economic development is not just about developing buildings and businesses.* Rather, it is about developing the talent, skills, and living conditions of the people who live in those buildings, the people who own those businesses, and the people who become their customers. Community economic development is not a vision of exchanging one group of people with lower incomes for another group of people with higher incomes. It is about assisting an entire community to rise up, helping people to live better individually and as neighbors.

From the Field

"Community economic development is connecting the dots between people, land, and money. It's building on your local assets to improve your local economy. It's both assisting businesses to grow and residents to improve their income."

TED WYSOCKI, current president and CEO of Local Economic and Employment Development (LEED) Council and past CEO of the Chicago Association of Neighborhood Development Organizations (CANDO)

Two Goals of Community Economic Development

Before going further, consider this definition of community economic development:

Actions taken by an organization representing an urban neighborhood or rural community in order to

1. Improve the economic situation of local residents (disposable income and assets) and local businesses (profitability and growth); and

2. Enhance the community's quality of life as a whole (appearance, safety, networks, gathering places, and sense of positive momentum)

This definition captures the two key goals of community economic development.

Most community residents focus on their individual and family well-being. Certain questions guide their daily economic life: Do they have the material goods needed to make their life comfortable, or are they always desperately trying to stay one step ahead of the bill collector? When they are done paying for the necessities of life, do they have any money left to spend on anything else? Do they accumulate any savings to be used for larger purchases or for that "rainy day" that always comes?[1]

This measure of how individuals and families are doing financially in your community is half of the picture. The other half is how the community is doing as a whole. Certain questions arise here as well: Do people believe the community is declining or rising into the future? Does it feel safe and attractive? Do people have a strong sense of knowing one another, of being connected to one another, because of living in the same neighborhood?

In short, the two primary goals of community economic development in low-income communities are to improve conditions for individuals and families on the one hand and for the community as a whole on the other. Community economic development is both people-based and place-based.

Individual and family impact means increasing the economic standard of living for low-income persons in low-income neighborhoods. This includes increasing residents' discretionary income (income available after paying necessities) and wealth (assets and savings).

Community impact means rebuilding the prosperity and livability of an entire community for the benefit of existing residents and businesses. This can include rebuilding the community's social fabric through economic means such as

- Creating new community gathering places—restaurants, child care centers, and coffee shops

---

[1] For a groundbreaking discussion of wealth (assets) as a crucial measure of and barrier to community economic development, read *Black Wealth/White Wealth* by Melvin L. Oliver and Thomas M. Shapiro (see Appendix A: Resources).

- Strengthening community pride and confidence through continual, visible improvements
- Providing long-term stability and affordability through local ownership of businesses and properties
- Generating inspiring new role models through local entrepreneur development and employment career development

Community economic development differs from development projects led by the private or public sector alone. One of the main distinctions is this dual purpose: individual and community impact. Another distinction is the long-term focus on a particular neighborhood—a persistent effort that is concerned about one community. The third main distinction is that community economic development is carried out in accord with a plan (and often by an organization) created and controlled by neighborhood residents, businesses, and institutions themselves. (See also the sidebar Traditional Economic Development Versus Community Economic Development, on page 9.)

From the Field

"Look at community economic development holistically. Don't just develop any type of business without taking into consideration the makeup of the neighborhood, the job skills of the residents, and your overall community development goals."

GUS NEWPORT, former mayor of Berkeley, California, and former executive director of Dudley Street Neighborhood Initiative, Boston; currently program consultant with Urban Strategies Council in Oakland

Community economic development, then, takes place in a particular neighborhood, directed by the citizens of that community, with the goal of improving their own neighborhood for the sake of existing residents and businesses.

Your Vehicle to Meet Those Goals— an Organization

Starting from a can-do attitude and strong local roots and networks, community groups have taken two primary tracks to improve their neighborhoods.

One is "action organizing"—leaning on the powers-that-be for solutions. This path has forced corporations, banks, and government at all levels to be more inclusive and responsive with practices that affect low-income neighborhoods. Through action organizing, groups often take on large-scale issues such as urban sprawl, poor-quality schools, or mortgage discrimination by banks who "redline" low-income communities out of their lending areas. One outstanding product of action organizing (led by Gale Cincotta and the National People's Action in Chicago) is the federal Community Reinvestment Act of 1977, which requires all banks to affirmatively meet the credit needs of all communities within their market areas.

The second track for community groups has been to solve their problems themselves. These groups tend to take on smaller-scale problems and seek many small solutions rather than one big resolution from an outside force. They identify and utilize many resources within their own community, and they seek resources from beyond their boundaries to help with their work. Hands-on activities such as housing or business development are characteristic of such groups.

This book focuses on the second type of community group, those that use neighborhood assets and elbow grease to work directly on solving community problems themselves. Some of these groups are known as *community development corporations (CDCs)*; others are *neighborhood business associations*. Some are *faith-based organizations* that grew out of local churches; others are led by members of *specific ethnic groups*.

In particular, this book targets groups that harness the strength and potential of local entrepreneurs and small-to-midsize businesses to reach their goals. This focus is a fairly recent addition to the community development field. Prior to 1980, relatively few community-based organizations did economic development directly. It wasn't until the mid-1980s and early 1990s that this focus began to proliferate and achieve successes across the country.

From the Field

"There will be a trade-off between economic feasibility and social goals. The ability to achieve that balance is the magic of community economic development."

JOE MCNEELY, executive director, Development Training Institute, Baltimore

Four Pivot-Point Strategies

As mentioned above, community economic development focuses on four pivot points, turning them into economic engines for family and community impact. These economic pivot points are the community's

1. Commercial district
2. Microbusinesses
3. Workforce
4. Job opportunities

Because these pivot points are so crucial to neighborhood economies, many community groups use them as primary strategies for community economic development. Let's look at each.

Revitalizing your commercial district

A neighborhood's "Main Street" represents the "face" of the community—what most people know of a community. This street forms perceptions, and perceptions—be they negative or positive—often lead to reality. In the eyes of customers and businesses, highly visible commercial districts that deteriorate are undesirable. For low-income communities, therefore, commercial district revitalization is critical. Neighborhood business and resident groups have had great success with revitalizing commercial districts.

Consistent storefront design sends a positive message of revitalization. Following are before and after shots of a facade improvement project in the Fruitvale Commercial District of Oakland, California. This project was completed by the Unity Council Main Street Facade Improvement Program. Project coordinator and design: Raquel Contreras. Muralist/Artist: Juan Zagal. Funded by the City of Oakland Neighborhood Commercial Revitalization Program.

Before

Photograph by Evelyn Johnson. Used with permission.

After

Photograph by Raquel Contreras. Used with permission.

Developing microbusinesses

"Microbusinesses" are often defined as having five or fewer employees. Most low-income communities lack opportunities and assistance for local entrepreneurs to start and grow these tiny businesses. These entrepreneurs, if nurtured, can generate substantial economic activity in a community. Equally important, they can fill vacant storefronts, serve as positive role models and gathering places, bring in new goods and services, create local jobs, and bring positive momentum to all community economic development efforts. Community economic development groups can do a great deal to find and support these valuable neighborhood assets.

Developing the community workforce

The largest single economic problem in low-income neighborhoods is unemployed or underemployed residents. Many of these people lack the skills, connections, or support necessary to get and keep good jobs. For most residents, the best path to economic development is training and placement in jobs with decent pay and prospects for advancement. Community economic development groups can do much to increase the numbers of residents who land such jobs.

Growing good neighborhood jobs

Certain types of growing businesses create a steady stream of jobs that low-income residents can obtain at their level of work experience and education, that pay above minimum wage, and that provide some job benefits and career advancement opportunities. Community economic development groups can work to identify which businesses these are, both inside their neighborhood and in their metropolitan economy. In addition to attracting more of these businesses to their neighborhood, development groups can help them overcome obstacles that restrict their growth, so they can produce more good jobs for neighborhood residents.

A note on other strategies

Defining exactly which strategies are included in the term *community economic development* is an ongoing debate. Many excellent public and nonprofit strategies contribute directly or indirectly to improving the economic status of neighborhood residents or businesses or contribute to the overall quality of life within a community.

Many people consider housing development in low-income neighborhoods as an economic development strategy. This strategy creates many short-term construction jobs and a few long-term maintenance jobs. Further, it can reduce a basic cost of living for low-income families, thus improving their economic well-being. Indeed, home ownership is a primary way for low-income persons to build their wealth. Housing development also improves the appearance of the neighborhood, thus improving perceptions and, potentially, investment decisions.

From the Field

"Approach this endeavor as a business, even though you have social and human objectives. You must apply basic business principles to all of your projects."

ABDUL SM RASHEED, chair, National Congress for Community Economic Development, and president/CEO, North Carolina Community Development Initiative

Yet, in spite of its economic impact, housing development is often considered a different industry from economic development within the broader community development world. Being a larger and older part of community development, it has a considerable amount of "how-to" material already available.[2]

Other community development strategies have a specific economic goal, such as building personal assets (focusing on savings and individual development accounts, or IDAs), establishing community development credit unions, and fighting predatory lending practices common in low-income communities.[3] Still other

---

[2] Excellent starting resources for housing efforts include *Shelterforce* magazine and national organizations such as the Neighborhood Reinvestment Corporation, the Local Initiatives Support Corporation, and the Fannie Mae Foundation's Knowledge-Plex web site (see Appendix A: Resources).

[3] Contact the National Federation for Community Development Credit Unions and the Woodstock Institute (see Appendix A: Resources).

[4] For two superb models of communities utilizing land-use planning and zoning

strategies have an indirect but definite community economic benefit. Examples are developing neighborhood health clinics, co-op grocery stores, and public arts projects and utilizing neighborhood planning and land-use control efforts.[4]

This book does not suggest limits to the ways in which a community group can approach the goals of improving the economic situation of residents or the overall economic quality of a neighborhood. Instead, *this book presents the four most common and potentially powerful approaches that community-based groups can use* to change the economy of their neighborhood. These approaches harness the strength and potential of businesses—from start-up, low-income "microentrepreneurs" to midsize, fast-growing businesses, from neighborhood retailers to businesses looking for more employees—to achieve the goals of community economic development. When these types of businesses begin to thrive in a low-income community, the benefits to the entire community are tremendous and widespread.

These four strategies, therefore, are not intended to simply help a few businesses or individuals do better. They are intended to be catalytic, a means to an end, with the ultimate goal being a stronger, healthier, more prosperous population and community.

Groups that work with small-to-midsize businesses to redevelop their neighborhood now represent a major component of the community development industry in the United States. This book teaches their techniques.

> **From the Field**
>
> "A viable community should be a good place to live, work, shop, and do business. Mixed-use creates economic vitality. Thus, industrial corridors and commercial strips are as important as decent, affordable housing. One's strategy for community development must have an economic development component to be successful."
>
> TED WYSOCKI

A Four-Step Process

Whether your organization chooses to work with just one of the pivot points—revitalizing your commercial district, supporting microbusinesses, helping businesses that grow good neighborhood jobs, developing your community workforce—or all four, you can use a simple process to promote your success. There are four essential steps in this process:

1. Assess current conditions
2. Create a vision and strategic plan
3. Implement your plan
4. Evaluate and improve your work

These four steps are repeated often in every community organization, generally in the order shown here. They apply not only to the organization's overall direction but also to every new economic development initiative that the group undertakes. This basic four-step dance will give structure to your organization's work.

controls to further the local economy, contact the Dudley Street Neighborhood Initiative in Boston and the Local Economic and Employment Development Council in Chicago (see Appendix A: Resources).

Traditional economic development versus community economic development

Inner-city economic development is pursued not just by community groups, of course. It is undertaken regularly by the private sector, often with help from the government. What distinguishes this more traditional form of economic development from community economic development? In general, community economic development is characterized by

- Long-term focus within one targeted area versus moving on after a project or two
- Ongoing, multiple projects connected by a common plan and goals versus one-time, unconnected projects
- Two goals—community impact *and* financial viability—versus one goal—financial viability
- Smaller-scale solutions versus large-scale solutions

Not all development in your neighborhood will be driven by your organization, nor should it—you need lots of investors and actors to rebuild your economy. Closely evaluate private-sector opportunities that come to you, using goals and measures that guide your own projects. Negotiate where possible for additional community benefits from private developers and businesses, but remember some basic, common-sense rules of thumb:

- You can't do it all yourself.
- As a nonprofit developer, you can take more time and tolerate more risk and lower returns than for-profit businesses, since you can raise charitable funds to cover overhead.
- Your group can also enhance a private project to increase community benefit.

1. Assess current conditions

Begin any economic development effort in your community by mapping out the current economic conditions and trends. If you don't know where you are now, you can't effectively determine where you want to go. In addition to assessing conditions in your community, you'll need to assess your own organization's capacity to conduct each economic development strategy.

2. Create a vision and strategic plan

After you get a clear sense of your current economic conditions, the next step is to create a vision for your community based on the pivot point you choose to tackle. This means painting a detailed picture of what you want your community to be like in five or ten years. You'll want to involve as many people in your community as possible in creating the vision so that it enjoys widespread support. To finish this step, you'll lay out three-year goals, one-year goals, and a detailed work plan to guide your vision into action.

3. Implement your plan

Now that you've planned your work, you can work your plan. Depending on your goals and work plan, you'll start to change the face of your commercial district, support microbusinesses, grow job-producing businesses, and/or upgrade the employment skills of the people in your neighborhood.

4. Evaluate and improve your work

The last step of the process prompts you to monitor the outcomes of your work. You'll take time to celebrate your success. You'll also analyze your results in order to improve your efforts. Even if your organization works perfectly today, it won't be perfect tomorrow unless you keep learning and adapting to new conditions.

Opening Your Toolbox

Much of what it takes to succeed at community economic development is common sense, persistence, good community organizing, skilled communication, and solid neighborhood networks. However, your organization will also need to wield some common tools of the trade. Some of them—such as real estate development, architectural design, small business lending, market analysis, and marketing and promotion—can get very technical.

Notice that each of these more technical tools represents a profession in which highly skilled people can spend an entire career. Fortunately, you do not need to become an expert in any of these areas. But depending on which pivot point your group tackles, you will need to learn something about one or more of these tools to succeed.

You can certainly hire competent professionals to do this work for you; in many cases this is exactly what you *should* do. Be sure to hire solid professionals when you need them: architects, attorneys, market analysts, real estate developers, bankers, contractors, and others along the way.

However, it will also help you to understand the basics of what these people do. That way you can do much of the technical work yourself on smaller projects and supervise the professionals you hire for larger ones.

Getting the Most from This Book

You're close to the end of this overview chapter. Chapter 2 gives suggestions for setting up an organization devoted to community economic development. And Chapter 3 explains how your organization can choose its first pivot point to tackle.

The next four chapters offer detailed instructions for working with specific pivot points. Chapter 4 focuses on revitalizing a commercial district. Chapter 5 offers ways to support microbusinesses. Chapter 6 explains ways to develop a community workforce. And Chapter 7 walks you through well-tested and new ways that community groups and expanding businesses are using to grow more good jobs for neighborhood residents.

What to do about gentrification

Gentrification happens in a community when lower-income residents and businesses are replaced by higher-income residents and businesses. This change is often driven by a strong appetite among professionals for older, solid houses located close to downtown business districts, with their accompanying employment opportunities and amenities. Even with the cost of substantial renovation, such housing is affordable to persons of middle-to-high income.

There's a downside, however: Gentrification displaces existing residents and businesses that can no longer afford the rising rents and taxes, or who are evicted to make way for new owners. This often has a racial overtone, as persons of color are frequently displaced by higher-income whites.

Many community groups do not need to worry about gentrification in their early years. Their community may be perceived as too run-down or too dangerous for wealthier outsiders. But as groups succeed in increasing the safety, attractiveness, and economic viability of the community, gentrification can become an issue.

Gentrification is often a market-driven reality. Still, many groups devoted to community economic development

debate what they can do about it. Some of the key questions to consider:

• Even if we do not aim to bring people with higher incomes into our community, what is the risk that gentrification will result from our work?

• Is some level of gentrification good for our community? If so, how do we control the spread of gentrification?

• How do we retain long-time residents when they start to earn more, perhaps because of our programs?

Each group that does community economic development needs to answer these questions for itself. However, most groups opt for local ownership of property and businesses as one response to this concern. These groups tend to share a core value: The people who benefit most from community economic development efforts should be existing residents and businesses— particularly low-income residents and small businesses.

Your group can do a great deal to encourage and assist local ownership. Of course, you can't control what new owners eventually do with their property. But at least these owners will get to decide for themselves rather than being pushed out by forces they can't control.

For more discussion about gentrification, visit the web site for PolicyLink's Gentrification Toolkit at www.policylink.org/gentrification.

Appendix A contains a list of organizations and government agencies you can contact to learn more about community economic development. Contact information is given for all of the examples cited in this book. This appendix also includes a list of helpful publications.

Appendix B contains information on how to do Internet research on your regional economy. It is intended primarily as a supplement to Chapter 7, but you may find it useful for other chapters as well.

Appendix C contains worksheets your organization might use in researching and planning your community economic development strategy. The worksheets are referred to throughout the book. Using the worksheets will help you make the transition from reading about community economic development to *doing* it. For your convenience, these worksheets are available online. Purchasers of this book may download the worksheets at no additional cost and adapt them to fit their organization's specific needs. The worksheets may be downloaded from the following Internet address. The access code is W369CEd02.

http://www.FieldstoneAlliance.org/worksheets

Take what you need and leave the rest

Community economic development is a subject that attracts a diverse audience. You may have little experience in community organization and little background in business. Or you may already be part of a thriving neighborhood organization or have a practical grasp of economics through years of owning and operating a business.

This book can work for you no matter what your level of knowledge and experience. If you are new to this field, most of the material will serve as a foundation for your work. If you are experienced in the field, use the basic information as a review and checklist, and then jump ahead to the new strategies that you are starting to consider.

Adapt these strategies to your unique community

The primary focus of this book is on revitalizing low-income neighborhoods in the inner city. In spite of this urban focus, the book should have much information that is useful in other settings. People interested in rural economic development and those focused on declining inner-ring suburbs should be able to utilize much that they find here, even though their setting has significant and very challenging differences from inner-city neighborhoods. Similarly, people working with particular ethnic groups should find much that is useful to guide their efforts, although they may need to adapt some details to fit their community.

Some seriously declining urban neighborhoods have seen a remarkable comeback because of a hot real estate market. This often threatens the affordability of the neighborhood for its existing residents and businesses (see the sidebar What to Do about Gentrification, on page 11). Rather than working to reverse negative perceptions or attract new businesses into the area, groups in these situations may focus on how to preserve the character of their community or how to ensure that existing residents and businesses can get a "piece of the pie." Significant portions of the four pivot-point strategies will be useful to these groups while other portions will need to be adapted.

Take one pivot point at a time

If all of the pivot points were effectively developed in your community, imagine the change that would take place. Good jobs would be available in or near your neighborhood, and people in your community would develop the skills that employers demand. Your commercial district would bustle with businesses and customers. In addition, local residents would have money to spend on more than just the essentials of survival. (See the sidebar When All Four Pivot-Point Strategies Are Working, below.)

However, no community group starts out working on all of the pivot points at once. The key to *starting* community economic development is to succeed at one pivot point. The key to *broader* economic development is to take on additional pivot points. This can happen as your organization grows in size and capability.

Again, Chapter 3 discusses how to choose the right starting point for your group. Basic considerations will include the most pressing economic problems and opportunities, and the assets your organization can bring to each strategy.

Bear in mind that no group can do everything, and that it is much more effective to be great at one thing than mediocre at many. If you become skilled at one or two of the pivot points, your reputation will grow as your accomplishments add up. You can then take on or at least influence other economic pivot points. In addition to gradually adding staff members, organizations typically develop this kind of clout by forming partnerships and coalitions with other groups. This is one way for your organization to expand its reach without getting stretched too thin.

Give it time

Revitalizing your local economy does not happen overnight, nor is it a solo effort. Your economy has many moving parts, all interrelated. The most obvious parts are your neighborhood businesses, buildings, workers, and consumers, and their

When all four pivot-point strategies are working

Many community economic development organizations across the United States have grown to the size and capacity where they are now successful with three or even all four pivot-point strategies. It is inspirational to see the sheer numbers of people, buildings, businesses, and public spaces that they have impacted over the years, and how their community is stronger and more unified as a result.

When the four pivot points are all being addressed effectively, the result is greater than the sum of the parts. New investment coming from within and from outside the community is far greater than the dollars directly spent or leveraged by the community economic development group itself. The combined strategies have a catalytic effect, as the neighborhood exports goods and services and attracts customers from outside its own boundaries. New money comes *into* the local economy, rather than draining out. The neighborhood successfully rejoins the regional economy. Most importantly, much of this new investment takes place according to a plan laid out by the community and its community economic development group, thus benefiting existing residents and businesses.

Two such groups are the Greater Southwest Development Corporation in Chicago and the New Community Corporation in Newark. Contact information for these groups is found in Appendix A: Resources. Take time to find out about these organizations.

condition, capabilities, histories, and plans. Beyond these, however, are the impacts of the regional, national, and international economies. There's also a complex of cultural influences—the automobile and suburban sprawl, changing consumer preferences, racial and ethnic tensions, rough local politics, factories that move overseas, immigrants that move into your community and young people who move out, and even social trends such as the shift toward households headed by a single person.

The complex and shifting landscape can seem too difficult for a small nonprofit organization to influence in any meaningful way. There are certainly community groups that do *not* succeed at revitalizing their local economy, often because they lack organizational basics or a tight focus, or because they trip over brutal local politics or lack of funding. But a great many groups *have* been successful, and your group can be too. The rewards are well worth the struggle. By breaking down the challenge into the pivot points and tackling these with persistence and every partner you can find, you can make a difference. Just take it one piece at a time. Learn to crawl before you walk and walk before you run, and you'll move steadily toward success.

Summary

This chapter introduces some building blocks that will be the foundation for your new effort to improve your local economy:

- Two primary goals of most community economic development: to increase the wealth and disposable income of families, and to rebuild the prosperity and livability of your community as a whole.
- The vehicle for all these efforts: a community-based economic development organization, well grounded and supported in your neighborhood.
- Four economic pivot points: commercial district revitalization, microbusiness development, workforce development, and businesses that grow good neighborhood jobs.
- A four-step community economic development process: assess current conditions, create a vision and strategic plan, implement your plan, and evaluate and improve your work.

Take inspiration from mature community economic development groups that work on all four pivot-point strategies. Community economic development is hard but well worth it. In the next chapter, you'll learn about getting started on this rewarding work.

Chapter 2

Develop Your Organization

B efore you can start working on any of the pivot points involved in community economic development, you need to understand the foundation for such efforts—your organization.

If your organization has been up and running for a number of years, you may want to simply scan this chapter. Treat it as a quick checklist of the organizational basics that you already know. If you're part of a young or start-up organization, however, then give this chapter some careful study. Establishing a solid organization is crucial to all four pivot points and greatly affects the outcome of your work.

Review the Types of Community Economic Development Organizations

Community economic development is typically done by community-based, nonprofit economic development organizations. These organizations are made up of local businesses, local residents, or both.

Your organization is where your community comes to analyze the local economy, to learn options for action, to create a plan based on the best options, and to implement strategies that achieve the plan. Your organization is also the place that attracts capable partners to help you succeed. Your organization is the economic "make-it-happen" place.

A community-based organization is generally defined as an organization whose boundaries are a geographic neighborhood; whose membership is typically open to all residents, property owners, businesses, and institutions within those boundaries; and whose board of directors is elected at open and well-publicized annual meetings of the membership.

Chapter 2 at a Glance

Chapter 2 helps you take steps to make your organization effective at community economic development. In this chapter, you'll find ways to

- Handle basic start-up tasks
- Establish basic operating principles
- Build your funding
- Build your staff
- Develop and maintain strong relationships
- Create effective partnerships
- Gain visibility and credibility

Such organizations use a decision-making process that is open to and guided by the surrounding community. Their decisions typically derive authority from their open connection to a broad base of people.

Beyond these basics, organizations involved in community economic development differ a great deal. Some are start-up organizations formed just for community economic development. More often, existing organizations—local businesses, local residents, local churches, ethnic organizations, or other community-based entities—add economic development to their set of goals.

From the Field

"You, too, must be an entrepreneur and have the persistence and tenacity to add value to your community."

TED WYSOCKI

Handle Basic Start-up Tasks

You've been inspired to start a community organization that works on economic development in your neighborhood. Great. So what's next?

Start by covering the basics. Set up your organization to represent the community it will serve, and to meet the requirements of the law. Meeting these goals generally leads neighborhood groups to organize as a nonprofit corporation. This corporation includes a board of directors to guide the group's direction and a staff hired to carry out the group's day-to-day tasks.

Entire books have been written on the subject of setting up nonprofit corporations.[5] This section briefly lays out a way to begin. Along with proper legal advice, it should be enough to get you started.

The first tasks you must undertake to start a community economic development organization are to

- Establish your board of directors
- Incorporate
- Get good insurance
- Obtain your tax-exempt status
- Use a fiscal agent
- Set up payroll and tax filings
- Set up bank accounts
- Set up annual audits and bookkeeping
- Start keeping board minutes

---

[5] Two useful books are *Starting and Running a Nonprofit Organization* by Joan M. Hummel and *How to Form a Nonprofit Corporation* by Anthony Mancuso.

Establish your board of directors

Your first step is to gather a board of directors. This board will evolve over time. In fact, it can serve just as an incorporating board for a few months until you hold your first annual meeting and select a full board of directors.

Most groups have between seven and fifteen members on their board. Fewer is easier to work with than more; however, more gives you broader representation, more volunteers to tap, and more skills to draw from. The number can start small and grow a bit over time.

When inviting board members, look for people who have strong credibility with different sectors of your community, especially in the sectors you will be working on. These people can include small business owners from your commercial district and other microentrepreneurs. Also consider people involved in workforce development—those creating jobs, looking for jobs, and helping people get jobs. Look for people with strong amounts of common sense and energy, people who are results-oriented and more prone to decisions than oration. Find people whose prime concern is for what's best for the whole community—who are "we" oriented rather than "me" oriented. (Read the next major section of this chapter—Establish Basic Operating Principles—for more ideas about board members.)

A quick word on finding and keeping volunteers, whether for your board, your committees, or other activities: You will attract dynamic, results-oriented people with a dynamic, results-oriented organization. Build that kind of reputation and you will get top-notch people. Communication with these folks, once on board, is a key to retaining them, as are results. Emphasize results that they can see— results that flowed from their involvement, their plans, and their decisions. Show these people each month how their time and thoughts matter in guiding your organization, and they will keep coming to your meetings.

Incorporate

The basic documents involved in incorporating are bylaws and articles of incorporation. Bylaws set out the geographic boundaries that you will work in, the types of people who can be members, the size of the board, the frequency of board meetings, how board members are chosen, and other details about the board, its committees, and its officers. Articles of incorporation state your general purpose (your "mission"), your convening board of directors, your legal address, and related details.

Try to get attorneys who work in corporate law (especially ones with experience filing for tax-exempt status) to donate help with incorporation. They will have the required documents and can walk you through the types of decisions needed to use these documents properly.

If you can't find a pro bono (free) attorney, borrow the bylaws and articles of a good nonprofit organization in your community and follow their format to develop your own. Pay an attorney to review what you come up with before you file the documents with your secretary of state's office.

Get good insurance

Incorporation may protect board and staff members from personal liability. However, there is no absolute protection from personal liability, since anyone can be sued for almost anything. Even with the protection of being incorporated, board and staff members can be found liable under the law, as can the corporation as a whole, if found to be negligent in their duties.

For all these reasons, having strong liability insurance is a must. Also maintain director and officer liability insurance ("D and O"), which covers misdeeds of the board acting as a whole and pays legal defense costs. Make sure your D and O also provides employment practices liability and will pay damages if your group or individuals covered are found guilty. Many groups add employee dishonesty insurance, and it's a good idea to add a rider covering any potential misdeeds of board members. To protect in the event of cash or checks being stolen, some groups buy money and securities insurance. As an extra level of protection, some board members carry an umbrella on their personal insurance policies, covering them for their volunteer activities such as serving on a board.

With proper insurance maintained at all times and strong management by both the board and staff, people do not need to be afraid of serving on the boards of community organizations like yours. Be sure that your start-up organization gets sound guidance from a reputable insurance agent as well as from your attorney on this matter.

Obtain your tax-exempt status

In order to raise charitable funds from foundations, corporations, and individuals, most organizations devoted to community economic development are set up as nonprofit corporations under Section 501(c)(3) of the IRS Code. Such a classification permits all donors to your organization to take a tax deduction for their contributions.

Talk to an attorney familiar with nonprofit law about this filing. You will need to get the appropriate IRS form and pay a filing fee. Your attorney may suggest a different status, such as 501(c)(4) (typical of lobbying groups or homeowner associations) or 501(c)(6) (typical for local business associations or chambers), depending on the nature of your group and what you want to do. Be aware that these classifications will not allow you to raise tax-exempt dollars, unless you are specifically permitted to do so by the IRS.

The IRS does not approve all requests. You will have to prove that your organization is intended to benefit an entire low-income community, not just a group of businesses. Again, it's a very good idea to ask an attorney experienced in such filings to assist you in filling out the forms or at least review the forms before you submit them.

A related note: Remember to obtain a federal tax identification number.

Use a fiscal agent

If you are trying to raise funds and start work while you wait for your tax-exempt ruling by the IRS, you may need to ask another local nonprofit organization to serve as your fiscal agent. This is a fairly common request, and many organizations will consider accommodating you.

Essentially, you use this organization's tax-exempt status until you receive your tax-exempt certification letter from the IRS. Any grants that you are awarded or contributions you receive go into your fiscal agent's bank accounts and onto its balance sheet as restricted fiduciary funds. Your fiscal agent then disburses the funds to your group per your written request. For the best results, make your board responsible for any request for these funds; treat this as you would the signature authority on your organization's bank accounts (see the section Set Up Bank Accounts on the next page).

To make all this happen, you need a written fiscal-agent agreement approved by the boards of both your organization and the fiscal-agent organization. This agreement spells out the duration of the relationship, the responsibilities of the fiscal agent, the limits on its liability, the fee you will pay, and the manner in which you can request your funds.

It's common to pay a fee to a fiscal agent—between 4 percent and 10 percent of your funds that go through the fiscal agent's accounts. Remember that your fiscal agent has to track these funds and show them on its books (explaining to its funders that these funds are really not the fiscal agent's own money). And, your fiscal agent has to worry about whether you're spending the money properly. While this organization is seldom liable under a properly written and executed fiscal-agent agreement and process, it still has a legitimate concern until the relationship is terminated.

You should carefully check out the bookkeeping system and track record of the group you ask to be your fiscal agent. Though rare, it does happen that a fiscal agent misappropriates funds for its own purposes.

Most foundations will consider grant requests that utilize a fiscal agent. But not all do, so check first with any foundation you are approaching for money.

Set up payroll and tax filings

If you have paid staff, then handling the payroll properly is a must. This involves taking out all of the mandated and optional withholdings: federal income taxes, state income taxes, unemployment taxes, health insurance, retirement funds, and others. It also involves recording the withholdings properly, filling out the correct forms, and sending them in on time—every month, quarter, and year. The easiest and safest thing to do is to hire a reputable payroll service, which charges reasonable fees to handle most or all of this for you.

Please take this responsibility seriously. Sadly, the number of neighborhood groups and small businesses that failed to do so—and that are no longer with us because of it—is quite large. Honest mistakes are easy to make and painful to correct; dishonest ones are worse. Get it right the first time.

Set up bank accounts

Set up your checking and savings accounts at a convenient local bank, ideally one that will be involved in your efforts. The bank will ask you to name the authorized signers for these accounts and give you a card to record those signatures. Choosing authorized signers is a decision for your board, and one to be recorded in your board minutes.

It's common to require two signatures on every checking and savings account withdrawal made by an organization. Many groups require only one signature for small amounts (say, up to $250 or $500). Generally groups have four authorized signers, in case one or two are unavailable when needed. Many groups name their executive director as one of the authorized signers; some do not.

Set up annual audits and bookkeeping

Once your organization has been in business for a year, most funders will require an independent annual audit of your finances. So, plan to put the cost of this audit (usually $2,000 to $4,000) in your second-year budget.

It is a good idea to hire your auditing firm right away. Bring it in early during your first year to help you set up your bookkeeping system properly. If the firm likes how you run your books for the year, its audit will go much easier and the cost to you will go down. In addition, you will have a good bookkeeping system in place, one that was established with professional oversight. Best of all, you shouldn't have to pay the firm until it does that first audit, one year down the road.

If you are like most start-up groups, with one staff person doing a hundred tasks every day, you'll probably find that keeping track of every penny you spend and receive is a pain. But you *must* do it! So, either start with a simple paper system or load up your computer with accounting software recommended by local accountants. If these options don't appeal to you, hire an accountant to do the work from the beginning. You face an enormous headache if you ignore basic bookkeeping.

A balance sheet and an income statement must be presented to your board of directors at each meeting. If you use computer software for accounting, it will format these statements automatically. If you use paper, you will have to set up these statements yourself. Ask your auditing firm to teach you.

Keep board minutes

Take minutes of every formal board meeting you hold, right from day one. Include a listing of all persons present and note every formal action taken by the board (motions, seconds, and votes). Send out these minutes to all board members within a week or two of the meeting. Then start the next board meeting by reviewing those minutes and voting to accept or amend them.

Board minutes become an important corporate document and must be kept in a special place. Most groups store the originals in a three-ring notebook and keep a second complete set elsewhere as a backup.

Establish Basic Operating Principles

There are economic development goals that most people can agree on: improved employment opportunities, renovated buildings, and stronger businesses in your community. Beyond these broad outcomes are a good many details that will need to be worked out—details that can generate honest debate. Often the debate results from a lack of clarity about the core values and operating principles of your organization. Therefore, it's important to establish basic operating principles early on.

Get people involved

Each organization needs to decide whom to involve in the meetings and discussions that will guide its economic development activities. Generally, it's better to involve more people than fewer, particularly in early stages.

The logic for involving greater numbers of people is simple: Your community is shared by everyone who passes through there, lives there, works there, shops there, and owns property or businesses there. All of these people have a stake in what happens to your community, and all will have opinions.

The challenge for some organizations is to get enough people to participate, attend meetings, and express their thoughts. For other organizations, the battle is having too many people with conflicting opinions. To succeed, you need to handle both situations.

A good rule of thumb is to include the entire community early on. Get as much input as possible when you create your overall vision and when you develop large projects with wide impact, such as streetscape projects and large commercial developments. Next, ask your board and committees to consider this input along with other relevant information and formulate a draft proposal. Finally, involve the entire community a second time as you present this draft proposal at community meetings. During these meetings, tell people how their input was included in your plan and why (or why not).

Working on broad, high-impact issues with only one community group—only business owners or only homeowners, for example—often causes other groups to feel left out on an issue that matters to them. Conflict ensues. Valuable time is wasted. Relationships get strained and projects get threatened. As a matter of respect and expediency, abide by the principle of high inclusion in the early stages. Once you've gained widespread input from the community and seriously considered it, your plans will have much more credibility—even for most people who don't agree with those plans.

Create community ownership

Right from the start, establish who needs to feel ownership of your organization and its decisions. That sounds simple enough. However, the concept of organizational ownership is a bit tricky to define.

In general, ownership is the feeling that people have about who really drives your organization, controls its decisions, and takes credit for its accomplishments. If too

A good rule of thumb is to include your entire community early on, especially when developing large projects. Once you've gained widespread input from the community, your plans will have much more credibility. Here people from the University Avenue commercial district of St. Paul discuss plans to renovate a number of buildings for commercial use.

Photograph by Petronella Ytsma for the Neighborhood Development Center, Inc. Used with permission.

many people in your community feel that someone else is making decisions for them, you'll encounter resistance rather than support for your ideas.

The feeling of ownership is first a function of involvement. The more time that people spend at meetings, the more they feel their opinions matter. The more decisions that people help to make, the more they feel ownership in your group. And the less people are involved, the more they will wonder, *Who made that decision, and was it really in my best interest?*

Secondly, a sense of ownership has to do with group identification: *Is it my group or some other group that controls this organization?* Group identification cuts many different ways. People commonly think of it in terms of "us" versus "them," which can mean

- Businesses versus residents
- My race versus other races
- Newcomers versus long-time residents
- Local people versus people from outside the community
- Male versus female
- Young versus old
- Downtown versus neighborhood people
- Large business versus small business
- Rich versus poor
- Government agencies and corporations versus "the people"

To get past these oppositions, apply a basic principle: *The people most affected by your actions and the people you most need to take future actions should be the people that feel a high degree of ownership.* Ideally, these people will feel that they are the ones, and not someone else, who are coming up with all the great ideas that affect their wallet, their business, or their property.

So, if you are focused on economic development and expect local small business owners to participate in your upcoming initiatives, they need to feel a sense of ownership. If you are interested in developing job skills and job opportunities for residents, then area residents need to feel a sense of ownership also. Residents also need to feel ownership if you must acquire a house or two for future parking development.

There's one common way for an economic development organization that is largely made up of local small businesses to achieve ownership balance: Add a few seats on the board of directors for strong, local resident organizations. Conversely, a resident-controlled group can add seats for local business owners or representatives of the local business association. In any case, the people you place on the board must feel that their involvement is more than a token commitment by your group. Rather, these people must feel that they hold a meaningful leadership position.

Committees of the board offer another opportunity for achieving balance of ownership. Membership on committees is generally not restricted to board members, and it is common to recruit non-board members who can represent a broader set of viewpoints and skills to do your work. A business-led group is likely to get lots of residents to participate on committees that will impact them, such as a committee to plan design standards for storefront improvements or a committee to create a job training program.

Another rule of thumb: *Early and frequent communication and invitations to meetings give people a sense that they are being included in the beginning of a process,* rather than being asked to rubber-stamp a deal after it is already finalized.

Beyond common manifestations of the "us-versus-them" mentality is the "insider" phenomenon. Over time, some people will say, "Our group is run by a clique." People naturally feel this way when they're unhappy about a decision (and, at times, because it may be true). The best approach to counter this phenomenon has already been mentioned: lots of early communication and lots of open, publicized meetings.

Diversity on your board, committees, and staff is also crucial. You must enlist strong representatives from each group of people in your community who will be affected by your organization's work.

Avoid gridlock and solve conflicts quickly

Ultimately, a small group—your board—will have to make decisions, and not everyone will agree with them. The ensuing debates may be difficult. However, a lack of consensus should not stop your organization from making and carrying out plans.

Again, a reasonable and common solution has been mentioned earlier: Involve as many people as possible in your strategic planning process. Then take a vote and move ahead with the majority opinion. If you wait for a consensus, you may decide nothing and change nothing in your community.

If conflict becomes ongoing, you may need to learn some conflict resolution techniques to get past it. There are thousands of conflict resolution centers and web sites to learn from, and many good books on the subject.[6]

---

6 See *Resolving Conflict in Nonprofit Organizations: The Leader's Guide to Finding Constructive Solutions* by Marion Peters Angelica.

Build Your Funding

You will need to raise money for your daily operations and for your programs. The amount of money you'll be able to raise depends on many factors. One is the number of likely funders in your area. Others include your organization's community impact, the thoroughness of your management practices, and the level of support you generate from your community, your city government, foundations, and other funders. To make the most of these factors, keep the following suggestions in mind.

Make the most of a lean budget

First, remember that most community organizations start out small, keeping their costs low and gradually building up their results and their budgets. Besides being prudent, this path impresses both community members and funders, since it's usually better to operate on a lean budget and produce visible results than to have a fat budget and produce only plans and studies.

Focus locally

You will have a hard time raising money from national-level foundations and corporations for your local neighborhood effort. One reason is the sheer number of requests that national entities get. Another is that they tend to fund larger efforts with regional or national scope.[7]

As an alternative, approach local banks, corporations, foundations, and government agencies. These organizations have a strong stake in the future of your neighborhood. Many of these funders will be attracted to the four pivot-point strategies found in this book, since these strategies harness the energy and investment of so many residents, businesses, and entrepreneurs in tangible and dynamic ways.

Banks in particular have a stake in business development; business owners are current or future customers. Also, as mentioned in Chapter 1, banks have an obligation under the Community Reinvestment Act of 1977 to "affirmatively meet the credit needs of all parts of their market area." Under this law, banks with over $250 million in assets have an obligation to make investments in their low-income communities as well as provide loans; this requirement can translate into grants for your organization.[8]

Your local government should give serious consideration to your work, if for no other reason than the new taxes that will be generated as you build the economy of your community. Work at getting Community Development Block Grant (CDBG) funds as well as Empowerment Zones and Enterprise Communities funds, both of which are federal funds controlled by your city government. Also pursue locally

---

[7] An excellent resource for learning about the focus of foundations throughout the United States is www.fdncenter.org, the web site of the Foundation Center. You can search by topic for foundations that are interested in your type of work.

[8] For more information on this resource, contact the National Community Reinvestment Coalition.

generated money from tax increment financing (TIF) and general revenues. Some cities raise additional funds with local sales taxes or related measures.

You may also get strong support from insurance companies, public utilities, newspapers, corporate donors, private foundations, and community foundations. Most people in these organizations will gladly talk with you, at least for the purpose of explaining their guidelines and funding focus.

Finally, talk to the religious congregations in your area, both individual congregations and their regional and national affiliates. Many of these entities have funds specifically for assisting community development efforts, and will consider funding community economic development.

Remember the "feds"

Even while courting local funders, remember that federal agencies have a wide array of valuable programs. It can take some time to investigate and apply for these programs, but they are one of the best options for funding your work. Here are a few examples:

- Agencies within the Department of Health and Human Services have funds available:
  - Office of Community Services for real estate projects that produce jobs for low-income residents, for grants for workforce development (Job Opportunities for Low-Income Individuals Program, or JOLI grants), and for Empowerment Zones/Enterprise Communities funding in select cities. This office also administers Community Services Block Grants (CSBG) for microenterprise and workforce development.
  - Office of Refugee Resettlement for working with refugee-status immigrants.
- Community Development Block Grants (CDBG) come to your city government from the Department of Housing and Urban Development.
- The Small Business Administration offers microenterprise loan and technical assistance programs.
- The Economic Development Agency in the Department of Commerce funds a variety of projects.
- Obtaining a designation as a "community development financial institution" (CDFI) from the U. S. Treasury Department can open funding opportunities from the Treasury Department (New Markets Tax Credit Program) and from local banks.

To explore more federal funding opportunities, search the official web site of the U.S. government: www.firstgov.gov. Also, ask the staff of your congressional representatives to assist you with applications to such funding sources. You can register to receive notices of funding availability (NOFAs) from most of these agencies. See the resource list in Appendix A for contact information.

Build relationships with funders

Personal relationships with funders are important. Starting with your first phone call, explain briefly to a program officer what your group does. (*Briefly* means three or four sentences!) Then ask if this type of work fits with the funder's guidelines. You may even ask what range of funding requests would be appropriate to submit.

After this initial contact, maintain relationships with potential and active funders. Invite them to visit your community and office. The more funders hear from you and about you, the more comfortable they are considering your grant requests. Also, listen closely to their advice; funders often have a deep knowledge of community development.

Remember some other pointers

Here are some more things to keep in mind when approaching funders:

- Most funders have a few focus areas that they consider when deciding where to contribute money. To save time, learn about these areas before submitting proposals.

- Concrete results count. Talk about your group's impact in terms of real people, real businesses, and real buildings.

- Strong management practices are critical. Have current financial statements, timely annual audits, updated annual budgets, and detailed strategic plans readily available.

- The makeup of your board is crucial. Demonstrate that board members are competent, highly involved in managing your organization, and representative of your community.

- Demonstrate that you have a broad base of support within your community, and from other funders.

- Stability is important. Point out the stability of the people on your staff and on your board, as well as the stability in project focus.

Build Your Staff

People who volunteer for boards and committees are the foundation of all good community organizations. However, community economic development requires a great deal of work—getting new awnings up, getting residents connected to jobs, answering the phone thirty times a day, and much more. For a volunteer with other job commitments, this level of activity is rarely sustainable for any length of time.

Therefore, your organization must aim at hiring a good staff person or two. Most groups that succeed at community economic development have a paid professional staff in the office. Many groups begin with one staff person, usually the executive director. Some even start with a half-time staff person for a few months. As your organization gets established and your funding and volunteer base gets stronger, you can add staff members.

When hiring, know what to look for

Hiring staff requires a tremendous amount of work, as those who have been through the process can testify. The trick is to know whom you will need when it does come time to hire—what sort of skills you're looking for. Consider the following qualities:

- Honesty and integrity
- Respect for community members and board process
- Exceptional work ethic
- High energy
- Great problem-solving ability
- Results-oriented
- Very comfortable with numbers
- Well organized, with ability to do many tasks at once
- Able to sort through complex situations
- Excellent listener
- Excellent communicator (written and verbal)
- Good balance of people skills and detail skills

A person lacking these qualities may not be highly effective in community economic development. Admittedly, this list describes an unusual person with an uncommon mix of traits. Few people are both people-oriented and detail-oriented, for instance.

Notice that one thing you do *not* see on this list is "strong business background." A person with the qualities listed above will be able to learn the ropes of small business and economic development. In contrast, a person strong in business skills but short on these fundamental traits will have a hard time generating the confidence needed to move many people in the same direction.

Clarify the relationship of board members to staff members

To prevent needless conflict, remember two basic points about the respective roles and responsibilities of board members and staff members:

1. The board, acting as a whole at board meetings, creates the mission and sets the goals of the organization. The staff is responsible for carrying out the mission and goals on a daily basis, and for thoroughly informing the board of staff

actions. Any changes from the overall direction laid out by the board need to be brought back to the board—promptly.

2. Board members are generally not advised to get involved in the daily operations of an organization. Such operations are the job of the executive director.

Community groups grind to a halt when board members get overly involved in day-to-day work, when executive directors leave board members in the dark, or when executive directors stray from the organization's mission.

Use consultants wisely

Consultants can extend the capacity of a community economic development organization. They can bring expertise and guidance, or they can simply be a way to get more people-power working on your effort.

As with any other type of hiring, be very clear about what you need a consultant to do, and use a fair and open selection process. Put your expectations in writing, state the due date for the required tasks, and specify how and when you will pay. It is generally a good idea to have shorter rather than longer time frames on a consultant's work—contracts can always be extended if necessary.

Develop and Maintain Strong Relationships

No single factor is more important to your work than strong relationships with a wide range of key individuals, organizations, businesses, and government agencies. This concept is embedded in virtually every page of this book. Good relationships are at the heart of your ability to form your group, to get funding, to form partnerships that expand your capacities, and, most importantly, to work effectively with the people within your community.

Strong relationships take honest and frequent communication and prompt follow-up on commitments. They take respect and understanding of the daily realities of the other party. They require open-mindedness and forgiveness of old grievances, as well as acknowledgment of your own mistakes.

Strong relationships are not, first and foremost, about what your group can get out of the relationship. They are about two people or two organizations gaining an understanding, a respect, and a concern for each other. From that base come knowledge, support, and opportunities of all kinds. Therefore, the more relationships you build and maintain, the more knowledge, support, and opportunities you can rely on down the road.

Create Effective Partnerships

Whether your organization is a start-up or an existing group that expands into community economic development, you will need resources beyond your own staff and board. *Strong partnerships and positive working relationships with local businesses and organizations, government agencies, foundations, corporations, and citywide nonprofit organizations are essential to this work.* Without the advice, expertise, funding, staff capacity, networks, and cooperation of partner organizations, you'll find that turning your local economy around is more than you can handle. The sidebar below provides tips for creating effective partnerships.

Look to nonprofits and city agencies

Start by looking at other strong nonprofit groups—those who can bring the resources you'll need to work on the pivot points you select. Consider groups that excel at job training, job counseling, or job placement for unemployed people. Also seek out groups that train people to start microbusinesses. Groups that offer funds to these people could stretch your capacity, providing "backroom" lending services while your staff is out on the street interacting with more potential borrowers.

Partnerships with city agencies such as the police and the public works department are often critical in accomplishing your goals. You will need a close working relation with your city's community development staff, since you likely share goals and are also likely to seek funding from this office on occasion. Many groups have close working relationships with county, state, and federal agencies as well.

Look to the private sector

The private sector offers another pool of potential partners. Knock on the door of your local business school for interested professors and MBA students. Look into law firms for pro bono lawyers. Ask local architectural firms for a little free design work. Remember that local corporations may be willing to "loan" you employees with the special expertise you need. Add banks to your list; they may be eager to work as your partner in generating more commercial loans.

Many groups make significant partnerships with large institutions in or near their community. These may include major corporations with nearby plants or headquarters,

---

Partners: What to offer and what to ask for

What can your organization offer to attract potential partners? Answers include

- A clear vision for what you want the partner to do
- Strong community support of this vision
- Strong networks within your community—the ability to reach many people
- Consistent and timely follow-through on the tasks you agree to complete
- Open and honest communication, especially if problems develop

And what should you require from your partners? Most important are

- Consistent and timely follow-through on the tasks they agree to complete
- Good communication
- Respect for community processes

Think through any partnership carefully and put the details of your agreed-to relationship on paper, either as a contract or something less formal. The key is that parties clearly understand their mutual goals, their respective roles, and their tasks and timelines.

or major nonprofits such as hospitals and universities. It takes extra effort to find the right person "on the inside" of such an institution, but he or she can bring enormous resources.[9]

Finally, cultivate partnerships with the media. Involve newspapers, radio stations, television stations, and web site developers in your efforts. Change people's perceptions by spreading the word about positive developments in your community.

Gain Visibility and Credibility

The first three purchases made by your organization should be a coffee maker, a phone line with conference calling capability, and a calculator. In other words, establish your organization as a make-it-happen place—the friendly convener of neighborhood folks, the local maker of deals.

To begin, get on the street and visit local businesses every day. Listen to what every business owner tells you, even those that seem to be a bit off the wall. This effort on your part will not only convince businesspeople that their voice matters—it will give you tremendous amounts of valuable information.

You can provide information as well. Tell people what else is happening on the avenue. Talk about other businesses that are starting or finishing a community development project. Get businesses enthused about doing a project of their own—painting their building, getting that new sign up, starting a new ad campaign, or adding a new line of clothing to their inventory.

Project optimism

Your most important organizational assets are visibility, listening skills, and a can-do attitude. The personality of your organization will convey excitement and confidence in the future—or skepticism and lack of interest.

A unified voice that is upbeat and results-oriented, led by your board and staff, will create a positive momentum that attracts others. An organization that does everything it can to help businesses will create support for community economic development. Focus especially on the little things—assisting businesses to cut red tape, responding quickly to inquiries and requests, and maintaining a professional appearance as you do your group's work.

Find the most important resources you need inside your community

Don't join the chorus of people complaining about what *isn't* being done for your community by the government, the banks, the corporations, or whomever. While all low-income neighborhoods could use more help from such institutions, there

---

[9] For information regarding community partnerships with universities, contact Seedco.

are enough resources within your community for many successes and sustainable progress in community economic development.

The resources and opportunities you need most lie within the skills and energy of your residents and businesses. They lie in the quality of your commercial and residential buildings. They include your parks, playgrounds, and other amenities. You will find them in your schools, churches, and community organizations. Opportunities can be found in your proximity to customers and businesses in other parts of your city, and in the vast network of people, organizations, and ideas that you have access to, via your internal community networks.

While you will always seek resources outside your community, the main ingredients for economic development progress are within your grasp, inside your community. Your job as an organization is to find these resources and make the best possible use of them. If you do this well, your argument for help from the "big institutions" is stronger too.

Highlight accomplishments

Ultimately, your work aims to change widespread negative beliefs about your community into positive beliefs. You will do this only with continual, visible results, and only if people understand that this is an ongoing community effort.

This is why you need to highlight your accomplishments. Spread the message that momentum is building in your neighborhood, that your organization is a crucial part of this momentum, and that these projects represent a growing confidence in the community on the part of many. People will talk to their friends and their business associates about your community and your group, and they'll talk in positive terms instead of negative terms. Word-of-mouth communication is one of your most valuable, if hidden, tools.

Put a three-by-three-foot sign in the window of every project you assist to promote your organization to local businesses and help customers spot a unified movement in your neighborhood. However, be careful that the sign doesn't promote your group over the business investment in the project. The signs can simply say *Project assisted by [name of your organization]* and show your phone number. Finally, become skilled at sending press releases to your local newspapers and radio and TV stations. They will often give you some space and highlight what you have done, since it is both newsworthy and a counter-balance to the day's less positive stories.

The San Antonio Unity

March, 2002   SERVING THE SAN ANTONIO DISTRICT   **FREE**

Eastlake's Makeover

By Fernan Ramirez

Eastlake has changed significantly in the past few years but the transformation soon to come will make it a very different place than what it is today. A $2 million streetscape project will bring dramatic improvements to the area around Clinton Park including enhanced sidewalks and streetlights as well as additions of trees, bus-stop shelters and bike racks. The East Bay Asian Local Development Corporation (EBALDC) and the Eastlake Merchants Association (ELMA) are working in partnership to better the area for residents and merchants.

Formerly known as The New Chinatown, Eastlake is located in the lower section of the San Antonio district just east of Lake Merritt. Years ago EBALDC and ELMA put together a team committed to improving the area. In order to acknowledge the diversity of the area the team gave Eastlake its new name. The commercial corridor of Eastlake runs along International Blvd (formerly East 14th Street) and East 12th Street between 1st Avenue and 14th Avenue. There are auto repair shops and dealerships, as well as ethnic restaurants and grocery stores that serve the multicultural working class neighborhood.

The Eastlake team leads the effort to improve the Eastlake district by enhancing economic development, infrastructure, promotion, and services for residents. The driving force of the economic development effort is business development and attraction. The Eastlake team helps local merchants improve their businesses by providing technical assistance. Also, the team aspires to bring new businesses to Eastlake, especially those currently not represented, like banking services.

As for the physical condition of the district, according to senior project coordinator Monica Angeles, "the Eastlake team is working to create a 'sense of place' in the area so that people can recognize when they have arrived to the neighborhood. We are working to make the district safer as well as more vibrant and attractive". The Eastlake team is currently working with the City of Oakland on a façades program aimed at embellishing local storefronts. The $2 million streetscape improvement project will break ground in August 2002.

If you are interested in participating in the revitalization efforts, please call (510) 287-5353 x327 or email Eastlake@ebaldc.com. ELMA always welcomes new members, and together with EBALDC, it strongly encourages residents and others to get involved.

A family spot in the neighborhood.

Send press releases to your local newspapers and radio and TV stations. They will often give you some space and highlight what you have done, since it is both newsworthy and a counterbalance to the day's less positive stories. This article, in *The San Antonio Unity*, highlights the work of the East Bay Asian Local Development Corporation and the Eastlake Merchants Association, both of which serve the San Antonio neighborhood of Oakland, California.

Don't oversell

Don't promise businesses or residents more than your organization can realistically deliver. Overselling will create skepticism on the front end; it will also sound like more of the same old broken promises and failed dreams that abound in inner-city neighborhoods. Small business owners are a "show-me" bunch. Remember, they are already masters of the sales pitch and will generally believe what you say only when they see visible results.

Prove to these people over and over again that your organization can deliver on what it sets out to do. Develop a track record right outside their door. Even those who start out with negative beliefs about your efforts can have a change of heart and begin to work with you.

Take time to celebrate your accomplishments

Sometimes the best thing you can do to build positive momentum with any of the strategies in this book is to have a party, a dance, a banquet, a block party, a potluck, or a picnic. You will be asking a lot of people in your community to participate in long meetings, to invest in buildings and businesses, and to take on a positive attitude about your community's future. All these folks need to have fun once in a while, to feel good about each step of the way, and to feel like the rest of the community appreciates what they have done. Make celebrations an important and regular part of your economic development work.

Summary

Before tackling any of the pivot points discussed in this book, take steps to make your organization effective at community economic development:

- Handle basic start-up tasks, such as establishing a board of directors, incorporating, getting tax-exempt status, setting up ways to manage money, and keeping board minutes.
- Adopt basic principles to get people involved in your organization, give them a sense of ownership, and avoid gridlock in decision making.
- Get sources of continuing funding in place.
- Decide how many people will staff your organization and what to look for in staff members.
- Build strong relationships through honest and frequent communication and prompt follow-up on commitments.
- Create partnerships with organizations that can help you work with the pivot point you select.
- As you take action on a pivot point, highlight your successes in ways that make your organization visible and credible.

With the organization in place, it is time to get to work. Chapter 3 helps you pick a pivot point that best matches your goals and capacity.

Chapter 3

Pick a Pivot Point and Get Started

Now that your organization is set up for success (the subject of Chapter 2), it's time to choose the first pivot point that you want to work on.

Every neighborhood is unique, and each community organization has different capabilities. For this reason, organizations choose different pivot points when they begin community economic development.

Any of the pivot points discussed in this book can become a complete focus for your organization. Over time, as your organization grows, you can tackle two, three, or all four of these pivot points if that makes sense. But you need to start with one strategy.

Two questions guide this choice: What are the most pressing economic needs in your community? Which pivot point is the most doable with the resources, skills, and partners you can obtain?

This chapter will help you get answers. You will

- Assess current economic conditions in your community
- Assess your organization's current resources
- Choose your first pivot point based on these assessments

Assessment is Step 1 of the process for working on any pivot point. The rest of this chapter will give you general tips on the remaining steps: creating a vision and strategic plan, implementing your plan, and evaluating and improving your work. These general tips apply to any pivot point and form the basis for the more specific suggestions given in later chapters.

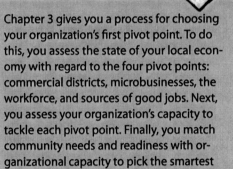

Chapter 3 at a Glance

Chapter 3 gives you a process for choosing your organization's first pivot point. To do this, you assess the state of your local economy with regard to the four pivot points: commercial districts, microbusinesses, the workforce, and sources of good jobs. Next, you assess your organization's capacity to tackle each pivot point. Finally, you match community needs and readiness with organizational capacity to pick the smartest starting point.

In addition, Chapter 3 provides tips for creating, implementing, and evaluating a strategic plan. You'll learn what planning means, how to set realistic goals, how to set time frames for steps in the process, and how to implement your plans in a way that builds momentum and success. Worksheets 1 through 4 will help you pick a pivot point.

Assess Current Economic Conditions

When considering which pivot point to do first, you will look at the four key underlying economic pivot points in your community: the condition of your commercial district, the employment status of residents, the ability of microbusinesses to start up and grow, and the number of businesses growing good neighborhood jobs in your community. You will also research the regional and national economy to understand the larger economic context in which your neighborhood operates.

This assessment is a general one—your first investigation of current conditions. The purpose of this assessment is simply to help choose your first pivot point. Once you've done that, you will do a second, more specific assessment of conditions relevant to that pivot point.

For now, the idea is to capture some numerical facts, such as unemployment rates and commercial vacancy rates. You also want to gauge the feeling of the community—people's perceptions of the neighborhood and its future. Your sources are the library, public agencies, simple observation, and conversation with local residents and businesses.

This level of assessment should not be a major, six-month research project. Instead, it can be a fun exercise in community building with a bit of Internet and library research thrown in. Talk to lots of people and capture the information as thoroughly as you can.

From the Field

"The challenge is finding the best place to intervene in your local market. It may be helping an existing business to grow. It may be assisting an entrepreneur to start a restaurant in an empty storefront. It may be turning an eyesore vacant lot into a new productive use for the community, or changing city zoning ordinances to permit small manufacturers to expand. The key is building local leadership and partners in the process so your organization can initiate and pursue all opportunities as they arise."

TED WYSOCKI

If you are a start-up organization, you can do some economic-assessment work while recruiting members and developing a network of supporters. If you are an existing group, simply use the following sections to research a pivot point you are thinking about getting into. Engage many different people from the neighborhood to give input and to gather information. You can arm them with checklists if they are willing to do some investigation. You can also hold meetings or attend any neighborhood function to ask people for their opinions and observations.

While assessing current economic conditions, also ask people what changes they would like to see in these conditions over the next five years. This will save time in your next step, the planning stage.

Survey your neighborhood's main commercial district

Start by making a simple map that shows the names and types of businesses on every commercial property in your area, block by block. Indicate which properties are vacant, which lots are abandoned, and which are owned by the city or county.

Color-code each building according to its physical condition—from good to seriously deteriorated. You might ask a local architect to draw this map for you.

To dig a bit deeper into the trends in your district and discover the types of businesses that were there in the past, go to your library and ask for a *reverse directory* from five, ten, and twenty years ago. (Reverse directories enable you to look up a person using either an address or a phone number. Two types are the *Polk Directory* and *Cole Directory*. Most librarians keep older editions on file.) Also talk to the local historical society.

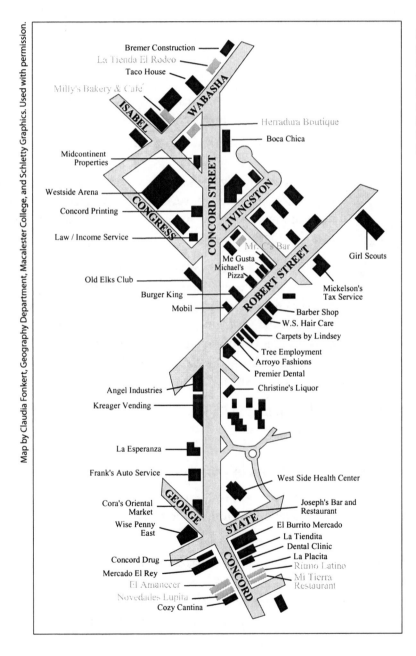

Map by Claudia Fonkert, Geography Department, Macalester College, and Schletty Graphics. Used with permission.

Create a simple map of your commercial district. Show the names and types of businesses on every commercial property in your area. This map of St. Paul's West Side shows each commercial property in the area. The gray properties indicate the Neighborhood Development Center's alumni businesses.

Talk to business owners and residents to find out how they feel about "Main Street"—its past, its current health, and its future prospects. Ask the questions listed in Worksheet 1: Survey Your Commercial District, on page 217, along with other questions that you devise. Use the worksheet to summarize their responses.

Survey your neighborhood's microbusinesses

There are various ways to investigate this part of your neighborhood economy. These tiny businesses (defined as having five or fewer employees) are sometimes hard to find, so using community networks will be important. Seek answers to three questions:

1. Is a new supply of local microbusinesses needed to fill vacant commercial space, generate a few jobs, or bring certain goods and services into the community?

2. How many residents want to start businesses in the community by building up their part-time, "on-the-side" entrepreneurial activity?

3. What prevents residents from starting or expanding businesses?

From the Field

"Work hard to connect your neighborhood economy to the regional economy."

GUS NEWPORT

Talk with as many people as you can about these factors. Contact local bankers, government agencies that do economic development, business instructors from local colleges, and local business owners.

Community organizations often survey their residents to find out how many want to start a business. Whether you conduct a survey now or later, get your neighborhood network to ask residents the three questions listed above. This can be done with a formal survey, via articles in your community newspaper, or in questionnaires left at businesses and local organizations. (The Asset-Based Community Development Institute is an excellent resource for community surveys.)

See Worksheet 2: Survey Current Conditions for Microbusiness, on page 219, for specific criteria to consider.

Survey workforce conditions in your neighborhood

Next, find out if your neighborhood residents are getting—and keeping—jobs that pay livable wages and offer opportunities for advancement. Ask the following questions:

- What is a living wage in your community, and what would it take to get more people working at or above that wage?
- Which specific groups of residents (such as single mothers or recent immigrants to the United States) are most affected by employment problems?

- Why are residents not getting the jobs that are available in your area?
- What agencies and organizations are working on unemployment in your community, and in what way?
- What type of employment services (recruitment, job training, placement, and support) do local employers want?

Pose these questions directly to people who live and work in the neighborhood. Visit local social services agencies and local employers. Visit nonprofit and government agencies that specialize in workforce development and ask them what they know about the employment situation in your neighborhood. Check employment data from the U.S. Census.

Use Worksheet 3: Survey Workforce Conditions and Good Neighborhood Jobs, on page 221, to guide your research and summarize your findings. The first six questions on that worksheet pertain to workforce conditions.

Research businesses that are growing good jobs

Take a quick look at how your neighborhood fits into the regional and national economy. You can do this by visiting the library, by talking with the city development agency staff, and by visiting two powerful and easy-to-use federal government web sites:

- The U.S. Census site: www.census.gov
- America's Career InfoNet: www.acinet.org/acinet

Find out which business sectors and subsectors offer the most jobs to people with skills similar to those of your neighborhood residents. *Sectors* are large categories such as *manufacturing* or *service*. Subsectors are categories within those larger categories. For example, the service sector includes businesses such as day care and home health care.

Find out which of these subsectors are growing and which are stagnant or declining, especially in your region.[10] When you have this information, determine how many businesses in your neighborhood are part of sectors that are growing good jobs in your region.

Also find out how many small and midsize manufacturing firms are located in your neighborhood. (Historically, these businesses have created many excellent jobs for people with limited formal education.) Determine how much land you have to allow these businesses to grow. Finally, see whether your community

From the Field

"Do solid market research before you start—first, to understand who is operating small-scale enterprises in your community and, second, to find out what services they need to survive and grow."

ELAINE EDGCOMB, director, FIELD Program, Aspen Institute, Washington, DC

---

[10] See, especially, Economic Census (conducted every five years) and County Business Patterns at the U.S. Census web site for this information.

includes firms that could represent a dynamic cluster of related businesses, with opportunities for businesses to work together to reach common goals.

Once you start identifying businesses in your community that have strong potential to grow good jobs for your residents, you can talk to them to find out about their plans. Most importantly, ask what is preventing them from growing, and think about how your group can help.

Turn to Worksheet 3: Survey Workforce Conditions and Good Neighborhood Jobs, on page 221, to guide your research and summarize your findings. The last three questions on that worksheet pertain to growing good neighborhood jobs.

Assess Your Organization's Resources

You now have completed the first half of your assessment step: discovering your community's current economic situation, where the local economy is going, what opportunities exist for improving it, and what local people feel about it.

The second half of your assessment is an inward look at your own organization's capacity to take on one of the pivot points. Any of these pivot-point strategies can be done by a neighborhood organization. But each pivot point requires different resources, different skills, and different networks. Each by itself represents a serious challenge for your organization as it strives to assemble all that is required to succeed. While you can certainly build on existing capabilities, do not take this challenge too lightly as you consider entering into a new strategy.

> **From the Field**
>
> "Make sure you have the right information, expertise, and capacity to make your projects successful, even in a very difficult environment."
>
> ABDUL SM RASHEED

Consider whether your staff members already have the skills and time to succeed at one or more of these strategies. If you have to add staff, how much would this add to your budget, and where do you think you can raise this money? Are there any organizations that could help you succeed at one of these strategies? Does your board have strong skills and time available to make one or another of these strategies potentially successful? Does your local government or a citywide nonprofit offer a program that could have a better impact on one of these pivot points in your community if your group gave it time and local support?

You can use Worksheet 4: Assess Your Organization's Ability to Succeed with Pivot Points, on page 223, to think through these issues.

Assess resources for revitalizing your commercial district

A common starting point for a neighborhood economic development organization is commercial district revitalization. Your commercial district is the most visible part of your community. When it is run-down, the whole neighborhood seems hopeless. And when improvements are made, they are so visible that they inspire other people to make additional investments.

Using lots of elbow grease and shoe leather—and a few tools such as loans, small grants, and good design suggestions—neighborhood organizations often succeed with this strategy. These groups help building owners fix up property and assist existing businesses to expand. They attract new businesses to fill vacancies and market the avenue to new customers. Commercial district revitalization often aims to create a theme for the street, developing a cluster of similar or related businesses. With consistent design and ongoing promotions, these efforts create a sense of identity and vitality.

This pivot point is well suited to a small or start-up community organization. Commercial district revitalization gets visible improvements and positive momentum happening with a modest budget and simple skills. One or two energetic staff persons with excellent communication skills and persistence can succeed with this strategy. They do not need a strong business background, assuming that your board of directors has those skills.

Commercial district revitalization is well suited to a small or start-up community organization. It gets visible improvements and positive momentum happening with a modest budget, simple skills, and the persistence of one or two energetic staff.

Assess resources for developing microbusinesses

Assisting microbusinesses to start and expand is a starting point for many neighborhood groups. This pivot point can also evolve from a commercial district revitalization program, since small businesses are common in neighborhood commercial districts.

Work on this pivot point involves training, financial lending, and support of all kinds for start-up businesses, all with a focus on increasing neighborhood economic activity. Often called *microbusiness development,* this strategy is also common for organizations that work in areas larger than just one neighborhood, especially overseas in developing countries.

The task of developing microbusinesses matches the typical skills of community-based organizations well. Your links to people throughout the community are the basis for this work, since start-up low- or moderate-income entrepreneurs often are most comfortable working close to home. And much of this strategy can be done with a partner organization providing the business sophistication. Such partnerships allow you to tackle this pivot point as a young organization, with deep community networks as your main asset.

The strategy of developing microbusinesses involves training, lending, and support for start-up businesses. This strategy is common for organizations that work in areas larger than just one neighborhood. It is also a typical next step for organizations involved in commercial district revitalization.

Many neighborhood groups eventually develop these business and lending skills in-house. This requires a larger budget than working with partner groups. Staff with strong business and lending skills typically requires a higher salary, and you may need to finance your own loan fund. Your organization may need a few years of development to get to this point.

Assess resources for developing your community workforce

Workforce development helps unemployed or underemployed residents find and keep good jobs. This pivot point includes offering a variety of training and counseling programs, connecting residents to jobs, and helping them do well on the job.

Most neighborhood organizations conduct work-force development in partnership with a larger organization that operates citywide training and placement programs. Tackling this strategy without an experienced partner is a difficult first strategy for a small start-up organization, but it can be done.

Most neighborhood organizations approach this strategy in partnership with a larger organization that operates training and placement programs citywide. Neighborhood-level groups bring a trusted reputation and access to community networks to such partnerships—qualities needed to bring your unemployed residents in the door and ensure a comfortable, high-quality training and placement experience.

If you can find a reputable, experienced nonprofit or government organization willing to be your partner, your group can undertake this strategy early in its history and with a small staff. As in all partnerships, clear roles and responsibilities are critical.

Some neighborhood organizations take on this pivot point themselves, without a partner group, if they can't find the right partner. This obviously requires a larger staff, more money, and more skills within your staff. For these reasons, taking on workforce development on your own, without a strong, experienced partner, is a difficult first strategy for a small start-up organization, but it can be done.

Assess resources for growing good neighborhood jobs

Depending on which form of assistance your local job-producing businesses need, your community development organization can take on the strategy of growing good neighborhood jobs early or later in its history. It can start with planning, organizing, and advocacy, and add a direct service program later on.

Depending on which form of assistance your job-producing businesses need, your group can take on this strategy early or later in your history. Many groups have added good jobs by using their organizing and planning skills to help local businesses prosper. These community groups have convened business owners and residents to develop networks and set plans for a future that includes more local employment. They have connected local businesses to local workers and to growth resources from outside the neighborhood. Your group only needs to have good planning, organizing, and advocacy skills to bring these valuable services to businesses targeted for job growth.

Sometimes such skills aren't enough to overcome obstacles to local business growth. Specialized loan funds, real estate development, and other complex efforts require advanced skills and resources, and are thus generally taken on by more mature community development organizations. New organizations could begin with planning, organizing, and advocacy—building relationships with local businesses in the process, and add a direct service or program later on, if it is needed.

Choose a Pivot-Point Strategy

Now that you've assessed your local economy and your organization, you have the information needed to choose your first pivot-point strategy. In addition, think about the possibility of taking on additional strategies later.

Pick your first strategy based on two conditions

To begin, pick the strategy that does the best job of satisfying *both* of the following conditions.

First, working on this pivot point will significantly improve the economy of your community because

- The strategy addresses a major problem immediately.
- You have some strong potential resources to work with—for example, a commercial district rich with impressive buildings ready for rehab; a thriving culture of microbusinesses ripe for development; or a wealth of small manufacturing businesses that could expand and grow new local jobs.

Second, your organization can succeed with this pivot point by using its current resources and by taking advantage of opportunities on the horizon. You must come to this conclusion after an assessment that includes the

- Skills and available time of staff and board members, relative to each pivot-point strategy
- Potential of support by funders for certain strategies
- Potential of strong partnerships that can make one strategy or another successful
- Presence of existing programs that could do more with a boost from your group

Consider additional strategies

Down the road, you may get to the point where you are ready to add a second pivot-point strategy. You will do this in much the same way you picked your first strategy, looking closely at the two conditions above. However, you will want to factor in an additional consideration: Which new strategy connects best to the one you are already using?

In some cases, this choice is based on what your neighborhood needs. Was work on your commercial district frustrated by a lack of outside businesses willing to move into empty storefronts? Some groups take up microbusiness development for this reason, since local entrepreneurs are usually willing to occupy local space. Did you start with a workforce development program and find there were not many good jobs for your neighborhood residents? Your network of employers in that program may be precisely the type of businesses that could grow more jobs—if your group could help them over a hump or two.

In other cases, your second strategy may evolve from your group's strengths. You may run a great loan program for retailers and be able to expand it to industrial businesses quite smoothly. Perhaps your staff has mastered real estate development skills that could be useful in redeveloping old industrial land. Your second strategy should evolve from such considerations and be fairly evident from the perspectives of neighborhood need and internal resources.

A note before moving on

With your pivot-point strategy chosen, you are ready for the four steps of community economic development:

Step 1. Assess current conditions in your community relating to this pivot point.

Step 2. Create a vision for this pivot point and strategic plan to achieve it.

Step 3. Implement your plan.

Step 4. Monitor, evaluate, and improve your work.

Doing the assessments described so far in this chapter has given you experience with Step 1: Assess current conditions. The rest of this chapter offers an overview of the remaining steps and general tips for completing them. Specific instructions relating to each strategy are provided in Chapters 4 through 7.

Tips for Creating Your Vision and Strategic Plan

There are many books on strategic planning, some of them designed specifically for nonprofit organizations. Several themes run throughout these works: Be sure the organization is ready to plan; involve the people who will be affected by the plan and who must implement the plan in the planning process; set aside time that is dedicated to planning; be sure your goals are clear and realistic; and be accountable to the strategic plan and the goals you've set. These planning tips are described on the next pages.[11]

---

[11] The process described here was inspired by *Strategic Planning Workbook for Nonprofit Organizations* by Bryan Barry.

Prepare to plan

Make sure your organization is ready to plan. Start by getting a commitment from your organization's leaders—executive director, board members, and staff members.

With a commitment to planning in place, you can "plan to plan"—that is, make some choices up front about how to proceed with the process:

- Choose whether to get help. Some nonprofits hire a consultant who specializes in strategic planning to guide them at every step of the way. Another option is to hire a consultant for one part of the process, such as conducting a planning retreat (as explained on page 46).

- Choose how much time you'll devote to planning. Typically, nonprofit organizations first gather and summarize the information they'll need to plan. (This is the information described in the Assess Current Conditions sections of Chapters 4 through 7.) Next, they schedule a four- to eight-hour planning retreat to review this information and reach agreement on the key points of their plan. Finally, they schedule two or three shorter meetings to review and finalize their plan.

- Choose a format for your plan. A plan does not have to be long, just complete. At a minimum, include three sections: a mission statement for your organization, three-year goals that relate to the pivot point you choose, and one-year goals that lead to your three-year goals. Many groups also add a three-year projection for budget and staffing to their plan, and other sections as they see fit.

Get input from community residents

Engage your community by holding open meetings. Show slides and present maps of the neighborhood showing what's good and what's bad. Stimulate discussion by providing examples of neighborhoods with stronger economies. Capture people's visions of a better economy in specific, concrete terms. Bring their visions to life in words and pictures.

Here are typical visions for a healthy commercial district:

- The district is filled with thriving businesses and storefronts that are well maintained.
- Vacant lots are developed into something useful, such as buildings, houses, or parks.

- Buildings stay vacant for a month or less when businesses or residents move out.
- Area residents can buy everyday necessities right in their community.
- Community gathering places such as restaurants and coffee shops give people places to be with their families and neighbors.
- Businesses, customers, and residents want to come to your community because it has a positive reputation as a place to live, shop, and do business.

Gather up these preferences and visions in writing and in visuals where possible. Consider using an architect to capture people's ideas as they speak in the meetings. This technique is called a *design charrette* and can significantly enhance a community discussion. See www.charrettecenter.com for more information.

Organize a planning retreat

Organizations generally take on the task of creating a vision and strategic plan at a board retreat, or at a few board meetings dedicated to that purpose. Some groups send their entire staff to a retreat; others just bring their senior manager, and then stage a full staff retreat at a different time.

Board retreats can be as short as two or three hours or as long as two or three days. They can take place where you regularly meet, or at a relaxing site away from the neighborhood.

In any case, you will accomplish more at retreats if the following criteria are met.

- *They are well planned.* Be clear about what you want to accomplish by the end of the retreat and what agenda will get you there. If you finish with a crisp mission statement and a prioritized list of one-year goals and three-year goals, you will be ahead of most groups. (Fleshing out a work plan is typically done later by staff members.)
- *You are well prepared.* Collect all the information you've gathered during the assessment step and summarize it in ways that your board members can easily digest. Study this information yourself so that you have an opinion on where to start and how to proceed.
- *Board members are well prepared.* Arm them with the summary information before the retreat, so they have time to develop some thoughts in advance.
- *A professional outside facilitator runs the retreat.* Your own staff and board members can certainly run a retreat, but they are rarely experts on group facilitation and strategic planning. Furthermore, you are all "players" at this event and will want to state your opinions early and often. Taking the role of a neutral facilitator isn't much fun for any of your members and can present a conflict of interest at certain times during the retreat.

- *The retreat is seen as useful.* This happens when participants know three things: that their input will be quickly worked into a draft plan, that they will see the plan again to finalize it, and that the plan will, in fact, become the organization's road map.

Set clear, doable goals

With your vision statement in hand, begin thinking long-range. Three years down the road, what will be different if your organization succeeds? Be specific, use numbers where possible, and include at least three different categories of goals: impact goals, program goals, and organization goals.

Impact goals describe what will be different in your community (such as the numbers of storefronts renovated or residents placed in good jobs).

Program goals describe what programs your organization will operate and how many results will be achieved (for example, how many loans or grants will be made).

Organization goals specify what your organization will look like in three years and how it will be managed. These goals can describe the size of your staff, the size of your budget, the type of financial management and controls that are in place, the function of your board, the type of office space you will have, and the kinds of office equipment you will use.

Don't set unrealistically ambitious goals. You certainly want to aim high and make a quick impact in your community. But be aware that it's far better to exceed expectations than to come up way short.

One-year goals are of the same nature as the three-year goals; they're just aimed one year down the road. It's even more important to prioritize your one-year goals than your three-year goals, because one-year goals give a clearer picture of the load you're placing on your staff and your volunteers.

As you break down goals into a work plan—a list of tasks to accomplish each month—you'll get more clarity on how much you can realistically hope to achieve in your one- and three-year time frames. So come back to your goals for further debate on priorities.

Your one-year goals can be broken down into a detailed plan that states specifically what you will do to reach each goal: a list of tasks, who will do each task, and when the task will get done (or when your organization will reach various benchmarks). This is a basic work plan, a valuable tool for measuring your progress and for prioritizing your work.

Review your strategic plan with your board

Bring your goals and work plan back to your board at least every six months (and at least every three months to your staff). Show how your work is following the plan, and admit where you are off track. Your work will improve if you do this, and your board members will know their time and guidance are worthwhile.

Tips for Implementing Your Plan

After your group takes the time needed to create a vision and strategic plan for working on your first pivot point, many of your members will be more than ready to move into action: *Enough planning, already,* they'll probably say. *Let's start producing results.* Use the following tips to build momentum.

Start with as many people as you can

You are in the people business. Your work must be important to and supported by a wide range of people, both inside and outside your community. You cannot operate alone or as a small group of "insiders" for the sake of efficiency or conflict avoidance.

Your success requires many different people to make decisions about where they will invest and where they will shop; whether they will fund your organization, come to your meetings, and speak in favor of or against your efforts; or whether they come to your meetings at all. You have to bring many people with you as you begin this journey.

Focus on economic results

People need to see results from your work early and often. In community organizing terms, results are called *victories* because they build enthusiasm and momentum. In the business world, results are called *profits* or *growth* or *satisfied customers and employees*, and are also highly motivational.

In the field of community economic development, positive results cover a wide range: attractive storefront windows that were once boarded up, new businesses that move into a vacant building, or a young person who lands a decent job and sticks with it. Beyond accomplishing your organization's vision, such results will keep volunteers coming to meetings and promote your organization as a dynamic agent of change.

It's easy to spend most of your time on organizational issues—assembling a board, volunteers, and committees; planning; fundraising; and hiring staff. While these crucial tasks take a lot of time, they are ultimately not what inspire people to invest their time, faith, and money in your community or your organization. Nor will organizational tasks turn your community's economy around. You can only accomplish that with economic results.

To keep results coming, have many small projects in your pipeline, and perhaps a few medium- or large-size projects as well. Too often, an organization's projects will have twists and turns that derail them. Plant many seeds, and some will come up.

Be visible

Seeing is believing. People in low-income communities hold negative beliefs about their neighborhoods because they've seen mostly negative trends for years. Therefore, your results need to be visible to everyone who lives, works, and passes through your neighborhood. This is a long haul, and people generally will not participate in meeting after meeting that fails to produce changes they can see. This is particularly true of small business owners, who as a group tend to be action-oriented and short on time. Most people get charged up by visible results, continually flowing from a solid organization.

Create catalytic projects

Your neighborhood economy is a big place. It will never be revitalized by your organization alone. But it will change when many people start viewing it differently.

From the Field

"Do your development work in a way that not only meets the needs of your residents, but also attracts more businesses, bankers, and investors into your neighborhood."

GUS NEWPORT

Perhaps there are 5,000 or 10,000 households and 50 to 200 businesses in your community. Imagine that 10 percent of them decided next summer to fix up their home or business property because they felt better about the direction of your neighborhood. And imagine if they bought all their supplies from local paint, hardware, furniture, and carpet stores. Your ultimate goal is to get all these decision makers to shop, start a business, improve their property, or create a few jobs in your community. This will happen when people believe that something positive is happening and will continue to happen.

You get more of these decisions with highly visible, catalytic projects. Examples include renovating a key corner building that has been vacant and deteriorated for many years and getting good press about the first ten young people you place in well-paying jobs. Pick projects that are symbolic as well as visible—projects that reverse long-standing symbols of your community's deterioration.

Highlight private investments

Most of your projects will involve a combination of public and private investment. Both are crucial to your success, since private investment seldom happens without public subsidy in badly deteriorated communities. However, in order to change perceptions and eventually stimulate private investment that comes into your community *without* a public subsidy, the message of community reinvestment should highlight the investment decisions made by business and building owners and customers, mentioning the public investment second.

In order to create a bandwagon effect with private investments, you must convince people that their peers are starting to believe in this community by making private investments. How you publicize your successes and to whom you give credit really matter. Give most of the credit to the people who reached into their own pockets because they believed in your community.

Start small

For purposes of creating and maintaining a momentum of private decisions, more results are better than fewer. And smaller, less complicated projects will happen more regularly than large, complex projects.

So, do the doable. Five new awnings on storefronts and ten residents in better jobs will make a wonderful impression on your community. Bringing in a small family restaurant or a video store, if you've been missing such a business, will do the same. Working for three or five years on the 40,000-square-foot shopping center can be a fantastic cherry on top of the sundae, but the shopping center packs more punch if every other storefront nearby has a new look as well.

Set realistic time frames

How long does it take to start an organization and get your first visible results? The following chart gives general time estimates for common tasks. Note that many tasks can overlap.

Timelines

Task	Timeline
Forming the founding committee around an initial vision statement	Two to four months, depending on local politics, organizational landscape, and need for this focus
Handling organizational basics—bylaws, articles, registration with state, filing for 501(c)(3) status	Two to four months
Getting input on plans, capabilities, problems, perceptions, and vision	Two to six months
Creating your first draft of a strategic plan	One half-day retreat to two months of shorter meetings and rewrites
Getting feedback from community on this draft	One meeting to many, depending on the level of interest and contention
Raising initial funds for overhead and programs	Four to eight months
Getting first visible results—such as completing storefront improvements, starting a training class for microbusiness, or placing a few residents into a customized job training program	Six to twelve months after convening

Balance implementation and planning

Don't get bogged down in planning. If you do, you'll start to lose action-oriented participants. The important thing with a plan is not that everyone agrees with all its details. What matters is that everyone has a say, that their comments are respectfully considered, and that a majority feels the plan incorporates the best ideas.

However, it's a mistake to get too far along with your efforts until you have a good sense of your basic direction. You could be attracting businesses into your district that you later regret because they don't fit into a cluster you are trying to develop. Or you could be helping to renovate storefronts in ways that clash with design themes that you adopt later.

So, after your initial planning and set-up period of two to six months, do planning and implementation concurrently. Set your direction early. Get to work. And then keep refining your plans as you go, using a beginning track record of completed projects as your motivation to continue.

Build community every day

This list of tips began with a focus on people. It ends on the same note. A common criticism of organizations doing community economic development is that they're too focused on technical matters—"brick-and-mortar" projects, loan criteria, development budgets, and the like—to the exclusion of building a solid base of regular community folks.

Your purpose is not just to fix up buildings, add some businesses, and place a few people in jobs. Rather, your organization must catalyze improvements throughout the community. Your community includes people as well as buildings, families and circles of friends as well as businesses. Furthermore, connected and supportive people are your number one asset—the network that provides you with timely information and support for your work.

How do you build community?[12] There are many ways, but to begin:

- Keep the focus on making a difference to regular people in your community.
- Keep your organization open and inclusive, and remember to have fun.
- Keep momentum going by spreading the word about your results.
- Get past conflicts as quickly as possible.
- Do the basic management of your organization well, so you don't get bogged down in it.
- Make things happen that many people can take credit for and take pride in. For example, invite the whole community to help design the benches or signs you are installing on your avenue.
- Focus on projects that bring people together, such as creating restaurants, coffee shops, or day care centers that represent the community's heritage.

---

[12] For a comprehensive list of factors that influence successful community building, see *Community Building: What Makes It Work* by Paul Mattessich and Barbara Monsey.

Tips for Evaluating and Improving Your Work

The most important thing to remember about evaluating your work on any pivot point is this: Evaluate regularly, honestly, and openly. The following tips explain ways to make effective evaluation happen.

Track activities and results

Effective evaluation begins with solid monitoring and documenting systems that are in place from the beginning of your work. Track results, large and small—from the numbers of people who attend meetings to the numbers of storefronts renovated and persons trained and placed in jobs. Use simple forms to record these facts as they occur. Then use simple spreadsheet or database software to track them monthly, annually, and historically.

Get solid organizational documentation from day one. The following are vital: complete minutes of all board and committee meetings, solid budgets, regular and complete financial statements, and annual audits. These are basic, day-to-day management tools that allow you to monitor the effectiveness of your decision making and the cost-effectiveness of your results.

Get visual recordings. Taking before and after pictures of your projects is a must. Have a camera in the office right from the start. Use maps to give an instant picture of the number and location of your results.

Evaluate results from four perspectives

Evaluate the work you do for specific, measurable results—and for the intangible impact it is making on your community's attitudes and individual decisions. To do this, look at your work from four perspectives.

First and foremost, take the perspective of the residents and business owners in your community. Ask these questions:

- How many results have you accomplished that are visible to them?
- Do your results affect lives and businesses in significant ways?
- Are their attitudes about their community and its future more positive, and are they more likely to stay?
- Do they feel involved in your organization's decision making? Do they believe that the organization is run by and accountable to neighborhood businesses and residents? Do they refer to the organization proudly as "our" organization?
- Can they count on your good results continuing into the future?
- Are there ways to bring even more positive results to the businesses and residents in your community?

Second, look through the eyes of your board, volunteers, staff members, and partner organizations. After you're well into a project, ask these players to assess the current state of your organization's work and your local economy. This assessment is often called a *SWOT analysis*—an acronym for Strengths, Weaknesses, Opportunities, and Threats—and is usually done to prepare for an annual board meeting or planning retreat.

The results of this SWOT survey are often compiled for board review, along with a comparison of actual results to the goals laid out in your strategic plan.

Third, look at your work from the perspective of your budget and your funders. Study what you spend on administration and program expenses, and compare these to the results you have accomplished. The basic question is simple: Are there ways to get more results within your limited budget? If possible, compare these costs to similar efforts by other organizations, locally and nationally, and run a salary comparison to similar organizations to ensure that you are paying competitive (but not outrageous) wages.

Equally important, measure your *impact* in quantifiable terms. Examples are the numbers of new businesses and jobs assisted by your efforts, the salary paid at these new jobs, the taxes paid by new businesses and workers, and the new dollars spent in your community. Collect as many of these figures as possible from the beginning of your work; they are vital to your reputation and your future funding.

Finally, compare expense figures to impact figures. Such cost/benefit figures are widely used, for instance, to look at public expenditures per each job created or each new business created. In this way, you can see how your group stacks up against other economic development projects. Just make sure you are really comparing apples to apples when you do this.

Fourth, get a perspective from outside your organization. As community organizations mature, they often pay an outside research firm to conduct an evaluation of their work every two to four years. This external evaluation serves a similar purpose to your annual financial audit and can focus on program results as well as internal management practices and systems. While pricey—anywhere from $5,000 to $30,000 depending on the size of your organization and what you are evaluating—there are major benefits to an outside evaluation. Funders and others see outside evaluations as more objective than evaluations done internally. Outside evaluations will generally be more valuable to you for the same reason. Some foundations think so highly of an outside, in-depth perspective on your organization that they have special funds you can apply to this cost.

Be willing to improve

Your strength as an organization will grow from a sincere belief in evaluation and improvement. The core attitude is that everyone can get better at what they do.

Even if you were perfect yesterday, the world is changing so fast that you won't be perfect tomorrow. You must keep learning.

Most change takes time and patience. So consider ways to improve your work in small, incremental steps as well as major, overall reforms. Most people don't like change, but they will warm to something new through their own involvement and in small steps.

Often program improvements begin as pilot programs—small scale with low costs and limited time commitments. As you work out the bugs from your pilot program and get staff, board, and community to buy in, you can increase the scale of the program.

The bottom line in community economic development: What you are trying to do is difficult, and there are few road maps. Since you are dealing with a unique community and unique personalities, much of your work will be innovative and experimental. You can face failure without fear if you are committed to constantly look hard at your results and change for the better.

Summary

This chapter has walked you through a process for choosing your organization's first pivot point. The aim is to start your work with your eyes open. To do this, assess the current state of the four pivot points in your local economy and your organization's capacities to tackle each pivot point.

In addition, you gained tips for creating a strategic plan as well as pointers for implementation and evaluation:

- Prepare to plan
- Organize a planning retreat
- Set clear, doable goals
- Review your strategic plan with your board
- Focus on economic results
- Be visible
- Highlight private investments
- Start small
- Set realistic time frames
- Balance implementation and planning
- Build community every day
- Track activities and results
- Evaluate results from four perspectives
- Be willing to improve

The next four chapters go into detail on each pivot point. If you are still not sure which pivot point is right for your group to tackle now, then read all four chapters to get a better sense of your options. If you are certain about which pivot point to tackle first, then go to the corresponding chapter and get started!

Chapter 4

Revitalize Your Commercial District

The face of your neighborhood is your commercial district. More people look at your commercial district each day than any other part of your community. These people drive down "the avenue," walk the sidewalks, shop, eat, go to work, and open up the doors of a business.

Typically there is three to five times as much traffic on your main commercial street as on any surrounding residential street. Day after day, more people will notice positive changes on this street than positive changes on a quiet, residential street.

To a large extent, financial actions follow perceptions. Suppose that your district is filled with boarded-up buildings, vacant lots, businesses that close at 5:00 P.M., and buildings that haven't seen a paintbrush since 1950. People will form the perception that this area is dying, and they will stay away. But, if your commercial district bustles with a healthy mix of businesses, appealing storefronts, and lots of customers, then things will change. People will want to come to your community as shoppers, business owners, homebuyers, and renters. Their investments will start a positive snowball effect on your local economy.

Overview

For these reasons, hundreds of community organizations around the country focus their efforts on revitalizing their run-down, worn-out commercial district (often called the *commercial corridor*). They don't do this work simply to help a few businesses, or even just to improve the district itself. They do it because it is the ideal way to stimulate confidence and reinvestment in the entire community because of the district's visibility and role in the neighborhood.

Chapter 4 at a Glance

Revitalizing your commercial district is the ideal way to stimulate confidence and reinvestment in the entire community because of its visibility and role in the neighborhood. The key to revitalizing your commercial district is a four-step process:

1. Assess current conditions in your commercial district, using Worksheets 5 through 9 as a guide.

2. With input from community members, create a vision for your commercial district; translate that vision into three-year goals, one-year goals, and a work plan for the next twelve months. Worksheets 10 through 12 can aid your planning.

3. Implement your work plan by choosing from the tools discussed in this chapter.

4. Monitor, evaluate, and improve your results.

Their work starts with assessing current conditions in their district. Next comes a clear vision for the district's future and efforts to get as many people from the community behind that vision as possible. Then they carefully set goals to achieve this vision, assemble revitalization tools, implement their plans, and evaluate their work.

Implementation involves many small, visible steps that add up to a rapid swell of momentum. For example, neighborhood organizations can

- Create a small loan and grant fund to help businesses paint their storefronts and add fresh signs, windows, and awnings.
- Develop, resurface, or landscape parking lots.
- Help existing businesses with their expansion plans.
- Market empty buildings to targeted new businesses, those that add the right mix to the district to achieve the community's vision.
- Add benches, lighting fixtures, district signs, planters, and other streetscape elements to create a sense of unity and progress.
- Create a fresh new marketing "image" for the district, and use it to attract customers.

Sometimes organizations themselves buy empty, deteriorated commercial buildings and redevelop them. In other cases, organizations work with developers who share the same community vision. Larger developments—such as a new, small shopping center, antique mall, or ethnic market with many small businesses—often come later.

Bringing shoppers to your changing district is the ultimate test. For your work to succeed, your businesses must win the support of the marketplace. Special events, festivals, positive media coverage, ongoing advertising, and branding with a new district name and logo are some ways to market your district and attract shoppers.

Through all this work, community organizations hope to create a stronger economy *and* a stronger sense of community. Restaurants, laundromats, retailers, coffee shops, and other businesses provide community gathering places. Your organization can deliberately seek out such businesses.

This chapter makes the case for revitalizing your commercial district and explains a four-step process for doing so.

Forces That Drive Districts Down

Why do commercial districts all over the country decline in inner-city locations? Many of the reasons are obvious:

- The era of automobiles, freeways, suburban sprawl, and mass merchandising made inner-city business districts seem old, cramped, and unexciting.
- The decline of blue-collar industries devastated buying power in older neighborhoods around the country.

- Crime, especially the fear of crime, became synonymous with *inner city*.
- Racial prejudices and negative stereotypes clouded perceptions of newly arrived residents, often fueling white flight to the suburbs.
- The exodus of upwardly mobile young people to the suburbs created an enormous drain of entrepreneurs, homebuyers, renters, and customers for local businesses.

It seems like solutions for most of these problems should come from private business or the government. However, *the private sector by itself rarely can reverse these conditions.* The imperative in business is to make a profit; if you don't, you won't be in business for long. Going to where costs are high and customers are scarce is not a good formula for business success, and this is what the private sector sees when it looks at the inner city. *Nor will the public sector, by itself, reverse these conditions.* City and state governments simply have too many jurisdictions to give every neighborhood commercial district the necessary attention.

If anything is going to turn commercial districts around, it must be a long-term, persistent effort led by local businesses and residents that draws resources from the private and public sectors. This is where you come in.

Revitalizing Rice Street—the heart and soul of St. Paul's North End

The North End of St. Paul, Minnesota, an old and proud blue-collar neighborhood, watched hundreds of good jobs dry up from 1960 to 1990 as local industries closed down. The housing stock—basic, built for railroad workers early in the century—became some of the worst in the city.

The North End's commercial district, Rice Street, also declined dramatically. By the mid-1980s, two department stores, a pharmacy, a hardware store, a high school, and other longtime anchors were closed. Fully 40 percent of the commercial buildings in this one-mile heart of the commercial district were boarded up—some vacant, some used for warehousing. Buildings that were still open for retail business were hiding that fact well.

With these losses came a loss not only of shopping opportunities, but also of residents' pride and hope for the future. Local businessman Tom Huppert, owner of North End Machine, said it was like watching someone die, a little bit at a time, and everyone waited for it to die completely.

North End Area Revitalization, Inc. (NEAR), was founded in 1984 by the local business club and resident organization for the purpose of economic revitalization. It is still going strong today. In its first 18 years, NEAR helped business owners restore 80 percent of all buildings in the commercial district with loans, small grants, and design assistance. It reduced the percentage of buildings in the six-block heart of Rice Street that were vacant or boarded up from 40 percent to 5 percent. NEAR created visible changes that affect every resident and business in the North End, and promises more to come, with expanded programs for industrial, housing, and retail redevelopment.

The Case for Revitalizing Your Commercial District

Commercial district revitalization is a key part of economic development for several reasons. One has already been mentioned: Your commercial district is the window into your entire community. In addition, revitalization provides a tremendous catalyst for further private investment and develops a growing local marketplace.

Your commercial district is the marketplace closest to your residents—the most convenient place for them to work and buy what they need. It is also where residents run into their neighbors and build up social networks that provide friendship, advice, role modeling, and other kinds of help. Finally, it is a great place for local entrepreneurs to start their businesses.

A note about job creation: Community development groups don't usually see commercial district revitalization as a strong strategy for creating jobs. While many new jobs can be created through revitalization, these are typically low-paying retail jobs.

Yet there are reasons why your community may view these jobs favorably. A high percentage of them go to local residents. And, many people find that these positions serve well as a second job, a starter job, or a part-time job close to home. Every community group will look at this issue from its own perspective.

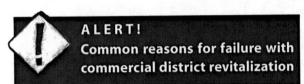

ALERT!
Common reasons for failure with commercial district revitalization

- Staff who are stuck in the office or in meetings rather than being on the avenue, getting projects lined up and completed
- Lack of capacity or resources needed to succeed at lending, marketing, or other implementation tools
- Lack of interest by business and building owners because of too much red tape or lack of meaningful incentives
- Lack of visible results, or results scattered over too large of an area to turn perceptions around (lack of geographic focus)
- Distrust or anger by business owners about the organization's program because of poor communication, lack of follow-through, or inconsistent treatment of businesses
- The organization ends the program too soon

Step 1: Assess Current Conditions

Revitalizing your commercial district begins with a clear assessment of current conditions and some sense of the opportunities for improvements. This assessment will take shoe leather, observation and research, and conversations with many people.

Consider the health of your commercial district as a whole

A vibrant commercial district looks unified and creates the impression that people are working together to give it a better future. The district serves the needs of residents, who patronize local businesses regularly and attract new businesses. In addition, individual businesses look like they're successful and growing.

In light of these general criteria, how does your commercial district stack up? Reflect on this question in writing. See Worksheet 5: Consider the Health of Your Commercial District, page 226.

Inventory existing property and businesses

List the properties and businesses presently in your district. On your list, include some relevant details about each business. Once you complete this list, keep it updated. It will come in handy often.

One of the primary reasons for making a property inventory is to list your vacancies. These are a major blighting influence on your district. Besides looking deteriorated and unsafe, vacancies send a loud message that the area is undesirable—the exact opposite of the message that you want to create.

Note that a small percentage of vacancies is normal in any business district for a limited time. Businesses close their doors or they move, resulting in vacancies. But you have a problem if vacant buildings stay empty for more than a few months, or if you have more than one small vacancy on every block or two at the same time.

Step 1 at a Glance

- Consider the health of your commercial district as a whole
- Inventory existing property and businesses
- Create a business map
- Talk to neighborhood business owners
- Visit other commercial districts
- Study successful shopping centers
- Do three levels of market research
- Find out the retail buying power of your community
- Create a targeted business list
- Consider your organization's capacity

Staying on top of vacancies (including knowing when a building is going to become vacant) gives your organization a valuable tool. With this information you can direct local entrepreneurs to available commercial space. You can actively seek people to fill these spaces with new types of shopping opportunities, renovated buildings, and shops that would complement your existing businesses by attracting similar customers.

Use Worksheet 6: Inventory Existing Property and Businesses, page 227, as a way to format your property inventory.

Create a business map

As a simple tool to focus discussion and consider alternatives for redevelopment, make a map of the businesses and other building uses in your commercial district. Block by block, map out each building, street, and alley. Try to get a local architect student or firm to do this at no cost, or just do it yourself neatly.

Identify on your map a few defining characteristics that will help your analysis. Plot key anchors in your district. Anchors bring people to your district every day. And people—customers and employees—are the basic ingredient in revitalizing your district. Anchors can be

- Large individual businesses, such as grocery stores or banks
- Clusters of similar small businesses that jointly attract high numbers of customers

- Major institutions—hospitals, government buildings, schools, libraries, or museums
- Large employers, such as factories and big companies in office buildings

Find out how many visits these businesses and institutions have every day, on average. These facts will prove the point that your district already has positive activity and will help you attract new businesses.

To complete this assessment, call the city traffic engineering department and get the traffic count map for your main commercial street. Determine where vehicles come from and what time of the day traffic moves in each direction. (The "going-to-work" side of the street is best for donut and coffee stores, for example; the "going-home" side is better for take-out food, videos, flower shops, and banks.) Put this information on your map.

For more tips, see Worksheet 7: Create a Business Map, page 228.

Create a map of businesses and other building uses in your commercial district as a tool to focus discussion and consider alternatives for redevelopment.

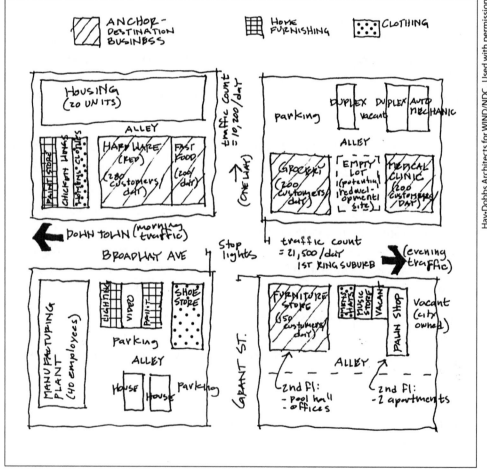

Hay-Dobbs Architects for WIND/NDC. Used with permission

Talk to neighborhood business owners

Now visit with every business owner in your district. Get to know who is doing well, who is not, and why. Find out who their customers are. Look for signs of excellent management and customer service in the successful businesses of your district; would similar practices help other businesses? The market has been expressing itself all along in your district, and businesses that work well today indicate what can work well in the future. Talk to local business owners to discover what motivates a person to locate or not locate in your community.

When talking to business owners, find out what their business plans are and how your organization can help. Do they need financial assistance to fix up their building or expand their business? Do they need business training on particular topics or help finding employees? Are they planning to move and need a buyer or renter for their present facility? You may know the expression "Everyone makes us happy here—some when they come, and some when they leave." A business owner who is planning to move may be a blow to your district, or it may be a great opportunity to replace a negative or neutral owner with a positive one.

Talking to business owners also gives you the opportunity to introduce and explain your organization. Take every opportunity possible to let people know what you're working on, how your work can benefit them and the whole district, and how they can get involved.

If you can get business owners talking, try to get the information requested on Worksheet 8: Talk to Business Owners, page 229. However, you may find that obtaining all this information is too much for one visit. These are busy folks, trying to survive financially every day. Focus on their business during the first visit. Then let them know that you will stop by again soon to get their general impressions of the district—its strengths and weaknesses, the direction the district is going, and the most important things your group can do to improve it.

Visit other commercial districts

Add to your knowledge by talking with business owners outside of your district. Drive through commercial districts in similar inner-city neighborhoods, and visit more upscale districts filled with specialty retailers. Make a list of what works well in each of these: which types of businesses succeed and which add the most to a sense of community.

Based on your observations, list the businesses that you would like to have on your street. Look at how much space these types of businesses use, and think about whether you have any space for a similar store. You may even visit with business owners for a minute and ask whether they would ever consider a second location in your district. No matter how they answer, you will learn a lot about how small business owners view your district and how to approach them in the future.

Also notice which districts appear unified. Look at their public space—sidewalks, streets, and parks. Notice benches, signs, street lighting, or other things that pull the district together. Some of these streetscape elements could be a good addition to your district. In this line of work, there are no rules against copying. If you see something that would enhance your district, then by all means consider ways to add it.

You can also research what other districts around the country have done to improve or re-create their image. An excellent source for this information is the National Trust Main Street Center, particularly in its partnership with Local Initiatives Support Corporation.

Study successful shopping centers

Commercial district revitalization is sometimes compared to shopping center management. Like the manager of a shopping center, you're working with a number of businesses to attract customers to your center or district. It is instructive to briefly look at shopping center techniques.

Why are shopping centers so appealing to modern customers, and how do the managers of shopping centers create this appeal? Here are a few of the pieces of the answer:

- Their stores have common hours, when it is convenient for people to shop. This assures customers that if they come, all the stores will be open.
- The center manages the mix of businesses so they complement one another and create a sense of cohesion. (They don't mix "dollar stores" with high-end furnishings, for instance.)
- The center advertises itself as a unit, with all businesses kicking in via their rent.
- The center is designed with one look, which is updated regularly for a fresh feel.
- Access and parking are convenient and easy to understand for the first-time customer. Customers may need to walk across a big parking lot, but the parking lot is hard to miss, and they can see the store from their parking spot.
- The center ensures constant litter pick up.
- Leases dictate the type of signs permitted and restrict the clutter of window signs.
- Customer behavior is controlled with security personnel.

Shopping centers can do these things because they are privately owned. All of these conditions are enforceable under the terms of their leases and under private property laws. You do not have this ability in your district. However, many of these lessons are valuable in understanding modern retailing and customer expectations; understanding them can help shape your vision and your practices for a district that is equally attractive to customers.

Do three levels of market research

Neighborhood market research seeks to identify who lives and shops in your district, what they shop for, how much they spend on it, what types of stores could be successful in your neighborhood, and who competes for customers. This information is valuable for your work. Since there is a great deal of information available and many ways to get it, it is important to understand what type of market information you need and for what purpose. This can change as your work progresses.

Many community groups start their work without conducting market research. They know they need to fix up old storefronts and clean up trash and graffiti. However, it is beneficial to *all* of your work in commercial district revitalization to have a basic understanding of where your district fits into the larger market around it, and what direction that larger market is moving in. Some of this research can be done by your staff; some of it may require hiring a professional firm.

Following are guidelines for three levels of market research: (1) shoe-leather research; (2) do-it-yourself research; and (3) professional market research. (See the sidebar Three Types of Market Research, below, for a quick summary.)

1. Shoe-leather research. The most basic ways to develop an understanding of your market have already been suggested: Talk to local business owners and residents. Also visit nearby shopping centers and neighborhood commercial districts—a great source of information for what may work in your district. Use these tours to create a map of nearby neighborhood shopping centers and business districts. List all the stores and what they sell, including a sense of whom they sell to (income, ethnicity, and age groupings). Estimate the square footage of these stores.

At a Glance... Three types of market research

It is beneficial to *all* of your work in commercial district revitalization to do market research—to identify who lives and shops in your district, what they shop for, how much they spend on it, what types of stores could be successful in your neighborhood, and who competes for customers. Three levels of market research are summarized below.

1. **Shoe-leather research**—talking to local residents, local business owners, and business owners from outside your community to learn what is needed and what might work in your district. Information gained directly from local decision makers and from direct observation is the most useful of all market research and should be done first.

2. **Do-it-yourself research**—finding basic demographic information and trends about your district at the library or on the Internet. This information may point to certain types of businesses that are badly needed in your community, or to certain opportunities to draw customers from outside your neighborhood.

3. **Professional market research**—paying a firm to look up and analyze national, regional, and local market research. Such firms analyze market data, and they usually have proprietary information to enrich the data.

You can get information about the shopping patterns and preferences of local residents via a survey placed in the neighborhood newspaper or at various community locations such as stores, libraries, and banks. You can also undertake an *intercept survey*, where interviewers stop people on the sidewalk and ask them a few pertinent questions.

Most workers in the field of community economic development will tell you that this level of information—gained directly from local decision makers and from direct observation—is the most useful of all market research. These are the people who ultimately need to shop or invest in your district, regardless of what market research says about trends. You need to be able to affect the decisions of business owners, and listening directly to them is the best way to learn how to do this.

2. Do-it-yourself research. There is a lot of information for your market research on the Internet, at the library, and through city and state government offices. This information may be useful simply to put your local economy into proper context with the broader economy. It could also lead you to new businesses and customers for your district.

First, define the market area. Define the boundaries of your market area, so you can look at information from inside these boundaries. There are three common ways to do this. The way you choose depends on the geographic layout of your market, and how you plan to get data for your market.

Many community groups start by using their own neighborhood boundaries as their market area. This is probably the easiest area to get demographic information about, since most cities maintain such information on a neighborhood level. In spite of the ease of this approach, it misses actual and potential shoppers from outside your area. Your market—areas that include potential shoppers for your district—is usually not the same as the boundaries of your neighborhood, however defined.

A second and better way to define your market area is to locate your commercial district on a city map and then draw three concentric circles around it. Draw these circles out to several distances—one mile, three miles, and five miles from your center point. This approach assumes that people will drive up to one mile for some types of shopping, three miles for other types, and five miles for still other goods and services.

A third and excellent way to define your market area is to draw the actual boundaries in your community that shoppers seldom cross—for example, a major body of water, a freeway, or your downtown area. With these boundaries identified on a map, lay out the same three concentric circles as above. This time, parts of some of these circles will be eliminated because of geographic boundaries.

Second, dig up demographics. Demographics tell you about who lives and shops in your market area. The types of demographic information most useful to understanding your market include

- Population data—numbers of individuals and their age, sex, race, and income
- Household data—household size, race, age, sex, and income
- Projections about what your population and households will look like in the future

This data comes from the U.S. Census information gathered every ten years and updated with projections every three years. You can get census tract information from the U.S. Census Bureau (www.census.gov) or the city planning department. The local library should have this data as well, often along with staff members who can help you find it.

While important, this information may be less useful to you than you hope. For one, it may be outdated; with a census only every ten years, you will have to rely on projections much of the time. Also the census information misses people; historically, the census has undercounted many low-income populations. There are sources of demographics that you can buy (as explained below), but most of these are based on the U.S. Census as well. Community surveys are sometimes used to catch undercounted populations, but these are complex to do and are not common.

If you define your market area with concentric circles that don't correspond to census tracts, however, you may have to buy the information you want from various demographic services. You can purchase this data, customized for your needs, for a few hundred dollars from firms like Claritas or Demographics Now. Some public libraries offer access to these services at no cost.

Next, research national and regional retail trends. Take a quick look at national and regional trends in retailing and office use. This information is quite easy to get on the Internet, and will give you the context within which your neighborhood district is competing for customers.

To start your research, turn to the home page for the U.S. Census Bureau—www.census.gov—and look at the main menu under the category Business. Click on Economic Census. The Economic Census is conducted by the Census Bureau every five years. Comparing the most current census data to previous census data will help you spot major trends. (For more hints on doing this research, see Step 1 in Chapter 7.)

Use this information to look at trends over the past few years. Businesses in sectors and subsectors that are growing will be more promising than those in declining subsectors. Of most interest to you will be the most local data possible (usually at the county or city level), and in subsector categories rather than large sector categories.

The International Council of Shopping Centers is another excellent resource to learn about retail trends. This organization's information, which is available for a fee to nonmembers, has been useful to many groups working on commercial district revitalization. To dig even deeper into the subject of market research, check out *American Demographics* magazine and web site (www.demographics.com), or any of the market analysis books listed in Appendix A.

Finally, study the information. The information you gather should be useful in its raw form to you and to business owners. You may find, for instance, that your market area contains a high percentage of children, or female-heads-of-households, or members of a certain ethnic or immigrant group. Or you may find that just beyond your neighborhood boundary—but well inside a three-mile circle—is a pocket of higher-income families. You may also find that you have more competition in certain types of products than in others.

This raw information may point to certain types of businesses that are badly needed in your community, or to certain opportunities to draw customers from outside your neighborhood. Maybe you could use a cluster of child-related businesses and services, or more stores to serve the Asian or Latino immigrant population. Maybe a nearby wealthy African American community could be attracted to a set of businesses that offer art, entertainment, books, fashion, music, and hair styling oriented to that market.

There are also ways to consider this information in more detail. Community groups will often leave deeper market analysis to hired professionals or teams of well-supervised MBA marketing students. You can take on a deeper analysis on your own (look at the next section, Find Out the Retail Buying Power of Your Community), but be aware that this is complex and time consuming. Also, good market analysis firms use proprietary data to supplement publicly available information.

Use Worksheet 9: Create a Targeted Business List, on page 230, to summarize the results of your market research.

3. Professional market research. Many firms do this type of work. Look for someone with local expertise, if possible, since the national data is already available to you at your library. These studies tend to run in the $10,000 to $25,000 range.

Such firms will start with much the same information as you can dig up on your own. However, they will have the capability to analyze this data in other ways that reveal additional useful information.

Find out the retail buying power of your community

From the basic demographic information you've gathered, you can discover the total income of all the people who live in your market area. A percentage of this income is spent on housing, a percentage on food, a percentage on clothes, and so on. This information defines the *buying power* of your population, by product—something you'll want to know when creating your targeted business list (explained in the next section). You can find this breakdown of household spending from sources mentioned earlier—commercial sources such as Demographics Now and Claritas or your local business library.

You can refine this analysis further with spending percentages sorted by the specific population in your market area. Again, this is useful, since your population has a unique profile of races, ages, income levels, and spending patterns—patterns that differ from the U.S. population as a whole.

Also determine the kinds of stores this buying power can support. Once you know how much money your market area spends on shoes, for example, you can translate this into the number and size of shoe stores that your area can support. (If you have contracted for market research, the firm you have hired will know industry standards for the dollar amount of shoe sales per square foot in a typical shoe store.)

If you want to look at this yourself, go to the library and get industry standards for sales per square foot from sources such as Dun and Bradstreet or Standard & Poor's. Ask the librarian for help, and try to get these standards for the smallest category of stores listed in these sources.

Marketing firms will extrapolate this figure to your entire market area, to show how many square feet of each type of store your community can support with its spending power. They can then see if there is a retail void in your neighborhood that could present an opportunity for a new store.

For instance, if your community can support 5,000 square feet of shoe-store space with its spending power for shoes, but has only one 2,000-square-foot store, you have a 3,000-square-foot retail shoe void in your neighborhood. This suggests an opportunity for a new business, since presumably more than half of your residents are buying their shoes outside of your area. The question is: What kind of shoe store can you use to get some of that business back—women's shoes, athletic shoes, men's dress shoes, or kids' shoes?

Again, this level of analysis is usually best left up to professionals, if you have the money to hire them, or to qualified teams of MBA students. Professionals can also consider the competing districts and shopping centers outside your neighborhood in some depth and evaluate opportunities stemming from differences in shopping patterns of various categories of shoppers by ethnicity, age, education, and other variables. This level of research and analysis is not needed early in your work, but it could become worth the cost later.

Create a targeted business list

Based on your market research, think about what specific *new* businesses would be a perfect addition to your district. A *targeted business list* lays out the best possible businesses to add to your district—the ones that would make the most powerful impact on your community and be economically viable.

If you have a great deal of vacant or underused property, your group will want to actively seek out new businesses. And as you become known for making good things happen on your street, people will come to you if they have space to rent or sell, or if they want to move to your district. In both cases, a targeted business list will help by defining which businesses would be the best addition to your district.

To start developing your targeted business list, answer these questions:

- What types of businesses are needed by the residents of your community and would be viable in your market?
- What types of businesses would complement some of your existing businesses by bringing in customers who would also shop at these stores?
- What types of businesses would fit into the vacant storefronts and office space, as identified in your property inventory?
- What types of businesses would add the most to your community well-being by serving as community gathering places, by adding entrepreneurs who can act as role models, or by providing goods and services your neighborhood needs the most?

Use all the assessment tools listed in Step 1 to begin creating a targeted business list. What new business ideas were mentioned most often by residents and existing business owners? What do competing districts and shopping centers offer that your district doesn't? What types of businesses does your market research suggest you consider?

Also look to see if you have any concentrations of businesses defined by the type of customers they attract or the type of product they sell. These business clusters give your district an image in the mind of the public. The image can be negative if you have tough bars, pawnshops, porn shops, and the like. Or it can be something positive that you can build on, such as a couple of furniture and appliance stores or several African American, Asian, or Latino retailers; these could become a home furnishings cluster or an ethnic cluster.

The last thing to look for is the mix of convenience businesses and destination businesses in your district. *Convenience businesses* serve customers on their daily routes and sell products that customers will not drive very far to get: gas, groceries, pharmacy items, flowers, donuts, videos, and the like. *Destination businesses* sell more expensive or specialty items that people will drive farther to get, such as lawn mowers, refrigerators, sports equipment, and furniture. Destination businesses offer an excellent foundation for your business district since they draw people in from far away to spend money with you. Convenience businesses can fill in around destination businesses to serve local traffic and the neighborhood.

Start simply. Your targeted business list will become more sophisticated over time. The final question on Worksheet 9: Create a Targeted Business List, page 231, provides a space for you to list the businesses you'd like to attract.

Consider your organization's capacity

Revitalizing a run-down inner-city commercial district is a realistic goal for a community-based economic development organization, but it takes time. *Set up for the long haul.* Your organization must be prepared to go hard at it every day for two to four years and produce constant, visible results on a small-to-medium scale (new signs and filled vacant storefronts rather than a large new mall). This is typically the minimum time required to start attracting private, unsubsidized investment into an inner-city commercial district. The effort takes good planning, adequate funding, good staffing, and a sense of humor to balance out the inevitable frustrations.

Step 2: Create a Vision and Strategic Plan

You are now armed with important information about your district—the information you need to create a community vision and a plan for revitalizing your Main Street. Review Tips for Creating Your Vision and Strategic Plan in Chapter 3, pages 44–48, and then get started. The major questions are: What do you want the street to look like in five years? And, how will you get it there? Your organization must build a picture of what you are working for and why. Then you can plan your effort and know when you've succeeded.

Build your vision on two pillars

The "why" of any revitalization vision rests on two pillars: what your community wants and what is economically viable.

Begin with what your community wants. Agreeing on a clear vision for what your commercial district should be like in five years is not easy. People in your community will disagree on this issue. Here are some common visions:

- "Let's make it the way it used to be. Bring back the hardware

Step 2 at a Glance

- Build your vision on two pillars: what your community wants and what is economically viable
- Get widespread input: go door to door, survey, publicize, talk to *everyone*
- Shape your vision and plan

stores, drugstores, dime stores, department stores, shoe stores, ice cream parlors, and family restaurants."

- "Let's make it look like a fancy historic district with lots of small, unique shops."
- "I want this street to bring our community together. Let's get a nice family restaurant (soul food restaurant, café, theater, or coffee shop) where we can see our neighbors once in a while."

These dreams must be balanced by the second pillar: the realities of actually attracting such businesses in today's world and having them succeed. Your district ought to look better *and* function better economically. Eventually it must attract a constant flow of cash-paying customers and private business investments—without the need for your organization's subsidies.

Presumably you are revitalizing your commercial district with and for *existing* residents and businesses rather than for a new wave of folks with money. Look hard at the type and number of businesses your residents actually can support and how residents' spending can be supplemented by shoppers who come from other neighborhoods.

Get widespread input

You can get community input and opinions in a variety of ways. Using several of the following techniques is better than using just one. At the very least, talk with all of the key groups in your community that are affected by the condition of your commercial district: businesses in the district; residents who live nearby; and nearby institutions such as schools, churches, libraries, and fraternal and charitable organizations.

For a second time, go door-to-door to all businesses in your district. When assessing conditions in your commercial district, you met with business owners to learn about their current operations and plans for the future. If you had enough time, you also asked for their impressions of the district as a whole. Now revisit the owners who didn't have time for this broader question. Ask them:

- What is your image of this district today?
- What would you prefer the district to be like in five years?
- What are the most important things needed to improve the district?
- How would you like to improve your own business if you could get a little help?
- Who shops at your business now? What type of customers would you like to attract? What other types of businesses would draw in customers who would also shop in your store?

- Would you be willing to attend a few meetings to help guide this revitalization effort?

Go to public meetings of residents and businesses. These take place at churches, local organizations, and schools. You can also hold your own special community meetings. Explain what your organization is doing, and give a few examples of what other communities have done.

Ask people to dream five years down the road and describe the businesses they would like to go to for a quick shopping trip or an outing with family or friends. Also ask people to dream about the appearance of their district—how the storefronts, sidewalks, and lighting could look better. In addition, get ideas for a theme that could tie the district together, such as an historical period or a prominent type of business.

Finally, ask people about specific conditions in your district as it exists today: parking, litter, graffiti, and safety. Find out where they go to shop (besides your commercial district) and what they enjoy about those places.

Use survey forms to get resident opinions. Knock on doors in your neighborhood and drop off written survey forms. On these forms, include the questions listed in the sidebar Sample Questions for Your Survey Form, on this page. Offer convenient ways for returning the survey if the person isn't home—a drop-off box at a handy place like a bank lobby or a self-addressed stamped envelope. Or go back to pick up the survey the next day.

Besides door-to-door distribution, you can put survey forms in your community paper, at local businesses, and at other neighborhood locations. Ask business owners to help get surveys filled out. Another option: Pay local teens to stand outside of businesses and ask people to fill out these surveys.

Publicize your effort. For example, place articles in the community newspaper about your revitalization effort and ask for input. Make it easy for people to respond. Include your organization's phone number, street address, and e-mail address.

Talk to key individuals in your community. Ask these people for their input, one on one: local elected officials, school leaders, church leaders, and leaders of nonprofit organizations, American Legions, Lions Clubs, and similar organizations. Talk with city planning and development officials to see what they've planned for your district in the next five to ten years.

Sample questions for your survey form

- How often do you shop on *[insert the name of your main commercial street]*?
- What do you shop for when you go there?
- What else would you buy there, if it were available?
- Where do you go to buy these items now?
- What is your impression of the street—its strengths and weaknesses?
- What's needed to make this district better—for example, new types of stores, new streetscape elements, or better safety?

Shape your vision and plan

Now write the first draft of a vision statement and long-term and short-term goals for your commercial district. Base these on the feedback from your neighborhood and the ideas from your research.

Review the assessment you conducted. Did the people you spoke with express a strong interest in removing a particularly bad building or bringing in a certain type of business? Did your property inventory reveal a number of run-down or empty buildings and vacant lots? Is litter and graffiti a major problem? How much did crime dominate your conversations? Did you learn about new businesses, new designs, or new district management techniques when you visited other areas? What did your market research reveal to you about strong trends in small-scale retailing? Where could these fit in on your street? What about mixed-use buildings, with housing above and retail below?[13]

An example of a vision statement could be: "Five years from now, our commercial district will be a major asset and driving force in our broader neighborhood development because of the continual improvements that take place there. Our organization's activities will be a major cause of this change." Long-term goals could include, for example, "We will fill half of our street-level vacancies with good retail businesses, attracting a family restaurant, and renovate half of all deteriorated facades." Short-term goals could include, "We will operate a consistent litter and graffiti cleanup campaign, conduct three storefront renovations, and obtain a beat cop for peak hours."

When you've got a draft vision statement and goals in hand, present them to the community and ask for reactions. Convene a special meeting of your organization just for this purpose and get on the agenda at other community meetings. Use architects and maps to stimulate thought and get everyone on the same page. Put your draft vision and goals in the local paper. Publicize them, explain them, discuss them.

Once you've conducted a widespread discussion with as much interest as you can generate, set up a meeting with your board members to discuss and finalize your vision, long-term (three-year) goals, and short-term (one-year) goals. From there, devise a work plan for the next twelve months.

For more detailed instructions on shaping your vision, see the following worksheets:

- Worksheet 10: Write a Vision Statement for Your Commercial District, page 232.
- Worksheet 11: Write Three-Year Goals for Your Commercial District, page 233.
- Worksheet 12: Write One-Year Goals for Your Commercial District, page 235.

---

[13] The Congress for New Urbanism is an excellent source for material on how urban commercial districts originally functioned and how many redevelopment strategists are returning to these concepts.

Step 3: Implement Your Plan

Now that you have a vision and goals for your commercial district and your organization is set up to achieve them, assemble your implementation tools—the services you will offer, the programs you will undertake, and the funds you have to work with. First take a minute to review the sidebar ALERT! Common Reasons for Failure with Commercial District Revitalization, on page 58.

Choose which tools to use first

What implementation tools should you develop first? The answer depends on your situation and what you hope to achieve. Here are a few tips for choosing your first tools.

Develop a coordinated set of tools to accomplish your plan. Over the next few years, your group will address a variety of problems in your district, as laid out in your vision and plan. These problems are connected to each other in significant ways, and each of the tools you use to solve them should be connected and coordinated as well.

For example, vacant storefronts result from people believing there is no opportunity to succeed in business in your district. This belief can come from a lack of customers, an overall run-down appearance of buildings and public space, or both these factors. To attract customers and fill these storefronts, many buildings may need to be fixed up first. However, their owners may not want to invest if they are highly concerned about crime in the district. Customers may also be staying away because of a negative image of your district, or simply because it isn't on their "map."

While there is no magic formula or ironclad rule about which tools to develop first and which come later, they should flow in a logical order from one to the next, and they should complement one another. Storefronts improved with the help of loans, grants, and design assistance should convey the same image as your customer-marketing and business-attraction campaigns—and vice versa. Your vision and plan are comprehensive and coordinated. Make sure your tools are as well.

Consider where other groups begin. Many inner-city commercial districts have to spend their first years dealing with the basics: litter, empty buildings, run-down storefronts, and a lack of good businesses. Some have to deal with crime reduction before anything else. Other districts are in shape to begin promotional efforts—special events and publicity—right away.

Step 3 at a Glance

In Step 3, you'll learn about thirteen tools you can use to help build your commercial district revitalization plan:

Tool 1: Cleanup campaigns

Tool 2: Partnering with existing loan funds

Tool 3: Operating your own loan fund

Tool 4:   Grant funds for storefront improvement

Tool 5: Storefront design

Tool 6: Streetscape projects

Tool 7: Business attraction

Tool 8: Marketing your district to consumers

Tool 9: Addressing crime

Tool 10: Lessons from shopping center management

Tool 11: Parking development

Tool 12: Real estate development

Tool 13: Business improvement districts

The goals of creating visible change and engaging existing business owners and residents lead many community organizations to begin with the following combination of tools:

- Improving general neighborhood appearance with a litter and graffiti clean-up campaign.
- Stimulating storefront improvements by partnering with existing loan funds, operating your own loan fund, using a grant fund for storefront improvements, and using storefront design.
- Filling empty storefronts through business attraction.

This mix of tools makes sense. A continual stream of storefront renovations will be eye-catching and make significant improvements. Renovations involve existing business and building owners, thereby convincing them that the revitalization effort includes them—in fact, that it begins with them. Offering a combination of favorable loans, small matching grants, and quick, customized storefront designs is a great way to build interest in such projects. And as these projects add up, district-wide design guidelines create a unified feel.

In the same light, assisting your existing businesses to improve connects your organization immediately to all of these business owners. If you bring them resources that are valuable to the survival and growth of their small business—such as a loan, grant, or free architectural design—they will speak well of your organization, speak well of the district, and be more inclined to volunteer for your board or committees.

Your first storefront improvement project, however, may take three to six months. Therefore, start immediately with a cleanup campaign to signal that something new and positive is happening—attack litter, weeds, and graffiti. The cleanup can involve many people in your community, which also creates ambassadors for your effort.

If you're faced with more than one small vacant storefront every block—or enough vacancies to create the impression of a half-dead district—then also undertake a business-attraction campaign right away. (Districts with only a few vacancies can put this tool off until later; even vibrant districts have some vacancies at any given moment.)

Consider your resources. How many hours do your staff members, board members, and volunteers have for revitalization efforts each month, and what skills can they apply? Also think about available funds. Talk with

- People from other community economic development organizations in your region. Find out where these organizations get their funding and ask about their budget for development activities. This will give you good insight into how much money you'll need.

- Program officers of local foundations and corporate contribution departments. If you can get these people on the phone, ask them in just a few sentences whether your goals and any of these tools are eligible for their funds.

- People in economic development at city and state levels. See if they'll fund any of your tools.

Finally, consider resources beyond your organization. Examples include local banks, which are often interested in partnerships with groups like yours and have in-depth knowledge about business conditions and lending programs. In addition, talk with other nonprofit organizations and appropriate government agencies to see if they can work with you on any implementation tools.

Tool 1: Cleanup campaigns

Consider a cleanup campaign early on in your revitalization effort. There is no easier way to tell the world that a new day has come than to pick up litter, clean off graffiti, get rid of junk, and pull out weeds. After you've done one cleanup campaign, keep doing it. Slowly you will convert skeptics into participants.

Community organizations all over America are great at doing cleanups. Some send out squads of school kids each week to pick up the litter. Others use Boy Scouts and Girl Scouts, college organizations, or religious groups. And some use "sentence-to-service" offenders from the court system. Clean up early and clean up often.

Beyond the basic pickup- and wipeout-approach, look into getting trash receptacles installed in your district. These become part of your streetscape (see Tool 5: Storefront design below). Put your district's logo on the receptacles; they'll serve a marketing function as well as a cleanup function.

Getting these receptacles emptied is part of the challenge. Many city governments will do this for neighborhood districts. Otherwise, enlist local businesses to adopt trash receptacles and keep them emptied.

Some community groups go in jointly for maintenance services, such as snow removal and power washing for sidewalks and buildings. This collaboration can be organized by your group and paid for by passing the hat each time. Or you can set up a business improvement district (Tool 13). This tool adds a small amount to all property tax bills along your commercial corridor, with the funds going for costs such as professional cleanup services.

Tool 2: Partnering with existing loan funds

An excellent way to get business and property owners to consider visible improvements or business expansion is to make these efforts affordable through favorable loan and grant programs. Often community groups offer both loans and grants in their district, but either program by itself can also be useful.

There are two basic ways your group can create a loan program: promote and facilitate the use of someone else's money (explained in this section), or create your own fund and do all the work of lending yourself (explained in Tool 3).

Look first for loan funds already available to local businesses from banks, other nonprofits, and the government. Many times these entities have excellent programs that you can work with rather than create and administer your own funds.

Discuss methods of making existing funds more useful in your area while tying your goals to these funds. One simple idea is for your organization to promote a particular loan program door-to-door to your businesses. In return, try to negotiate better lending terms and a faster turnaround time on loans for deals that help achieve your goals.

Loan packaging refers to steps that help a busy lender consider small or risky deals. It includes loan application preparation, preliminary analysis, assembling financing sources, and structuring the deal.

Loan application preparation consists of helping the business owner assemble and improve all the documents required by the bank—usually a business plan, cash flow projections, financial statements, tax returns, and the actual application form.

Preliminary analysis includes checking the assumptions, management systems, and numbers for obvious problems before the loan officer reviews the application in greater detail.

Assembling financing sources includes attracting multiple sources—such as a bank loan, government or nonprofit loan fund, and the owner's equity—into a joint finance package.

Structuring the deal is piecing together different amounts, terms, and interest rates from each of the financing sources to match the borrower's and the lenders' goals.

It is not necessary to do all these tasks. Just consider those tasks for which your organization is qualified. Also, your relationships with banks should be spread around to different banks, provided they are being helpful. You do not want to promote one particular bank to the exclusion of others.

Tool 3: Operating your own loan fund

After exploring partnerships with existing loan funds, many community groups decide that they really need to operate their own. Reasons for such a decision include the following:

- Local businesses may have a hard time getting loans for storefront improvement projects, even with the organizations' assistance. Their deals may be too small for banks or their "credit-worthiness" too thin.
- Interest rates and fees of other loan funds may be too high to entice businesses to use them.
- Organizations with their own fund are able to promote their community vision, since they can tie revitalization goals to the terms of the loan.

Typical uses of loan programs for commercial district revitalization include visible storefront improvements such as new awnings, large storefront windows that replace plywood or fake stone, a new coat of paint, and new signage. Parking lot development is also common, including landscaping, paving, and signage of lots. Many groups extend their loan funds to business expansion uses, such as working capital for new product lines, new equipment, or new buildings.

Typical constraints on these loan programs are that borrowers agree to make improvements that are visible to the main street and that follow the organization's design guidelines (no bright orange, metal buildings!). Business expansion loans will generally require adherence to the same design guidelines and give priority to expansions that meet the goals of the organization (for example, to build up targeted clusters of businesses).

Lending to existing businesses in your commercial district is generally less complicated than lending to new microbusinesses. However, you may benefit from jumping to the section in Chapter 5 on lending (pages 123–132), where you can find additional suggestions for operating a loan fund.

Find a source of funds. Finding sources of loan funds involves the same fundraising expeditions that you go on for overhead dollars. Look first to government agencies, foundations, and corporations.[14] Often these funders will be interested in your requests *if* you can prove competence in managing a loan fund, so get one or two experienced commercial lenders on your loan fund committee. Banks may also be a source of loan fund capital. Review the sections Focus Locally and Remember the "Feds" in Chapter 2 on pages 25–26 for more information.

Another option involves working with a group of banks to create a pool of loan funds, perhaps combined with some grant funds. The banks spread out the risk of these deals by each taking a part of every loan rather than the whole loan; if the deal goes bad, they lose only a small portion. By building grant funds into this pool, you can cover part of a loss for each bank, so the risk is reduced even further. In addition, each bank has a commercial lender on the loan committee and can opt out of deals if they choose. This is a good way to create a sizable loan fund without the need to raise most of the money for it.

---

[14] To search for government funding, start at www.firstgov.gov; for foundation funding, start at the Foundation Center, www.fdncenter.org.

Choose your lending terms. Among organizations dedicated to community economic development, lending terms vary quite a bit.

Loan size varies with a group's goals and with the size of the loan fund. Typical storefront improvement projects cost $5,000 to $25,000. Most groups will make loans up to $25,000. (If your entire loan fund is $100,000, however, you probably won't want to use one-fourth of it on one loan.) Be flexible enough to make small loans, down to $1,000 or less, to help the small projects. If you have the funds and have a goal of business expansion, then going up to $50,000 can leverage a good amount of other funds to assist a major business expansion on your avenue.

Leverage refers to the amount of other people's money that is required to go along with your funds on a deal. Most groups require at least a 10 percent or 20 percent cash participation by the business owner. In addition, some groups will only put in 50 percent of a deal from their funds, requiring the balance to come from another source. This is not a good idea if you are working on tough deals that banks are likely to avoid. It *is* a good way, however, to stretch your loan dollars if you have some projects that are nearly "bankable" that you can assist.

Collateral requirements also vary considerably. Some groups do not require any collateral for smaller loans of under $5,000. Some require 100 percent collateral coverage of their loan, while others will lower that somewhat to achieve their goals. In any case, most groups will accept a subordinated position on collateral to a participating bank—that is, the bank gets to recover its loan from the sale of collateral first, in the event of loan default, and your group gets any funds that are left from that sale to recoup your loss.

Credit histories and tax returns are usually examined before making a loan, although some groups skip this step for smaller loans of less than $5,000. As with much of this effort, you are in a narrow window between the very low risk that banks take in their lending and your own definition of unacceptably high risk. Each group treats this differently. As you design your standards, weigh your banker's advice against your mission statement.

Most groups require their loan to be paid off in full if borrowers move their business from the community. The typical language in a loan agreement states that the loan is "due and payable if the borrower moves within three or five years."

Use these administration tips. As you begin operating your own loan fund, keep the following in mind:

- *Operate with consistency.* Don't give one business a better interest rate or term than the next. If you build flexibility into your terms, be clear up front that the conditions for one loan may be different from the next one.
- *Operate with good process.* The decision-making process must be seen as fair, well informed, and impartial.

- *Operate with confidentiality.* Any time that you ask people to submit financial or other private information, maintain strict confidentiality. Your organization's credibility is at stake, and you would be in legal trouble if everyone on the street learns such information about a business. One option is for confidential material to be reviewed by one person only, such as an experienced banker.

- *Operate with quick response and turnaround time.* With banks giving one-hour loan decisions, people will not be impressed if your organization takes two months to deliberate on their loan application. Two to four weeks at the most should be the time between a complete loan application and a closed loan.

- *Keep it simple.* Business owners hate red tape. Now that you are creating your own loan fund, don't overbuild your paperwork and process requirements. This is especially true for loans that range from $1,000 to $5,000.

- *Promote your program to every eligible business on the same day,* if possible. Hand out a flyer to everyone at the same time so no one feels that other business owners got an unfair advantage.

- *Remember that choosing between eligible projects, particularly if you are running out of funds, can be tricky.* Stick with your vision. Fund projects that are most consistent with your plan and that will make the biggest impact on your revitalization effort. And state clearly in your marketing materials that you will do this!

> ### How much do you need for a loan fund?
>
> How much do you need for a loan fund? It depends both on the number of buildings and businesses you want to improve, and the average size loan you need to make to get good projects done. For example, consider a group with $120,000 in loan funds to be used for storefront improvement projects. The group can assist 24 projects with loans of $5,000 each the first cycle of lending. As the repayments come in, the funds can be lent a second and third time. This "revolving" feature of loan funds allows the group to have ongoing impact on a commercial district without the need for enormous amounts of capital up front.

Establish a loan committee. Generally, a loan committee consists of your organization's board of directors. Occasionally you can add a few outside persons with skills in particular areas, such as banking, construction, law, or architecture. An alternative is to set up your committee with all outside professionals.

Many loan committees consist mainly of board members who are also local business owners. This enhances local business owners' feeling of ownership of the program. In addition, loan committee members have local knowledge of each applicant. But it can also create problems of trust and confidentiality. Given that you are likely to have a committee with at least some neighbors deciding on loans to other neighbors, it is even more crucial that you set up your guidelines clearly, market your fund evenly, and operate it consistently. In addition, be sure to maintain clear and complete minutes from all loan committee meetings.

Train your staff and seek outside resources. Underwriting (evaluating and presenting) loan requests, closing loans, and servicing loans are a great deal of work and quite technical. Many neighborhood groups do these tasks and do them well. Staff should attend loan fund management training available from the National Development Council, the Association for Enterprise Opportunity, your state bankers association, and others. Any or all of this work can be outsourced, if you can find a bank or experienced nonprofit willing to do it for you. The banker on your loan committee will be key to helping you set up the necessary documents and procedures.

Consider whether any other entity can manage the "backroom" functions of your loan fund. While your group is out promoting the loans, some other group can do the work of underwriting loans, writing up reports to your loan committee, putting together the documents, closing the loan, and servicing it until it is repaid. All of these functions involve detailed and specialized work; contracting with a trusted organization to do them is an excellent option, if it is available.

Setting up loan procedures, guidelines, and forms requires a good deal of care. It is important to obtain solid banking and legal help. Find a commercial lender from a local bank who has experience with small loans, and who is known for being proactive and creative in lending to small businesses.

Tool 4: Grant funds for storefront improvement

Some city development agencies have grant programs for storefront improvement—programs that you can actively promote in your district. If no one offers business grants of any kind in your district, then consider raising funds for your own grant fund. Offering small grants for specific types of visible improvements is an excellent way to act on your strategic plan.

There are many similarities between starting and operating a grant fund and a loan fund, so review the previous section on partnering with existing loan funds closely. Look especially at the administration tips in that section; they apply to grant funds as well.

Most funds specify a maximum dollar amount for each grant. And most community groups offer matching grants, generally covering no more than 50 percent or 60 percent of the costs for a storefront improvement. The rest of the funds come from the business owner's pocket or debt that owners take out. Even if you grant only 25 percent of a project cost, this may stimulate many business owners to fix up their storefront. Owners often realize that their business ultimately benefits the most.

Sample exterior improvement loan structure

Following is a sample business loan for exterior improvement.

Uses of cash

$9,000	Paint building
$4,000	New awning
$8,000	Construct new storefront window
$9,000	Pave and landscape lot
$5,000	New signage
$2,000	Fees and permits
$3,000	Architect
$40,000	Total

Sources of cash

$8,000	Owner's equity
$22,000	Bank loan
$10,000	City or nonprofit loan (subordinated position on collateral)
$40,000	Total

Typical uses of a storefront improvement grant include

- New business signage
- Rebuilding or restoring storefront display windows
- Exterior lighting
- Cleaning and tuck-pointing brick
- Painting the exterior and installing new awnings
- Parking lot paving
- Landscaping

Building improvements that are not visible to the commercial street are often not eligible, except for security items, such as additional exterior lighting or security systems. While these are not visible items, they support the safety goals of most community groups and get the attention of business owners who care less about paint and more about crime.

Some groups offer higher matching grants—up to $50,000—on larger renovation projects of key buildings in their district. These still require at least 50 percent private investment of debt.

Typical constraints on storefront grant programs start with design. Most community groups require the business owner to follow certain design guidelines. This is done to develop a district that over time has some feel of unity. Most groups also require that the business remain in the building being renovated for three to five years; if the business moves out earlier, the owner repays a portion of the grant. (You could waive this repayment feature if the next user of this property retains the improvements.)

Tool 5: Storefront design

The design of storefront improvements is both a matter of unifying your commercial district and of private taste. So, approach this tool cautiously.

On the one hand, you don't want to anger property owners with too many dictates that are, after all, a matter of taste. Small business owners are an independent bunch. Often these people have a strong belief that no one should dictate to them the type of awnings to install or the colors to paint their building. Yes, it's important to have design guidelines. It's also important to be realistic in the eyes of business owners. You must sell your guidelines to these owners and maintain some flexibility in their application.

On the other hand, you will be sorely disappointed if the storefront project you just worked so hard on turns out to look ugly. It happens. Almost as bad are adjoining storefront projects that look fairly good on their own but clash with each other—for instance, when a plastic, backlit orange awning explodes next to an old-fashioned yellow canvas awning. Setting up storefront design guidelines for your district is a good way to keep such design clashes to a minimum and help building owners understand the overall look that your organization wants.

Create design guidelines with widespread input. Developing design guidelines should be a public process. Setting up a design committee offers a good opportunity to involve residents with business owners. (Such a committee could also work on streetscape design, Tool 6.)

Most community groups hire an architect to help set up design guidelines for their district, while some groups set up guidelines on their own. In either case, go back to your original vision statement. What look and feel are you trying to achieve in your district? What types of customers and businesses are you trying to attract into your area? What do the buildings need to look like in order to achieve that vision?

Design guidelines vary from group to group. In practice, most groups keep design guidelines fairly simple and affordable by emphasizing the original design and materials on every building. Most older commercial buildings were constructed using excellent materials and a design that would be expensive to replicate today and that seldom look better covered up with anything. Therefore, most groups have design guidelines that promote removing all cover-up materials—stucco, wood, metal—and returning to the original look as much as possible. Some groups also promote the use of a certain type of awning, color scheme, or type of sign that can tie the district together visually.

Furthermore, most groups promote restoration of the original, large storefront windows. This looks better and brings in more customers who can now see what the business offers. The windows also put more "eyes" on the street, contributing to safety. This is not the same as *historic restoration*: restoring every detail of the original building, from the cornices and placement of doors, windows, and chimneys to the color and style of the building trim. While beautiful and worthwhile in certain situations, restoration is mostly done in higher-income districts where the spending power of affluent customers justifies costly renovation.

Instead, establish guidelines that encourage a return to original materials and design and preserve elements that may have historic significance. In this way you respect the history of the buildings and make use of good original design and craftsmanship. You also keep the project attractive and affordable.

Promote your guidelines. Now that you have design guidelines, how do you make use of them? Typically, community groups incorporate the guidelines into their loan and grant programs. Rarely does an organization have any way to enforce design guidelines on businesses except through the "carrot" approach. This means using the lure of lower-interest loans and grants along with help in cutting through red tape to convince building owners to use your design guidelines.

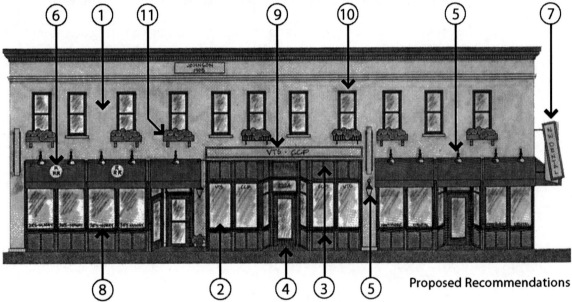

Proposed Recommendations

1 — Clean existing brick
2 — Anodized aluminum storefronts
3 — Wood bases and upper transom panels
4 — Tiled entries
5 — Goose-neck lighting above awnings
    and historical lights

6 — Awnings with signage
7 — Perpendicular signage
8 — Stenciled signage on windows and doors
9 — Wood sign above storefront
10 — New storm windows to match the new storefronts
11 — Wood or wrought-iron flower boxes

Design guidelines vary from group to group. In practice, most groups keep design guidelines fairly simple and affordable by emphasizing the original design and materials on every building. Above are design guidelines created by DJR Architecture, Inc., for the Central Avenue Mainstreet Project, a program of the Northeast Economic Development Council in Minneapolis, Minnesota. The architect used an existing building in the Central Avenue commercial district as an example.

Even with such a lure, you must sell your guidelines. You will get nowhere if you come on too strongly about what "we" want for "your" building. So talk about your guidelines as a help to business owners—a tool that makes the district look unified and makes their businesses more attractive to customers. The best approach is to actually get your architect to do a few sketches depicting what owners' buildings could look like. If this is done quickly and at no cost or obligation, most owners get interested—especially if your architect has incorporated many of the owners' ideas.

Tool 6: Streetscape projects

Streetscape projects are attractive visual additions made to the public spaces in your community, particularly its sidewalks and streets. Revitalization groups often take on these projects because they are an effective way to change the feel of their district in one large-scale project. Also, streetscape projects take place on public land, where community groups and city government are the key decision makers.

Streetscape projects typically involve items that lend a unifying design, color, logo, or graphic to your commercial district, such as:

- Banners
- Benches
- Wrought-iron fencing and bollards (short posts)
- Planters and landscaping
- Signage for parking, street names, business clusters, and related uses
- Decorative streetlights
- Pocket parks—interesting use of small empty spaces
- Gateway elements—design features that greet visitors at the entrances to your district
- Trees and other plantings
- Bus shelters
- Unique paving on sidewalks and streets at intersections
- Unique trash containers
- Pedestrian-friendly design for your street. Examples are sidewalk bump-outs or islands in the center of the street where pedestrians can wait if necessary. Bump-outs and center islands can also hold other streetscape elements.

Form a streetscape committee. Such committees commonly involve local businesses, residents, and other interested parties. Often the committee will also work on storefront design guidelines for the district.

Your streetscape committee may only exist for six to twelve months. Even so, this is an excellent time to get area residents involved with local businesses. After all,

Streetscape projects have a high visual impact. Little else will change the appearance of the street as dramatically as a well-designed streetscape. Here, the Riverview Economic Development Association used streetscape elements such as public art, benches, banners, and public gardens to help define District del Sol, a commercial district in St. Paul, Minnesota.

streetscape projects will be a visible addition to their community, and residents can have a major hand in creating these projects.

Consider inviting someone from your city public works department to the streetscape committee. Just like any interested party, public works officials appreciate being involved early. And this department will have a lot to say about anything put on public space. For example, sidewalks cover electrical, gas, and water lines; must be kept clear; and must be wide enough at every point to accommodate wheelchairs.

Most streetscape committees bring in an architect to assist in developing the project. (Some also use local artists in teams with an architect.) Have your committee interview several architectural firms. Look for an architect who has a good record of doing streetscape projects in commercial districts; visit these streets if possible to see how they look. Also look at the architect's track record in working with community groups and districts such as yours. When you have architects competing to do a project, describe the project clearly in writing. And check references!

Get the money together. Before you start designing streetscape projects, get some idea about where you can find the money and how much you can get. Funds for streetscape projects typically come from three sources:

1. Grants from foundations, corporations, and local businesses
2. Grants from public entities (city, state, and federal)
3. Self-taxation or business improvement districts

Streetscape projects are major undertakings, in part because they cost a considerable amount of money. Worse, there is no single interested party to pay the cost, as when you work on a building renovation with its owner. Besides buying the streetscape elements, the architect, installation, and ongoing maintenance and replacement must be paid for.

All told, these projects often run in the range of $100,000 to $500,000 or more for a one-mile district, even without streetlights and gateway projects. (These are the most expensive features to add; banners are probably the least expensive.)

Given the high cost of streetscape projects, it is fair to again ask, *Why are we doing this?* The answer is that streetscape projects have high visual impact. Little else will change the appearance of the street as much as a well-designed streetscape project. And as long as the city cooperates, you have control over these projects. Choosing what to do with a public space can be easier than convincing property owners to improve their buildings.

Rank your desired streetscape elements by priority, based on cost and visual impact. Implement streetscape changes in phases over a number of years. Finally, remember to tie your streetscape project into your other strategies—the image you may be developing with a branding and marketing campaign, and with your storefront design guidelines. Keep all of these visual and marketing messages consistent, and they will be much more powerful.

Budget to maintain your project. After your wonderful project has been up for a week, it will begin to age: Someone may skid off the road and hit a sign or bench. A banner may tear. Graffiti could mess up your new trash container.

For these reasons, you must have a replacement-and-repair fund built into your initial budget and a way to replenish it over time. This fund can go as high as 50 percent of the original purchase and installation budget, although usually it is much lower.

You might also buy a few extras of each streetscape element right away and store them for future use. Buy cans of touch-up paint from the manufacturer to cover inevitable scratches or graffiti.

Also look for no-cost ways to maintain your elements. Find out if your city public works department would empty your trash containers, as they do in many cities. Enlist nearby businesses, residents, retired people, and youth groups to adopt a planter for a summer.

Create and implement your design. The design of streetscape items is the most important aspect of this project—and the most fun. Hold a series of planning meetings so that your architect can find out what people want the district to look like in the near future. At this early point, do not limit your initial creative process by worrying about costs. This consideration will come into play soon enough.

As you gather ideas, draw heavily from the vision that you have already created for your district and any design guidelines you created for building renovation projects. Also develop a number of maps of your district that begin to analyze possible locations for some of these elements.

Your architect can then translate this input into a preliminary layout of streetscape elements. To get ideas and to see what these items cost, look at catalogs of benches, trash containers, streetlights, and other streetscape elements.[15] (Pre-made elements will cost considerably less than custom-made elements.) Consider ways to involve local youth to help with parts of designing or implementing this project.

Features of good streetscape projects often include

- Repetition of elements along the avenue to create a sense of unity for the district.
- Use of a simple colorful logo, graphic, or slogan to highlight your marketing identity. (See Tool 8: Marketing Your District to Consumers.)

---

[15] Two resources for streetscape elements are Sweet's Product Marketplace (www.sweets. construction.com) and Landscape Forms (www.landscapeforms.com).

- Major elements at the entry points to your commercial district—gateway signature pieces—to make people aware they are entering a unique district.
- Durability—for instance, metal banners instead of cloth ones.

When your streetscape committee has narrowed down its ideas to a few, put these ideas out to the community for review and comments. Also hold a community meeting to publicize your design options. Afterwards, meet with your streetscape committee and board to consider community reaction, finalize the plan, and get the project started.

Use public art. An excellent extension of a streetscape design is using public art as a tool. Forms of public art that are commonly used in commercial district revitalization include

- Murals painted on walls.
- Bridges and overpasses painted with designs.
- Gateway projects that are uniquely designed—distinct from, but compatible with, other streetscape elements.
- Art work in parks: fountains, sidewalk paving designs, plantings, and actual art pieces such as photo exhibits and sculpture gardens.

These projects are a great way to involve local youth and local artists, capture the spirit of the community, and share your group's vision. Youth of all ages from local schools are often recruited to work with an artist to help make individual pieces of the work of art—for example, individualized ceramic tiles that make up a sidewalk or wall. This brings kids and their families down to the avenue with a sense of ownership and pride, tying residents in with businesses.

You should note that maintenance of public art can be even harder than other streetscape elements, since these projects are one-of-a-kind. Careful consideration of this issue, in advance, with the original artist, is crucial.

Tool 7: Business attraction

One of the highest impact results you can get in commercial district revitalization occurs when you fill an empty building with a new business. This creates excitement and reaffirms the decision that your district is a good place to locate. And with a new business generally comes a building renovation that lights up the area.

Like most revitalization efforts, attracting new businesses to your district takes planning and persistence. Businesses do not establish new locations easily and have many options when they do.

Planning your business attraction effort begins with your property and business inventory list and your targeted business list. With these lists in hand, you know which buildings you are trying to fill and which businesses you are trying to bring in. Now put your business attraction pitch and materials together and get as much help as possible in reaching out to prospective businesses.

Review practical considerations. The planning and preparation outlined in this book should never prevent you from spontaneous action. At any point you can just pick up the phone and call the owner of a particular business that you feel would be perfect in your neighborhood.

Most revitalization groups never "steal" businesses from another low-income community by actively recruiting their businesses; your gain becomes the other neighborhood's loss. Instead, look for existing targeted businesses that want to start an additional location in your community. If a business you contact wants to move out of its present community altogether, inform the community group in that neighborhood immediately, so it has a chance to retain the business.

In business attraction you are marketing properties you don't own. Explain that your group is a nonprofit, that you cannot take a broker fee (unless you are a licensed real estate agent), and that you will reap no benefit when a business moves into your neighborhood. Furthermore, be clear that you are not vouching for the seller or the buyer, the renter or the landlord; and, by all means, stay out of the negotiations. You do not want to be blamed for an unfair price or some other unfortunate turn of events later.

Business attraction can be sold as a benefit that your organization provides to local property owners, and it offers a great way to engage them in your effort. But while you are trying to find the perfect targeted business for their space, building owners are usually looking for *anyone* who can pay the rent. This means you have to move quickly. Don't waste your time on properties where the building owner is uncooperative.

Things can get even trickier when an existing business owner vehemently opposes your bringing in a competing business. Retail experts believe that competition is good; it draws more customers into your district, gives the existing business more exposure, and forces everyone to improve. This argument does not always impress small business owners, however. The key is knowing why you are trying to bring in a competing business and, if you are, to work closely with the existing business owner to build up that store's competitive edge.

Review, refine, and update your targeted business list. If you haven't created your targeted business list, do so now (see pages 68–69 in this chapter). Try to match all the ideas for new businesses with actual spaces on your property inventory. Do a quick ranking of your targeted businesses and think about particular buildings and parts of your district that will match particular businesses on your list.

In the process, ask these questions:

- Can you weed out unpromising matches of available space and prospective businesses? For instance, most grocery stores today want either very large or very small spaces at low cost and at high-traffic locations. If you don't have such space available, you should save your time trying to attract a grocery store unless you have a good lead to follow.

- Are there any small clusters of similar businesses that you want to build upon, like home furnishings, Latino or Asian retailers, or antiques?

- Is there a desire for creating community gathering places, like a soul food restaurant or a coffee shop?

- Which types of retailers are growing in number (coffee shops, perhaps) and which kind are diminishing (rental videos)?[16]

- Are there any franchises you would like to see in your district? To find trends and details about possible franchises, look at *Franchising World*, an industry trade magazine. Some national business magazines have annual franchise editions that are worth looking at as well.

- Does your commercial district have any empty office space or light manufacturing space for businesses that can grow great jobs for your neighborhood? (See Chapter 7 for more information on this strategy.)

Keep building your list as you get new leads and information. You will use it continually to guide your business-attraction campaign.

Locate the people who own businesses you have targeted. Finding the owners of targeted businesses is the next trick. The easiest way is to take out the Yellow Pages phone book and go to a targeted category of businesses. Look for businesses with more than one location, often indicating an appetite for growth. Also look for those that are not in your market but located nearby, in markets that are roughly similar to yours.

Also use other ways to locate owners of targeted businesses:

- Use personal contacts from your board, other local business owners, and city agencies.

- Talk to commercial brokers.

- Drive through other similar commercial districts to find out which businesses are expanding and looking for new opportunities; contact the owners of these businesses.

Develop marketing materials. To catch the interest of prospective business owners, keep your first contact with them short and deliver only relevant information.

---

[16] For current information about retail trends, see International Council of Shopping Centers.

This is a good idea whether your contact is by phone, in person, or with a written ad or mailer. Business owners are busy, and they make judgments rapidly.

For a typical small business owner, the most relevant marketing information about your district includes

- Location
- Traffic count
- Access via freeway and other major routes
- Size of the prospective market within one-half, one, and two miles of your main street
- Proximity of competitive and complementary businesses
- Leading businesses in your area and their customer counts
- Availability of suitable sites
- Trends in your district—what your organization is doing and how momentum for improvements is building up

Sum up this information on an attractive flyer. Call a few realty firms to get a flyer showing one of their listed properties, and use this as a sample for yours. If you can afford it, spend a little money on a four-color brochure to capture the owners' attention and to convince them that you are professional.

When creating flyers, do *not* oversell your incentives, such as low-interest loans or grants. Mentioning them is fine. But if you lead with them in banner headlines, you may only reinforce the perception that your commercial district is in deep trouble and desperate to find anyone who will go in.

Prepare a stack of mailers, ready to go out immediately, to anyone who expresses an interest in your area. This could be simply your flyer, or it could be an envelope with your flyer, a newspaper article or two about recent projects or your organization, and perhaps a fact sheet about any property the owner expressed an interest in.

Use people power to reach targeted businesses. It's time to start marketing! There are many ways to do this. And the more you use, the better your chances for success.

Start by making cold calls to targeted business owners, avoiding their busiest time of the day. All staff members of your organization could call five or ten prospects every day. In addition, you can hire some folks from your community as telemarketers—a great way to get a lot of calls out and connect with more of your residents. However, limit your telemarketers' calling time to a few hours a day. Since most owners will reject your pitch within seconds, this can be grinding work.

Send out your mailer immediately to any owner who agreed to look at it. Follow up with calls within two or three working days after owners get the mailer. Your executive director should make these calls, not the telemarketers. The goal here is to get owners to visit a site or two on your avenue.

As you make these calls, you will develop a good understanding of how owners make location decisions, and about what is going on in various market segments in your region. Feed this information into your targeted business list, pointing your efforts into more and more realistic opportunities.

Beyond the telemarketer approach, there are some other excellent ways to reach business owners you've targeted:

- Share your marketing materials and property lists with city agencies and commercial brokers. Ask them to be on the lookout for prospective owners for your district.
- Give marketing materials to your board, local business owners, and other volunteers in your marketing. Ask them to solicit prospective owners from their networks. You can even offer a small incentive for leads that result in a new business.
- Take out ads for new businesses in newspapers and business journals (expensive), or write articles for your community paper, and get lots of news coverage (free).
- Offer incentives to brokers who know your area—a retainer fee and a bonus if they send you a targeted business. (This can be expensive, so have the building owner contribute a portion of the fee.)

Tool 8: Marketing your district to consumers

As you progress with new businesses, storefronts, streetscape elements, and improved parking, it is time to start promoting your district. If you don't promote, people will not come, and they won't know all that your district has to offer. People won't know about your drugstore's great new look, the one-of-a-kind antiques place, or the African art they can find only on your street.

Remember these foundations for a successful marketing effort:

- Get your message where the customer will notice it.
- Keep your message short and memorable.
- Promote the things that today's consumers demand: convenient access and parking, a variety of stores, quality and uniqueness of merchandise, and customer service that is friendly and helpful.
- Target existing customers and area residents for more visits, and target new customers for their first visit.
- Sell your whole vision for the commercial district—not just the individual businesses you want to promote.

- Make sure that your marketing message and theme are consistent with the vision that you developed at the beginning of your work.
- Cross-sell your businesses. ("Make one visit and find seven great home improvement stores.")

There are many ways to market your district to customers. Here are some of the most common marketing methods used in revitalizing commercial districts.

Brand your district with a new image. Go back to the vision statement for your commercial district. Think about how to put that vision into a simple, catchy form that the public can remember and get excited about. This is a good time to involve the whole community in some public meetings, since residents will have many good ideas and because their support of the new image will be crucial. "Eat Street" for a cluster of restaurants and "District del Sol" for a colorful Hispanic area are two examples in Minneapolis and St. Paul, respectively.

Many groups work on branding their commercial district with a new name or logo to shift attention away from negative perceptions. Try to connect to a name that the public may already know about and feel positive about, or to a name that sounds fresh and interesting. Most groups do not literally change the name of their street, but they do use this new branding and logo in all of their marketing materials.

Sponsor special events. Many inner-city communities are already known for festivals and events of all kinds. Neighborhoods across the country feature festivals such as the Fourth of July or Cinco de Mayo. These events draw tens of thousands of people each year to neighborhood commercial districts.

Many redevelopment groups build on these events. For example, they might add a "sidewalk sale extravaganza" to an existing festival to promote businesses. Other groups create new events to publicize their new image: antique or art crawls, antique car shows, and holiday lighting promotions. Most groups recoup some of their costs by charging street vendors a fee, selling dance tickets, or operating some sort of concession themselves. A few groups are good enough at this that they come out ahead and fund some of their other organizational expenses with these revenues.

Get free publicity. As every business owner and politician knows, nothing is as effective as a great feature story in the newspaper or on the evening news to promote your business. These stories reach a huge audience and carry more credibility than an ad, and they are *free.*

Your work is newsworthy! A series of storefront improvements, a new business or two, a streetscape project, or a mural painted by local kids—all are excellent local news stories. Get the attention of the media with press releases, tours of your district, or personal appeals. Invite your mayor or governor out for a visit and get some coverage.

There's a tendency among some reporters to want to tell neighborhood improvement stories as an heroic effort in a dismal neighborhood, perhaps focusing on how a few brave souls are toughing it out in the trenches. While you can't control reporters, you can pitch the story and work to steer the reporter clear of that clichéd, usually erroneous, approach. Explain that this is a wonderful neighborhood, perhaps a bit worn around the edges, and that it's time to look at all the positive energy that's going on here to capitalize on the great properties, excellent local market, and so forth; emphasize some of the very same points you use to attract new businesses. Sell the community-created vision to the reporters.

Advertise. Advertising costs money, so most community groups don't use it on a regular basis. However, there are strategic times when a paid ad will go a long way—for example, to get people to a festival or special event, or to promote a new district branding. Ask local newspapers or television stations for an advertising discount, given the nature of your effort and organization. Point out the number of businesses in your neighborhood that already buy advertising from them, and that the success of your work should result in more advertisers in the future. Remember to use your branding and logo in all ads.

Use billboards. Talk with local billboard companies about using billboards at the gateways to your neighborhood to advertise your commercial district. Often the companies will give you the space free for a limited time if you pay for the artwork.

Keep in mind the foundations of a good marketing message listed earlier. And, above all, keep your message short and memorable. On billboards, the rule of thumb is ten words or less! Finally, make sure that the billboard company commits to leaving your message up for at least sixty days, especially if you paid for the artwork.

Tool 9: Addressing crime

If customers and businesses stay away from your district because they do not feel safe there, you must deal with crime early on. Putting attractive awnings on storefronts is pointless if people are afraid to shop.

If you ignore this issue, you will lose the participation of many businesses for which crime is the number-one concern. Indeed, the topic of crime is an effective way to get people to a meeting and acquaint them with your organization.

There are two types of problems here: the *perception* of crime and the *reality* of crime.

Deal with the perception of crime. Quite often, areas that are perceived as dangerous have crime rates no higher than city averages. They suffer from the false impression of crime because of the association people make between run-down or empty buildings and crime. More sadly, districts can suffer this mistaken impression because of stereotypes about lower-income people and people of color.

It is your job to change these images. Promoting your new business investments and activity shows the world that this is not a dangerous place. If your crime statistics are no worse than the city average, you should build such facts into your ongoing promotions. (However, overemphasizing crime facts in your publicity can backfire by reinforcing the link people make between your community and crime.)

Talking to newspaper and television station editors about the problem of crime perception can also be helpful. The coverage they give to crimes in inner-city communities often adds to perceptions of danger. You have a right to balanced coverage in the media and should ask in meetings with their representatives for better coverage of positive developments. Also ask them to avoid casting their positive stories in a context of "this is even more amazing here on these hard streets, where crime is rampant."

Deal with the reality of crime. Many inner-city neighborhoods have more than a perception of crime, however. If your neighborhood is one such place, there are plenty of steps you can take to combat high crime rates.

Begin by forging a strong relationship with your police department. Consider hosting a satellite police desk in your office, and try to get a beat cop to walk your avenue daily. An alternative request of your police department is to intensify the squad car patrols in your district. Their presence will tend to push out much crime, especially if the officers get out of their cars and walk around a bit.

Try to get police officers to frequent your restaurants. These officers become effective at deterring crime and reasserting a sense of security because they soon get to know everyone by sight. A few commercial districts hire their own security patrols, but they are very expensive and have a less powerful presence than uniformed police officers with the full backup of their department.

Crime experts often say that the most effective crime deterrent is well-organized citizens. Team up with residential block club efforts to bring the eyes, ears, and voice of your businesses into this effort. Your businesses ought to support residential block clubs with funds, political support, and discounts for block club members. They might consider forming a business district block club.

Drug dealing, the activity of johns and prostitutes, graffiti "artists," loud and obnoxious behavior, public drinking and urination—such behavior is illegal and devastating to your businesses. Few customers will walk these gauntlets even if they *want* to spend money in your shops. One option is to provide training in *verbal judo* to your businesses—ways to handle unruly persons in their stores, on the sidewalks in front of their buildings, and in their parking lots. George Thompson, who originated verbal judo, describes it as "the gentle art of persuasion that redirects others' behavior with words and generates voluntary compliance."[17]

---

[17] See his book *Verbal Judo: The Gentle Art of Persuasion*. Also see his web site at www.verbaljudo.com.

In addition, police departments are usually happy to provide training to business owners and employees on how to handle troublesome situations safely and effectively. You can bring police officers into your meetings or set up a special meeting for this purpose.

Go further with telephone trees that give every business some other businesses to call to spread the word of an unsolved crime, whether it is passing bad checks, vandalism, assaults, or more. Train your businesses to call the police with all suspicious or criminal incidents, no matter how small. This builds a case against the perpetrators and keeps the eyes of the police on such actors.

In addition, many police departments can teach your organization about ways that building design can combat crime. This practice is called *crime prevention through environmental design* (CPTED). CPTED techniques call for eliminating or illuminating dark spaces where people can stay anonymous and conduct criminal activity. Controlling public phones that can be used for drug sales is another technique.[18]

Tool 10: Lessons from shopping center management

The assessment section of this chapter suggested studying shopping center management techniques. Here are a few specific suggestions:

- Talk to the owners of businesses that close early about staying open longer. Explain that almost all retail shopping in the United States takes place after 5:00 P.M. weekdays and on Saturdays.
- Talk to them about picking up litter in front of their stores.
- Show them pictures to illustrate the difference between homemade signs, which tend to look cluttered, and professional window displays.
- Offer workshops or handouts about modern merchandise display techniques and customer service standards.
- Consider the use of district-wide coupons. In every store of your district, place coupons that promote other local businesses; participating businesses can offer a discount after a certain number of purchases in the district.
- Create a map of all parking in your district and make the map available at all businesses.

Tool 11: Parking development

Lack of parking is an issue in virtually any large city. But it can be an acute problem in older, inner-city commercial districts that were built for trolleys and foot traffic instead of sport utility vehicles.

Your approach to creating more parking must be flexible and persistent. Comprehensive planning will be needed to look at your district as a whole and find

---

[18] You can get more information from the International CPTED Association.

every opportunity for expanded parking.

For an individual business to create new parking where none exists is often prohibitively difficult and expensive. The cost of purchasing property, relocating tenants, demolishing buildings, and paving and landscaping adds up quickly.

So, study your entire district over and over, with your board, with architects, with local businesses, and with the city. Search for where there is actual parking need, exactly when in the day and the week this need exists, and where there is any available parking that is underutilized. For example, do business owners or their employees park in front of their own store and then complain about lack of customer parking? Is there parking half a block off your district that they can use instead of prime customer spaces? Could a furniture store use the next-door bar's lot during the day? Would businesses with excess parking share their space with adjacent businesses?

After you have exhausted all options for more effective use of existing space with existing owners, you may have to look at ownership options. City ownership of parking lots in your district is an ideal situation, but few cities are willing to provide this to their neighborhoods. Another route was taken by the City of St. Paul in the 1980s, when it offered forgivable loans to create community-use parking lots in neighborhood commercial districts. Ownership by your organization is another option, with obvious burdens of liability, cost, and management.

Sometimes the lack of parking is more of a perceived problem than a real one. Your organization can help solve this perception problem in a few ways. Let customers know where parking is located; available space is often easy to miss. Every lot in your district, whether open to the public or not, could have the same parking sign on it. Tie this sign in to your streetscape plan. Some districts design maps that highlight all the parking for the whole district. They provide a stack of these maps at every business.

Tool 12: Real estate development

Real estate development is the set of activities needed to turn bare ground or a deteriorated building into a new or fully renovated building. These activities include

- Planning the building's potential use, including a thorough financial and risk analysis
- Obtaining financing from banks and investors

Community-use parking on private lots

Some groups offer partial grants for paving and landscaping parking lots as part of their overall commercial district grant program. You can offer larger grants (for example, $5,000 instead of $2,000) to any business that will open its lot for "community-use parking." Such an incentive is more likely a start than a permanent solution to the parking problems in a neighborhood, since the community-use feature often "sunsets" at some point down the road.

Some groups pay for signs telling the public of open parking lots and post the restricted hours of public use. If you try this idea, be clear in writing who has responsibility for proper maintenance (usually the owner, not your group), and that your group has no liability or responsibility for the lots, since you are neither an owner nor a renter. Check with your attorney about appropriate written agreements.

- Hiring and working with architects and contractors
- Filling the building with tenants

Business incubators—an interesting option

A fairly common goal for community economic development groups is the development of a *business incubator,* a building that nurtures a number of small firms in their early years. This concept is mentioned in other strategies in this book, but not discussed in detail, since it is essentially a mix of real estate development and business development. It can be a valuable strategy to consider, and good information is available. Contact the National Business Incubation Association for excellent information about this concept.

After taking these steps, developers may sell the property or hold it and manage it themselves.

Many community groups get involved with renovating old buildings and building new ones. Often these groups are faced with highly visible buildings in terrible shape but with great potential if renovated and filled with the right type of business. To this end, groups work with existing owners of buildings, attract outside developers, and sometimes become developers themselves.

There is a whole range of options here. Don't consider the hardest options (doing the development yourself) until you have exhausted all easier ones. Be clear with your board members about how much time they want staff to spend on such projects, and how much financial risk they are willing to take on. Such discussions take expert advice and usually a number of meetings to get through.

Work with existing owners. The first option is to work with the existing owner of the property, perhaps offering help with financing, architects, and leasing. Such assistance may be enough to entice some owners to take on a tough project, since much of the reluctance is based on the cost and time involved. Even with the incentives you have offered, however, there will be owners who can't or won't develop their buildings with your design guidelines in mind, nor will they commit to rent or sell to a targeted business from your list.

Usually this is because it makes no economic sense for owners to do so. Perfectly rational reasons for such an unhelpful attitude may include the following:

- The current use of the building doesn't benefit from renovation. (Customers may not come to this site, for instance, if it is a warehouse or factory.)
- The owners plan to retire in a few years.
- The renovation project would cost much more than the owners can afford or than they would ever get back from the level of market rents in your district.

Sometimes owners are just plain ornery and don't want anyone telling them what to do with their property. Others may simply not believe that your commercial district is improving.

Sometimes owners are willing to sell their buildings rather than fix them up and hold them. Your organization can get involved in two major ways with such owners: connecting the owner to a buyer who is able and willing to work with your group, or buying and renovating the building yourself.

Connect owners to buyers. Finding a developer to buy targeted buildings, renovate them, and fill them in accordance with your organization's vision is a matter of networking and searching, similar to searching for targeted businesses. You need to use the same basic pitch to these developers as you use with prospective businesses—that your district has turned the corner, shows positive momentum, and has good development opportunities.

Talk to as many people as you can about the opportunities in your commercial district. Commercial bankers, contractors, architects, city development staff, other community development groups, and commercial real estate brokers are all sources of names. Look for people who

- Have done commercial projects of this size successfully before
- Can obtain bank financing
- Are good at working with contractors and architects
- Are able to fill the building with good tenants
- Buy in to your organizational goals

There are major reasons why private sector developers and building owners can't take on these projects in the same fashion that a nonprofit group can. For example, some of the design and rehab that looks good isn't always necessary. Attractive signage or awnings, for instance, may not benefit the building owner or occupant and can be left off a building at a savings of $10,000 or more. Also, the level of rent revenue that lower-income business districts can generate is typically lower than elsewhere and will not support higher-end rehab efforts. And getting all the required approvals from your neighborhood and city adds time, expense, and risk.

Buy and renovate buildings yourself. If you are not able to find such a developer for your key projects, you may consider taking on the project yourself. But be warned that real estate development takes an enormous amount of staff time, costs a considerable amount of money, and can add a major new source of potential liability to your organization.

Understand another important thing before charging into this battle: The reason you can't get anyone else to do your project is that it's hard to survive financially because of

- *High costs.* Expenses come from assembling land that is already built up, from demolition costs, from lead and asbestos cleanup, from the high cost of renovating old buildings, and so on.
- *Long time frame.* The same factors that add cost add time. Plus, city and neigh-

borhood approval processes take time to navigate.

- *High risk.* Risk stems from the cost and time factors, plus an uncertain market once the project is done. Who knows whether new businesses will actually come into this building?
- *Low expected returns.* Rent levels or resale levels are lower than they would be in areas with a strong business climate.

However, there is a simple reason that many groups eventually take on real estate development themselves: *No one else will.* No one else has the economic incentive or patience to do the project "right," the way you want it done, with tenants and design that really make a positive difference to your district. The building may sit empty or deteriorated for many years, or someone may develop it in ways that are seriously in conflict with your goals and plans.

Because you are a nonprofit, you can try to get grants and low-interest financing for the project, and you don't have the same expenses as a typical owner. Nonprofit renovation may be the only option to redevelop a particularly bad or promising property in a way that furthers economic revitalization.

Start with these tips. A number of good books on real estate development are available.[19] Following are just a few basic tips.

Get professional advice. Pay for it if you have to; get it free if you can. Ask developers, brokers, attorneys, bankers, city development officials, and local and national community development groups for training and advice.

Get training. Groups such as the National Development Council, Development Training Institute, Neighborhood Reinvestment Corporation, and others offer excellent seminars on commercial real estate development in neighborhood settings.

Be clear about your goals for design and usage. Try to keep these goals on the front burner throughout the project, even when costs dictate compromises on each. Budget enough for these costs, and hold out for targeted businesses to fill your building that really will make a difference in your district.

Seek competent legal help. Get advice on the best way to protect your organization's nonprofit status and resources from the downside of developing properties. Typically this includes setting up a new corporation or a corporate subsidiary of your organization to own the property. If set up correctly, this entity will provide significant protection to your parent nonprofit corporation.

Begin discussions immediately with potential sources of funding for your project. These include banks, city, state, and federal government agencies, and charitable sources.

---

[19] For an in-depth education, read *Real Estate Development: Principles and Process* by Mike E. Miles et al.

Get great tenants. Most developers will tell you that the single most important and elusive element in owning and renovating a building is securing the right tenant. Therefore, consider this element early in your search, and make it a priority. Tenants hold the key to banks giving you a loan; banks will look at tenant strengths as being your strengths and their weaknesses as your weaknesses. Tenants also hold the key to your financial survival as long as you own the property, since their rent is your only source of income to pay your loans, insurance, taxes, and repairs.

Finally, as an organization that does community economic development, you are even more choosy about tenants than most developers. You are looking for a targeted business, one that really adds to your district. Therefore, a lawyer or chiropractor located in your prime first-floor retail space may not meet your goals, since an office with blinds pulled down all day may not be the look you want. Since you are after a smaller set of potential tenants than other developers, you really must make the job of finding the right tenant your top priority from day one.

Know the relevant requirements. Find out what your city and other funding sources require for on-site minority and female hiring goals. Learn which handicapped accessibility and lead or asbestos abatement requirements apply to your project. Ask about other requirements that come with your sources of funding, such as federal and state versions of the Davis-Bacon Act, which mandates the wage level to be paid on projects with some public funding. City development staff and experienced architects and contractors are good sources for information regarding requirements, but make sure to ask a number of these people to ensure you don't miss anything.

Assemble a team including an architect, a general contractor, a banker, and city officials as early as possible. Your board will typically get involved in hiring an architect and a general contractor. Carefully review architects' and contractors' track records on similar projects with similar requirements for wage levels or affirmative hiring practices. Have your attorney review contracts before they are signed, ensuring clarity about results, timelines, and payments.

Get the numbers right. You will work on two sets of numbers to lay out your project: a "sources and uses of cash" and a "ten-year operating budget." Be thorough and accurate with your numbers. Revise them again and again as you get more information from your contractor, banker, city staff, and potential tenants. If you are too cautious with all estimates (such as a 25 percent vacancy rate every year for 10 years), you will kill your project. But, if you are too optimistic about how the project will perform, you may kill your budget and perhaps your organization if it has to feed a runaway project.

Give careful thought to the ongoing management of the building once it is renovated and filled. Considerations include who will manage it, how much everything will cost, how often tenants will turn over, and how you will replace them with other targeted businesses. Consider managing the building yourself.

Start with healthy reserve funds. Set aside money for operations (to avoid cash-flow problems), maintenance (repainting walls, fixing toilets, and the like), and replacement (for larger items such as the carpet and roof). Set up a reserve from the first day for property taxes. Lay out a schedule showing when you anticipate needing to replace major items in the building, such as carpeting, the roof, the heating/cooling system, and so forth. Feed all reserve funds each month, setting aside enough money to meet this "capital replacement schedule"; if you can't, then your building is *not working.*

Get adequate insurance immediately, effective the minute you take ownership of the building. This includes coverage for a vacant building and builder's risk during construction, replacement in the event of fire and other major damage, and strong liability coverage. Name your parent nonprofit as well as your subsidiary and all your debt funders on the policy. Strongly consider director and officer liability insurance for the board of the subsidiary, if you have such a board.

Learn about site control options. Even if you never develop a building yourself, controlling key sites until you can find a cooperative developer can be a powerful revitalization tool. Learn how to use a "purchase option" and a "right of first refusal" in ways that give you time to assemble financing or find that developer without jeopardizing your organization's resources.

Finally, you must have a strong stomach for all this. Real estate development can be both the most rewarding and the most frustrating activity you take on. An old development adage is: *After the deal is finally and completely put together, it will typically fall apart only three more times.*

Tool 13: Business improvement districts

Creating business improvement districts (BIDs) is a fairly common way of coordinating services in inner-city business districts. BIDs are based on self-taxation, with a small amount of property tax assessment added to all properties in your district according to the amount of linear feet of storefront. These funds are used for specific improvement purposes, such as litter cleanup, streetscape maintenance, security, installing new banners, and promotional activities. The issue of what these funds will be used for, and by whom, must be resolved before the district is established.

BIDs are set up with city and state authorization and require a super-majority vote (usually 60 percent to 80 percent) by the property owners in your district to be implemented. The city collects the special assessment as part of its property tax and passes it along to the designated business group for use on the specified activities.

BIDs are not permitted in all cities and states; check with your local development agency about this. Also, BIDs often have an end date, after which another vote is required to extend the tax.

Step 4: Monitor, Evaluate, and Improve

Monitoring and evaluating your results is crucial to convincing prospective businesses and developers that your district has improved and will continue to get better. What's more, tracking what you've done and how well it worked can help you build on successful efforts, eliminate your unsuccessful ones, and be more cost-effective. Finally, current and future funders will be very interested in this information (and may require it).

To monitor specific results, simply track the number and type of physical improvement projects that you've had a hand in, and your costs over time. Then periodically compare staffing costs to tangible results in your district. Each year, compare your results to the goals in your strategic plan.

More difficult to track are overall improvements to your district and your community—economic impacts and community impacts, as described in Chapter 1.

Economic impacts can include

- Increased customer visits and sales at your businesses.
- Jobs that have been created for local residents by the new and expanding businesses assisted by your group.
- Increased valuation of properties and taxes paid by businesses (local government will like this one), which you can track at the local property tax department.

Community impact is a mix of visible change and less tangible but ultimately more important change in how people feel about your commercial district. Look for improvements in "social capital," such as more businesses where your residents can gather, an increased number of visible, inspiring role models, and more leaders emerging from your commercial district to push local organizations forward.

To track people's perceptions of your district, gather comments and stories from residents and business owners as they watch and participate in the successes your organization generates. Ultimately, your goal is to inspire many people to stay and put sweat and money into your community. Take time to find out if this is happening. If not, you may need more visible results and better ways to promote your successes.

Summary

Many community economic development organizations choose commercial district revitalization as a starting point. Commercial district revitalization involves efforts that fit the capabilities of local development organizations.

Because of its highly visible results, revitalizing a run-down commercial district is an excellent way to improve the local economy. When these results capture the community's vision, a self-fueling momentum builds that is exciting and contagious.

Your organization will have the greatest chance of success if it follows the steps presented in this chapter: (1) assess current conditions, (2) develop a community-wide vision for what success will look like and back it up with realistic goals, (3) put the plan into action, and (4) continually monitor your success in achieving your goals.

A wide variety of tools help organizations and communities revitalize commercial districts, including cleanup campaigns, loan funds, streetscape design, and the creation of business improvement districts. Success with one tool will build the confidence to move on to others. Use these tools to generate one visible result after another, and turn your community's vision into reality.

Chapter 5

Develop Microbusiness

An important element of your neighborhood economy is the collection of tiny businesses scattered throughout your community. Some are in storefronts on your main business district. Others are hidden inside homes. Some of these business owners work out of a truck or in their backyard or on the street corner, while others rent small spaces inside old industrial buildings. Some are long-standing enterprises, while others are start-ups. Such *microbusinesses* are usually owned and operated by neighborhood residents.

Microbusinesses seldom employ more than five workers, and generally have less than $100,000 in annual sales. Microbusinesses (run by *microentrepreneurs*) can exist in almost any sector, from retail to service to light manufacturing.

In the developing countries of South America, Asia, and Africa, an enormous industry to assist very poor microentrepreneurs has grown up over the past thirty years. Variously known as *microenterprise development*, *village banking*, *peer-group lending*, or *circle lending*, this industry began primarily as a rural model, focusing on women in small villages. Some programs now operate in urban settings as well. Developing microbusiness in your neighborhood as a strategy for economic development merges the strengths of community development corporations with the strengths of this international model. The three main elements of such a program are training, lending, and support.

Overview

Microbusinesses exist in every low-income community. Some operate "above ground" and others operate as part of the "underground economy"; that is, they usually avoid taxation, zoning, and regulation. (*Above ground* and *underground* are sometimes referred to as "formal" and "informal" sectors of microbusiness, respectively.) Both types can be developed into strong contributors to the local economy and the neighborhood.

Typical microbusinesses in inner-city communities are well known: the small flower store, the auto mechanic, the TV repair shop, the small restaurant, the office and housecleaning service, the caterer. Typical examples of "underground" microbusinesses include unlicensed street vendors selling legitimate goods they have purchased somewhere else, day care providers working in their own home, hair stylists working out of the home, backyard auto mechanics and painters, and lawn care or snowplowing businesses working out of a truck.

Chapter 5 at a Glance

Microbusiness development is an effective way to build your neighborhood economy from within. Yet tackling this pivot point presents many challenges because of the nature of microentrepreneurs. Your planning and implementation will hinge on attracting microentrepreneurs, training them effectively, connecting them with available space, and offering them financing and support. Use the four steps that apply to any of the pivot points discussed in this book:

1. Assess current conditions in your community, including the need to support microbusinesses, the supply of microentrepre- neurs, emerging business trends and opportunities, and your organization's capacity to support microentrepreneurs. Worksheets 13 through 15 will aid your assessment.

2. Create a vision and a strategic plan that will find microentrepreneurs and help them establish businesses that can grow and anchor your community. Worksheets 16 through 18 guide you in this planning.

3. Implement the five aspects of the microbusiness development program: attraction, training, connection, financing, and support. Using partner organizations is often the key to success with this strategy.

4. Monitor the results with a constant eye toward improvement.

Many times these enterprises are a sideline activity that supplements wages from another job. Sometimes these enterprises are the owner's sole income; they may be the only opportunity for a single mother with small children at home to earn enough to support her kids.

Most of these enterprises capitalize on people's unique skills and assets. The owners' personality adds flavor to the community, because such entrepreneurs are endlessly creative in the way they design their business, the way they treat customers and employees, the products and services they provide, and the way they try to grow their business. This combination of passion, creativity, hard work, and community connections makes microentrepreneurs a valuable resource for community developers.

Developing microbusinesses is a fairly new pivot point for neighborhood development groups. Even so, this is an excellent strategy. In this chapter, you'll find information on working with *microentrepreneurs*. You'll discover ways to bring them above ground through training, lending, and ongoing support.

This chapter explains

- Three reasons to see microbusiness as an economic pivot point
- Three important things to know about microentrepreneurs
- A four-step process for developing microbusiness

Three Reasons to See Microbusiness as an Economic Pivot Point

Microbusinesses are a pivot point in your neighborhood because they are a major hidden source of economic vitality, they benefit the community, and they are often a good match for community development organizations.[20]

---

[20] For additional information about the microenterprise field, contact the Association for Enterprise Opportunity and the Aspen Institute. Look specifically at Aspen for its FIELD study series and its Economic Opportunities Program.

Microbusiness and the Minneapolis Mercado Central—a success story

Interfaith Action, a group organizing Latino congregations in Minneapolis, conducted an "asset inventory" of parishioners in 1996. As a result, the group discovered many recent immigrants from Mexico, Central America, and South America with a business background and a desire to work in business. Language barriers and lack of knowledge about how to start a business in the United States prevented these people from realizing their dream.

This inventory led the Neighborhood Development Center (NDC), working with Interfaith Action and Whittier Community Development Corporation (CDC), to offer training in Spanish on how to write a business plan. Over seventy-five entrepreneurs participated in the training. These entrepreneurs and groups decided to create a *mercado*—a marketplace where many people could run their business under one roof. The entrepreneurs brought this concept from their homeland. A third nonprofit, Project for Pride in Living, carried out the real estate development, while NDC and Whittier CDC did extensive training, lending, and marketing and formed a cooperative of the entrepreneurs to run the mercado, all prior to opening.

As a result, the Minneapolis Mercado Central opened in July 1999, home to forty-seven Latino businesses. Most of the owners surfaced their business idea through the asset inventory and came through the NDC training program. Most received financing through NDC or Whittier CDC. NDC maintains a technical assistance office in the mercado, providing Spanish-language business assistance five days a week. In their first year, these businesses had over $2 million in combined sales.

The renovated mercado building is a major gathering place for the Latino community and for the low-income neighborhood of Powderhorn Park in South Minneapolis. This highly visible project has become a catalyst for further economic development, as other buildings at the same intersection have been redeveloped following the success of the mercado. Inspired by its success, NDC is working on a second mercado with another neighborhood group, and on a Somali *suuque* (market) with a private owner.

Photograph by Mihailo Temali. Used with permission.

The renovated Mercado building is a major gathering place for the Latino community and for the Powderhorn Park neighborhood of South Minneapolis.

Microbusinesses already exist in your neighborhood

Many community groups working on commercial district revitalization run into a wall of negative attitudes about their community when they try to attract outside businesses. These attitudes can be extremely hard to overcome in low-income white communities, and impossible to overcome in low-income communities of color.

Fortunately, these same neighborhoods have some formal and many informal microbusinesses already in operation. These entrepreneurs are generally not negative about their own community, since they are *part* of the community. They know from experience that money can be made doing business in the neighborhood. Your group can develop these businesses and fill the neighborhood's storefronts and office space with homegrown businesses instead of relying solely on attracting outsiders. (A combination of the two approaches is generally the best.)

Microbusinesses offer benefits

A healthy supply of microbusinesses benefits the local economy. Such businesses typically hire area residents, building incomes in the community. These businesses also bring goods and services into a community, so residents don't have to travel elsewhere to obtain them. Microbusinesses can fill otherwise empty storefronts. They pay property and income taxes and their employees pay income taxes as well.

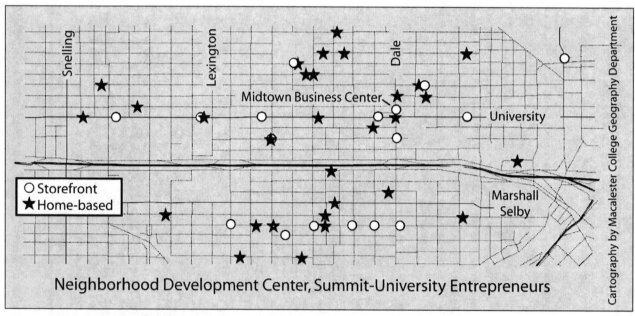

A healthy supply of microbusinesses offers many benefits to a local economy. The map above shows the concentration of microbusinesses in the Summit-University district of St. Paul, Minnesota.

Map by Claudia Fonkert, Geography Department, Macalester College, and provided by the Neighborhood Development Center, Inc. Used with permission.

One of the main benefits of this strategy is its multiplying effect. Even though they may hire only two or three people on average, fifty of these tiny businesses may jointly hire 100 to 150 people. Although they may occupy only small storefronts or offices, thirty of them can significantly revitalize a worn-out commercial district.

As small business owners, these residents become highly visible role models for local youth who see them at work day after day, slowly building up to success. These entrepreneurs often take leadership roles within the community and in churches, schools, and neighborhood organizations.

Finally, some of these microbusinesses grow to become larger businesses. Thus, building a base of microenterprises can ensure an ongoing supply of larger firms in the future.

Microbusinesses offer a match for your organization

Microbusiness development fits the skills and capacity of many community organizations. First, this is a strategy that you can control, because you work locally, with eager, neighborhood-based entrepreneurs. Second, this strategy includes a series of actions that many community organizations can carry out if they are persistent and careful; microbusiness does not put all your organization's eggs in one basket, as you might if you were trying to lure a major corporation to move in and hire 500 workers all at once. Third, most neighborhoods have more small spaces available to businesses than larger spaces. Finally, this strategy yields results that gradually multiply, creating momentum and renewed neighborhood confidence.

Understand Microentrepreneurs

Collectively, microentrepreneurs and local residents with entrepreneurial dreams represent a tremendous asset found in virtually every low-income community in America. Yet they are usually an untapped asset for several reasons.

Microentrepreneurs can be difficult to reach

While formal microbusinesses are tough to get into training because of time constraints, informal businesses are even harder to reach. One reason is that they purposely avoid attention. They are often hard for anyone to reach—whether to help them, buy from them, tax them, or shut them down. They stay in the shadows because of a complex set of factors:

- They operate on a cash or barter basis, and rarely volunteer this income to the tax authorities. If they did, in fact, pay taxes, many would not bother with their enterprise, since they don't make enough money to give any to the government.
- They may be in violation of city zoning codes or business regulations.

ALERT!
Common reasons for failure with microbusiness development

- Your organization lacks sufficient contact with community networks or a solid reputation, hindering its ability to attract microentrepreneurs.
- Your organization lacks the capacity or resources to offer all tools needed by microentrepreneurs to succeed—training, lending, and ongoing technical assistance.
- Local microentrepreneurs are unable or unwilling to use expert advice or basic management practices, particularly regarding bookkeeping and financial management.
- Your lending requirements are overly lax or overly restrictive.
- Your organization lacks the technical skills and sound procedures to succeed at lending.
- Your organization fails to connect the entrepreneurs you assist with other elements of your community economic development strategy, such as filling vacant storefronts or creating community gathering places.

- They are often owned by people who have limited education and limited success in the workforce and who may be uncomfortable in large, centralized education or training environments.
- They are often members of minority or immigrant communities, and may have had negative experiences interacting with larger institutions, such as the government, banks, or schools.
- They may have difficulty getting away from responsibilities of home and business to attend classes.
- They may have poor credit histories, limited savings, or little collateral, and may doubt that anyone would ever give them a business loan.
- They may believe that they know all there is to know about their business, and that any training is unnecessary.
- They may be uninterested in expanding their business.

You will never be able to assist all microentrepreneurs in your community. However, you can work with enough of them to have a positive impact on the local economy.

Microentrepreneurs need access to training

While training and other assistance are available to many small businesses, little has been provided at the neighborhood level in a manner that is accessible or comfortable to low-income residents. Further, it has been virtually impossible for microentrepreneurs to get loans for start-up businesses in low-income neighborhoods—either because their start-up plans are not well developed on paper or because their risk factors are considered high by traditional lenders.

Distinguish between microentrepreneurs and small business owners

Various definitions distinguish a microbusiness from a small business. The range is wide, with *microbusiness* often defined as businesses with less than $100,000 in annual sales and fewer than five employees and *small business* as having up to $5 million in annual sales.

To some extent, these definitions don't matter to you, since you want to work with any microentrepreneur or small business owner who could use your help. However, these distinctions can be important for a few reasons. First, some funding sources may restrict whom you can work with using their money. Examples are microloan and microtechnical assistance programs from the Small Business Administration (SBA). Second, the characteristics of microbusinesses and small businesses vary. The typical small business, with a history behind it and $1 million in annual sales, will have more sophisticated management, successful experience securing bank loans, prior experience with business seminars and training materials, and professional advisors such as accountants and lawyers. Small business entrepreneurs need a level of training and financing that is often beyond what most community organizations have to offer.

The approach in this chapter is aimed at the smaller end of the range: the formal and informal microbusinesses and smallest existing businesses in your neighborhood that need the kind of help your group can offer, including training, small loans, and business consulting.

There are four steps in developing your program to build microbusinesses:

1. Assess current conditions
2. Create a vision and strategic plan
3. Implement your plan
4. Monitor, evaluate, and improve

Step 1: Assess Current Conditions

During the assessment step of microbusiness development, you will look at four major areas:

1. The need to support microbusinesses in your community
2. The supply of microentrepreneurs in your community
3. Emerging business trends and opportunities
4. Your organization's capacity to support microentrepreneurs

Step 1 at a Glance

- Assess need
- Assess supply
- Assess trends and opportunities
- Assess your organization's capacity

Assess need

Study the commercial properties in your neighborhood. Do you have many vacant storefronts, offices, or industrial spaces? Is your neighborhood missing basic goods and services that your residents have to go elsewhere to purchase? Does your community lack the great gathering places that it used to have thirty years ago, like the drugstore soda counter or the sit-down family restaurant? Does your neighborhood lack locally owned businesses whose proprietors are leaders and role models for the community?

If you answered yes to some of these questions, you have a need for a microbusiness development. By developing a steady stream of microbusiness start-ups, and by expanding the smallest of your existing businesses, you will create many opportunities to fill those vacancies, to bring in the missing goods and services and role models, and to create community gathering places.

You can use Worksheet 13: Assess the Need to Develop Microbusiness, on page 237, to guide this part of your assessment.

Assess supply

The second part of your assessment is to learn about your supply of existing and potential microentrepreneurs. Some are already in business in commercial spaces or in homes; others are active in the underground economy, without any plan for getting above ground; and others are potentials—people with a strong business interest and concept who haven't started yet.

You can discover these existing and potential microentrepreneurs by surveying neighborhood residents. Surveys like this are sometimes called *asset inventories*. Made famous by John McKnight of Northwestern University, this approach focuses on the assets of low-income communities rather than their deficiencies ("the glass is half full, not half empty"). You can learn more about this approach through the Asset-Based Community Development Institute.[21]

For a list of questions to guide this part of your assessment, see Worksheet 14: Assess the Supply of Microentrepreneurs, page 238.

Assess trends and opportunities

To discover the fastest-growing types of businesses in your area, start by looking at the Economic Census section of the U.S. Census Bureau web site (www.census. gov) and by talking with a local small business banker or business professor. Also find out if any strong business clusters in your metro area could potentially need additional small-scale vendors and suppliers. Even if these are high-tech clusters, such as medical devices or telecommunications, they may have low-tech subcontracts that your entrepreneurs could obtain.

You may choose to offer training just in a few of these stronger business sectors, or you may consider a model where your group picks a business idea and literally seeks out a resident to be the owner. See the sidebar Pick Strong Business Ideas and Train Owners, on page 113, for examples.

If your organization is also conducting a commercial district revitalization strategy, look at your targeted business list. (See pages 68–69 and Worksheet 9: Create a Targeted Business List, on page 230.) Look for ways to help microentrepreneurs who have business ideas that match businesses you want in your main commercial district. You can also refer to any market analysis that you may have done for that strategy to identify missing businesses with strong market demand in your community. These offer good opportunities for local entrepreneurs with the right training.

---

[21] Information on asset inventories can also be found in *Building Communities from the Inside Out* by John P. Kretzmann and John L. McKnight.

Pick strong business ideas and train owners

Community Development Corporation of Kansas City (in Missouri) has approached microenterprise development from a different angle—picking business ideas that have high potential and then seeking out and training residents with entrepreneurial characteristics to take over ownership. Examples include a concrete block manufacturing firm, a plastic injection molding company, and construction companies. Several retail businesses have also been selected and placed into a shopping center operated by the community development organization as a business incubator.

These business ideas come from various sources: word of mouth, retiring business owners looking to pass their business along, and close observation of the local marketplace. Businesses are sought that can pay at least $7 per hour starting wage, and $12 to $13 per hour after training. The entrepreneurs are found via networking, including discussions with bankers. Skills are developed through individual consulting, adding experts to the board of the business, introductions to an extensive network of customers and professionals, and access to loans and ongoing technical assistance.

Like any strategy, this one has its pitfalls. More than half of the businesses developed in this fashion have not succeeded—in fact, even some of those in the shopping center didn't succeed. The chief difficulty has turned out to be getting people to accept expert advice—a similar problem in most microbusiness training programs. Nonetheless, this is still a very interesting model to consider.

Assess your organization's capacity

The final area to assess is your own organization's ability to put an effective microentrepreneur development program together. Succeeding at this strategy requires fairly high levels of staffing—both in terms of person hours and in terms of business and lending sophistication.

To begin, look at your networks and reputation within the community. Can you be effective at encouraging the "shy" underground entrepreneur to surface for assistance?

Look at the business skills and available time of your staff. If necessary, can you hire competent business consultants and trainers? Are these people available and do you have the funds to pay them? Talk to potential partner organizations with people who are skilled at certain parts of this program. Find out if these organizations are willing to come into your neighborhood to work with you on this strategy.

Finally, talk to potential funders and weigh their reaction to initial inquiries for funding a microbusiness program. Given the level of staffing needed for this strategy, it can require higher budgets than some other strategies. Contact the Association for Enterprise Opportunity, the SBA, and your local One-Stop Career Center for good leads on microenterprise funding.[22] For example, the SBA designated the

---

[22] To search for additional government funding opportunities, start at www.firstgov. gov. For your foundation search, start at the Foundation Center at www.fdncenter. org. For an explanation of One-Stop Career Centers, see Chapter 6 on workforce development, page 141.

Greater North-Pulaski Development Corporation in Chicago as a Small Business Development Center on the grounds that the organization reached a clientele not served by others and subsequently awarded it funding.

Use Worksheet 15: Assess Your Organization's Capacity to Support Microentrepreneurs, page 240, to think through this issue.

Step 2: Create a Vision and Strategic Plan

Now that you have a good understanding of where microbusinesses can help your local economy and roughly how many microentrepreneurs you have, plan how you will develop this rich resource within your community.

You need to consider three main things as you plan:

1. The focus of your program
2. The content of your program
3. A vision statement and set of goals expressed in writing

Focus your program

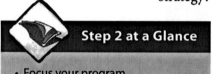

Step 2 at a Glance

• Focus your program
• Develop program content
• Write a vision statement and goals

The first step is to get agreement from your board on what you hope to achieve with this effort. How will your community be different after three or five years of this strategy? Is your top priority filling empty storefronts in your commercial district, or is it finding a particular type of retail business that would help your neighborhood the most (such as building on a cluster of Latino retailers, or antique dealers, or restaurants)? Or is it creating jobs for local residents in the manufacturing trades? Is your priority helping low-income single mothers find work, or is it developing businesses within a certain ethnic or immigrant group? Depending on how you answer these questions, you may choose to work with microretailers, manufacturers, home-based businesses, or ethnic-specific entrepreneurs.

Next, choose whether your organization will function as a generalist or specialist. Many organizations work with any and all microbus-inesses that will benefit their community; other organizations focus only on certain types of businesses. Your choice will depend on the community's greatest need, the greatest opportunities in your market, and your organization's capabilities.

For example, if you have many vacant retail storefronts, consider specialized training for entrepreneurs who want to start retail businesses. If you need places for the community to gather, consider helping coffee shops, restaurants, ethnic retail markets, farmer's markets, and ethnic delicatessens. If your priority is creating jobs for residents, then consider working with entrepreneurs who have manufacturing ideas. You might also consider assisting only businesses with high-growth potential. This will restrict the type and number of entrepreneurs you work with, since most underground entrepreneurs do not have the background to manage a rapidly growing company. However, there may certainly be some entrepreneurs in your community who are already in business and have such potential.

Finally, make decisions about the entrepreneurs you will work with. Some community development groups choose to work with any income level, while other groups work only with low- to moderate-income residents. These latter groups reason that higher-income entrepreneurs are more likely to seek and receive good business advice and financing at existing institutions such as the local business school, the SBA, and local banks.

However, while some low-income communities do not have many high-income residents, many do. Allowing higher-income entrepreneurs into your program might make sense for two reasons: (1) They may agree to start their business in the community (which is certainly a plus); and (2) they may have a greater chance for success (since they may have more assets or management experience). This is a discussion and decision your board should make.

Your funders and partners may influence your choice: They may not participate with you unless you focus on certain demographics. But ultimately, you need to focus on the people that make the most sense given your community's needs and your organization's capacity.

In any case, your choice of focus is important. Once you have made this choice, you will have to design your training and loan services to effectively serve your target entrepreneurs and to make the maximum impact on your community. Remember that when you do choose a focus, it can change over time as your needs, opportunities, and capabilities evolve.

Develop program content

Your next step is to determine what type of help your microentrepreneurs need, lay out exactly what you will provide to these entrepreneurs, and choose how you will go about it.

Community organizations usually assist microbusiness through five specific sets of activities:

1. *Attracting* these entrepreneurs to your training and financing programs through community publicity and networks.
2. *Training* these entrepreneurs to focus their business idea and write a solid business plan, either in group classes or in one-on-one consulting.

3. *Connecting* these entrepreneurs to properties in your neighborhood as they evolve from home- and street-based businesses to enterprises that need small commercial spaces.

4. *Lending* to these businesses, whether for start-up or for expansion.

5. *Supporting* these businesses in a wide variety of forms, including management and operations advice; assistance with marketing, accounting, and legal and other issues; and sometimes actually housing these entrepreneurs in business incubators.

These five activities are discussed in more detail under Step 3: Implement Your Plan.

Talk with microentrepreneurs directly to find out what program content and style would be useful for them. In addition to one-on-one conversations for this purpose, you can use surveys or small group discussions to learn what would help these people grow and succeed.

You can also talk with commercial lenders at local banks and the SBA, along with business instructors at local community colleges or universities. Asking small business accountants and employees of the IRS or the state business tax department about common pitfalls can help you develop program content. Talking with owners of strong existing businesses about what may have helped them in their early days is always a good idea.

Take ideas from all these people, categorizing their suggestions into the five elements of program content listed above. Also listen closely to any advice these people have for how to carry out each of these five activities.

While you're having these conversations, ask people if they are interested in being either a participant or partner in your program. Are any of the entrepreneurs po-

What about people without a clear business idea?

Many entrepreneurial residents may lack a clear business idea. To help them, offer two-hour workshops entitled "Picking the Right Business Idea." In such a workshop, you can lay out the realities of starting and operating a business, give guidance to selecting the right business idea, and direct participants to resources at the local library or bookstore on home-based businesses, hot franchises, and similar topics. Bring samples of resources to pass around.

Advise people to consider five main factors in this choice:

1. Business trends: Does this business have a strong future in this market?

2. Money: Can they afford the start-up and operations cost, or realistically get a loan for it?

3. Lifestyle: How many hours do they want to devote to their business and what sort of flexibility do they want in their life?

4. Skill: Do they have the skills required for this business?

5. Passion: Do they truly enjoy the activity called for in this business, since it will occupy most of their waking hours?

tential students for your classes or borrowers for your loans? Are any of them interested in finding a commercial site in your area? Could any of the existing business owners, accountants, or lenders you meet be a good trainer or advisor to start-up entrepreneurs? Would any of the bankers be willing to consider lending money to your training graduates? Use this information-gathering phase to start building the network of participants and partners for your microbusiness program.

While some community groups take on all parts of this strategy themselves, it is more common to form partnerships with other organizations. Many nonprofit, government, educational, and business organizations can take over pieces of this strategy. The role that the neighborhood organization must play, at minimum, is to bring these resources into the community and effectively connect them to local entrepreneurs. Organizations should also make sure that their businesses stay in the community, employ area residents, fill vacant storefronts, and create positive role models and community gathering places.

Write a vision statement and goals

Be sure to put all your choices about program focus and content into a strategic plan that includes a vision statement and list of goals. You can use the following worksheets for this purpose:

- Worksheet 16: Write a Vision Statement for Microbusiness, page 242.
- Worksheet 17: Write Three-Year Goals for Microbusiness, page 243.
- Worksheet 18: Write One-Year Goals for Microbusiness, page 245.

Also see Tips for Creating Your Vision and Strategic Plan in Chapter 3.

Step 3: Implement Your Plan

At this point, you should be clear about which type of microentrepreneur you are going to work with, what you will offer microentrepre-neurs, and what you hope to accomplish. You are now ready to implement the five aspects of your program mentioned above: attraction, training, connection, financing, and support.

Step 3 at a Glance

- Attract microentrepreneurs
- Train microentrepreneurs
- Connect microentrepreneurs to commercial space
- Lend to microbusinesses
- Support microentrepreneurs

Attract microentrepreneurs

Outreach to the microentrepreneurs in your community is your first step. You must get the word out to them that you are offering business training and support (either directly or through a partner). Fortunately, if your group is like most other community-based organizations, you are expert at reaching people. You have networks of community members who can spread the word. You can be regularly found in the community paper with articles and notices. People know where your office is, who your staff and board are, and how to connect to your activities and meetings.

To find microentrepreneurs, post flyers at banks, places of worship, and homes; put notices in the paper; and make announcements at various community meetings. Most important is word of mouth. Recruit everyone who may know of local residents interested in small business—bankers, small business owners, your own board members, and more. All these people can get the word out.

Train microentrepreneurs

It's often said that the two primary reasons small businesses fail in the United States are lack of knowledge and lack of capital. Business training is essential to solving the knowledge problem.

Positive publicity can attract more microbusinesses and resources to your efforts. Here, Marlon McGee, owner of LeMont's Gourmet BBQ Sauce, is featured on the cover of *Ventures,* a magazine for growing Twin Cities companies. McGee received one-on-one consulting and assistance training from the Neighborhood Development Center in St. Paul, Minnesota.

Running a business in the United States is complex. Even for the smallest of businesses, having a good business idea and putting in many hours of work are not enough. Entrepreneurs must navigate an endless stream of demands, first to start a business and then to sustain it. A comprehensive plan that anticipates these demands—from the customer, the landlord, the employees, the tax collector, the lender, and others—is a major help and predictor of success.

Business training can be obtained the hard way—from experience—if business owners can afford to lose money while learning the tricks of their trade, or if they are fortunate enough to work as a manager in a similar business before starting their own company. For many inner-city entrepreneurs, however, business experience is limited to running a part-time, underground business out of the home. These people may show an entrepreneurial spirit, but often they never really learn how to operate a sustainable business. Indeed, they easily learn many bad habits that are hard to shake. Effective training is what these talented people need most to bring their energy above ground and contribute more to their community.

Consider three training formats. The overall goal of business training is to help people produce a written business plan or to provide specific information about a business topic that will help a business get off to a good start or on a better footing. There are three basic formats for training microentrepreneurs and existing small businesses: classes on business planning and start-up, workshops on specific business topics, and one-on-one consulting.

Classes. Holding business planning and business start-up classes is the best way to convey a great deal of information to existing and potential entrepreneurs. Classes allow them to explore all the facets of their business idea and understand what it will really take to bring their business out to the avenue.

Typical start-up classes cover the sections of a business plan:

- Business concept and description
- Background and capabilities of the owners and management team
- Local and national industry trends
- Competition—who they are, what to learn from them, and how to survive against them
- Potential customers
- A marketing plan that fits the business, target market, and budget
- Start-up costs and sources of money
- Daily operations and management
- Month-by-month cash-flow projections for the first year, and quarterly projections for two more years

To develop the class curriculum, some groups hire trainers, give them the training goals, ask them to assemble a curriculum, and then review it prior to the class. Others use small business instructors at local colleges and the SBA's Small Business Development Center. Some groups shop for the best curriculum and purchase it. Finally, some groups develop their own curriculum after a few years of experience.[23]

Workshops. Brief workshops can be offered on business start-up or on more advanced topics. Business start-up workshops can lay out the reality of owning a small business in the United States. (Since few inner-city residents come from families with small businesses, they often hold many misconceptions about this subject.) Workshops can also guide people—particularly if they are new to this country—to actually select and refine a business idea (see the sidebar What about People Without a Clear Business Idea? on page 116).

Workshops on specific management topics can attract and train owners of existing small businesses. These owners have little time for any type of training but understand the importance of management skills more clearly than owners of start-up businesses.

---

[23] Sources of good curricula for microenterprise training include Association for Enterprise Opportunity, Northeast Entrepreneur Fund, Neighborhood Development Center, and the Small Business Administration.

Sample workshops for existing businesses include

- Setting up a bookkeeping system
- Financial management for small businesses
- Effective marketing
- Merchandising and displays for better profits
- Employee issues for small manufacturers
- How to manage a restaurant

Keep workshops to a few hours, and offer them at a convenient time and place for the business owners you want to assist.

One-on-one consulting. Working individually with your microentrepreneurs, whether owners of start-ups or existing businesses, is essential. Some community organizations use their own staff members, some use contracted trainers, and others use volunteers or experts from partner organizations for one-on-one consulting. Many people learn best through individual consulting; it is less intimidating and more private (to protect the business idea) and can progress at the individual's own pace.

However, consulting lacks the important peer support and networking available in classes, so it is best used in combination with some group learning. You can tie workshops specifically to one-on-one consulting, with the workshop trainer visiting each participating business owner before and after the workshop.

Set the right tone for your training program. Training opportunities for micro-entrepreneurs may already exist in your community. But these will fail to attract participants if they don't offer an atmosphere of *trust, comfort, value,* and *business* that appeals to potential and active microentrepreneurs.

Trust. First, local entrepreneurs need to see your organization as trustworthy and made up of people from their own community. Informal microentrepreneurs do not want to worry about being turned in to the tax collector. They may also worry about being in violation of zoning laws or other regulations. In addition, many low-income persons and persons of color have suspicions about the motives of public entities and other institutions.

The fact that your group is made up of their neighbors is the first step to gaining the trust of wary microentrepreneurs. Your ability to find these people, talk with them, and convince them that your program can help their business dream advance is crucial to tapping into this outstanding neighborhood asset.

Comfort. People also want to be in a training setting that is physically and psycho-logically *comfortable.* Their culture, educational level, language, and life experience must be understood and respected, preferably by people who share some of these traits. Your microentrepreneurs may feel intimidated by a setting that is too much like school: lots of students, lots of strangers, and boring lectures. But, if people believe that your organization is really made up of "us," they are likely to feel comfortable in your training.

Value. You must also convince microentrepreneurs that training will be *useful* to them—that it will actually help them achieve their dream of owning a business. Entrepreneurs often have little time for programs or classes and believe that they can just jump into business right now with a little bit of financing. Slowing these people down enough to listen to sound business guidance is not always easy. Convince them that you can deliver content that is directly relevant to their business and that your training will not drag out too long.

Business tone. You also want to set a business tone: Yours is not a "give-away" program but a place for highly motivated persons to turn a business dream into reality. Participants must commit to working hard, and they must get past the idea that anyone will "give" a business to them. This attitude reinforces a strong work ethic in participants and conveys a much stronger sense of pride and ownership when a business gets off the ground.

Select the trainers. Whether for a classroom setting, workshops, or one-on-one consulting, trainers must be

- *People with whom your residents feel a high degree of comfort and connection,* either because they come from the same ethnic group or because their communication style works across ethnic lines.
- *Experts at small business planning and management* whose knowledge and experience command the respect of your entrepreneurs. Often people who have owned their own small business are most successful at gaining this respect. They've "been there."
- *Good at effectively teaching complicated material.* This is a separate talent from good business skills.

Trainers who have all three qualities are hard to find. Look first for people who currently do such training, and bring them to your community. You can also find good candidates by advertising and by spreading the word through various business networks: banks, chambers of commerce, and government development agencies. Professionals who work with small businesses for a living—such as small business accountants, attorneys, and business consultants—can be good trainers.

Consider ways to train candidates who may be strong in business and able to relate well to your folks but who don't have a teaching background. By educating these people in teaching techniques and providing them with a prepared curriculum, you can develop a good trainer.

Another option is to put experienced trainers in teams with new trainers for a year or two to train the trainers. You can use this technique to train immigrant entrepreneurs in their own language. Pair an experienced trainer with a strong trainer prospect from the immigrant group; this prospect can translate and learn how to teach simultaneously.

Select trainees. Select trainees through written application forms and a twenty-minute interview with each applicant that involves the trainer and your program coordinator.

Selection can be based on a number of considerations, including

- *The likelihood that the trainee can carry out his or her business concept and raise the funds to finance it.* For instance, a person who has sold cookies at a church bazaar for five years and now wants to open a sit-down restaurant with $500 in savings is probably not a good prospect.

- *The potential for the business concept to succeed in your neighborhood.* Someone who wants to open a laundromat in a neighborhood that already has two well-run and affordable laundromats may have a poor chance for success.

- *The ability of the trainee to devote enough time to this effort.* For instance, a single person with a full-time job and three young children may not have the time to plan and start a business.

- *The willingness of the trainee to accept guidance from a trainer.* This characteristic is perhaps the number-one reason that microentrepreneurs succeed or fail. It is also very difficult to predict. Some people have the bull-headedness needed to succeed as an entrepreneur and are also hungry for suggestions on how to succeed. Others believe that they know everything before the class starts and are so stuck on their original business idea that any modification is unacceptable. There's a big difference between these two groups. To probe these differences, ask applicants to describe a failure they had early in life and what they learned from it. Also monitor their initial reactions to suggestions you make about their business concept.

Most training workshops and individual consulting offered by community groups are open to all interested entrepreneurs. With classroom training, however, you may get more applicants than you can handle in one class. Consider limiting class size to ten or twelve trainees. That way, the trainer has more time with each business owner and more ability to reduce intimidation.

What to include in an application form

A written application form is a simple and important way to begin selecting trainees. It also helps you collect evaluation information. Make certain that your application form captures the information you need to assess applicants and to evaluate your program's success, without being overwhelming or intimidating. Important items to capture include

- Basic demographics, such as age, gender, race, and income
- Their business concept
- Their expectations for the business—for example, the amount of income they expect and the personal satisfaction they expect to get from owning a small business
- How much time they have to devote to developing their business

Connect microentrepreneurs to commercial space

Connecting microentrepreneurs with available spaces in the community is the fun and easy part of your job. You can easily miss this part, however, in the flurry of daily office activities.

Stay abreast of available commercial space in your neighborhood, including space that will be vacant in the near future. As discussed in Chapter 4, many groups involved in community economic development keep up-to-date lists of available commercial space in their neighborhood. Start-up microbusinesses usually need rental space. Business incubators are often an ideal option for these businesses. (See pages 134–135 for more information on business incubators.)

Make sure entrepreneurs who receive your training are directed to the owners of available spaces at the right time. This is tricky. Start-up microentrepreneurs who lease too soon incur a major expense before they are earning money and their plans are mature; if they wait too long, they may lose their ideal site. So, giving advice on when to lease (and what lease terms to accept) will be a judgment call for your trainers and staff members. Make sure your microentrepreneurs know about available spaces in time to act with the best advice possible.

Lend to microbusinesses

Lending to microbusinesses is the next key step in your development strategy. Second only to the lack of business knowledge, the lack of money to start, expand, or stabilize a business is the major obstacle to entrepreneurial success in this country.

Look for sources of equity and debt. The typical ways that the U.S. economic system provides money to business—equity and debt—are not easily available to the microbusinesses with whom you work.

Equity is scarce if you are working with low- or moderate-income entrepreneurs in a low-income community. Some recent immigrant groups, such as the Hmong, have effective traditional ways of pooling savings into a loan fund that they make available to one another for business and other purposes. Some community development groups have drawn on individual development accounts (IDAs), which identify starting a business as an eligible use for these matched funds.[24] Residents who own their own home can tap into the equity in their house, although this is very risky.

While equity is scarce in low-income neighborhoods, low-income persons can usually save *some* amount of money toward their business, and friends or relatives may be willing to invest a little as well. Even when equity is only a few hundred dollars, it's important that microentrepreneurs contribute to their own business as much as possible.

---

[24] A good source of information for IDAs is found at www.acf.dhhs.gov/programs/ocs, a web site of the Office of Community Services in the Department of Health and Human Services. Web sites of the Association for Enterprise Opportunity and the Corporation for Enterprise Development have information about IDAs as well.

Debt for businesses comes from a variety of places, few of which are accessible to or appropriate for your microentrepreneurs. Credit cards are often used by people who can get them, but these generally carry high-interest rates that can cripple a small business. Banks rarely lend to these tiny start-up businesses because of the high cost and risk of such loans.

In fact, relatively few businesses of any kind start with loans from a bank. As a regulated industry, banks, on the one hand, are pushed to provide loans in low-income areas by the Community Reinvestment Act of 1977. On the other hand, banks are held to cautious lending standards by their examiners and high-profit goals by their shareholders. Few of the microbusinesses that you are likely to work with have the total package that banks require: strong business experience, significant equity, strong credit history and collateral, and a solid business plan.

Even so, bank loans can be coupled with government funds, nonprofit loan funds, or both to make some microbusinesses eligible. Any SBA, city, state, and nonprofit loan funds that exist in your community should be used to their maximum potential. Work with the staff of each of these funds to bring their resources to the microbusinesses in your community. Also meet with any local banker who is willing to take extra time to look at these small and difficult deals.

Package loan applications. Your organization can play a crucial role by packaging microentrepreneurs' loan applications for presentation to bankers and loan funds. *Loan packaging* is essential to commercial district revitalization and is discussed in Chapter 4 on page 76. Loan packaging includes

- Loan application preparation
- Preliminary analysis
- Assembling financing sources
- Structuring the deal

When loan officers at banks and public programs see all these things in place, they have a much easier time considering a loan to microentrepreneurs. However, only do those tasks for which your organization is qualified; any one of them will improve the loan application.

Create your own loan fund. Many community development organizations decide to start their own loan fund after watching a high percentage of their microentrepreneurs fail to get financing. Such failure could be due to a lack of governmental or nonprofit loan funds in the area or to the fact that the microentrepreneurs are considered too high risk for even those programs. In fact, community groups often create multipurpose loan funds that can be used with other pivot-point strategies in this book.

CAMBA develops microbusiness and small business in Flatbush

The Church Avenue Merchants Block Association (CAMBA) began in 1977 as a nonprofit merchants association in the Flatbush district of Brooklyn. Since then, it has evolved into a large community development organization providing a wide variety of services to young and old throughout the borough. In addition to American-born recipients of its services, CAMBA works with a high percentage of recent immigrants from various Caribbean countries, the former Soviet Union, and Asia.

One of CAMBA's services is to assist start-up and existing businesses. This service fits with the organization's mission to help individuals attain economic self-sufficiency and boost the economy of Brooklyn via business development. The program, which is called the "Entrepreneurial Assistance Program," offers training in workshops and in one-on-one counseling sessions and provides access to financing via mini-loans and start-up grants.

CAMBA's ability to work with start-up businesses is enhanced by its extensive networks and relationships with resources from throughout New York City and also by its hands-on involvement with a business improvement district on Church Avenue. The organization works directly with the 165 business owners in this district to fight crime and litter, provide business assistance, and decorate the district for the holiday shopping season.

Photograph by CAMBA, Inc. Used with permission.

Take advantage of your networks as you find and develop new microbusinesses. Here, Cynsations owner Ophilia Griffith poses in front of her store. Hers is one of many microbusinesses CAMBA has developed through its extensive networks and relationships throughout New York City.

However, starting and operating a successful loan fund takes considerable staff and board time, high levels of specialized expertise, and funding for the loans themselves and for their proper management. *Before you take this leap, be certain that no other loan funds in your area can work effectively with your microentrepreneurs.*

Don't start a loan fund if you are only going to make three or four loans each year. It is simply not worth the effort, nor will you gain the expertise needed to be successful. If you project low volume, try to find an existing nonprofit, city, state, or special bank loan fund that can get the job done for these businesses.

If you choose to go ahead, then study in-depth the loan procedures, documentation, and portfolio management techniques used by banks, solid nonprofit organizations, and government agencies in your area. You can also study the management techniques of national groups such as the Association for Enterprise Opportunity, the

National Community Capital Association, and the National Development Council. If possible, go to their conferences and trainings and talk to their staff.

Talk with a good banking attorney to make sure that your adaptations of documents and techniques achieve your goals and comply with state laws. Your attorney should also ensure that you are filing loan documents properly, have adequate collections procedures, and are protected from liability as much as possible.

To learn additional basics about administering a loan fund, see Tool 3: Operating Your Own Loan Fund in Chapter 4 (pages 76–80). In addition, review the following list of specific considerations when developing and managing a loan fund for microbusiness.

Consider sources of loan funds. A variety of government programs, foundations, and corporations have contributed to microloan funds operated by community organizations. Contact the Association for Enterprise Opportunity, National Community Capital Association, and SBA for information on national funding sources for microlending. Talk to local banks about a grant or an investment in your loan fund (such investments are now required for banks with over $250 million in assets to achieve the top ranking by the Community Reinvestment Act). Also take your plans to local funders. As with any request, these donors will be looking for your organization's clarity of purpose, the completeness of the plan, and the capacity to implement the plan.[25]

Once you have a strong lending track record, a few other options open up. As mentioned in Chapter 2, you can become certified by the U.S. Treasury Department as a community development financial institution (CDFI). As a CDFI, you can attract funds from banks and the Treasury Department for your work. This certification also enables you to sell new markets tax credits to corporations and individuals who need these credits. The proceeds of the sales can then be used for community economic development projects.

Consider your tolerance for risk. Most community organizations aim to finance microentrepreneurs that banks pass over because of high risk, small reward (small loans pay small fees), and time constraints (these deals take a considerable amount of the lender's time). Since you are setting up this fund to improve your community through entrepreneurs that have few (or no) other sources of funds, your loan program can generally accept significantly higher risk—along with higher delinquencies and higher default rates—than the local banker will accept.

In your loan guidelines, include your expectations for the number of delinquencies and defaults. Discuss this with your funders as well as your board and loan committee. While U.S banks aim at default rates of less than one-half of 1 percent, most community groups expect 3 percent to 10 percent in loan defaults. In your guidelines, define low-, medium-, and high-risk loans. Then set targets for how many loans you will make in each category.

---

[25] Contact the Association for Enterprise Opportunity and the Small Business Administration for funding suggestions.

You may want to include the type of ongoing technical assistance that your group will provide to the borrower. Such assistance can considerably lessen the risk of a default and the impact that a defaulting business will have on your community. Be careful that potential community benefit does not override all other considerations when you make a loan: A bad loan to a high-impact business will have even more negative community impact if the business goes under!

Consider the size of your loans. Lending to microbusinesses is typically done in small amounts, from $500 up to $25,000. While the low end of this scale may seem too small to deal with, remember that piling too much debt on a business can do more harm than good. Also, having the flexibility to make small loans is important.

Among groups that do community economic development, there is considerable variation on the upper end of the scale. Some groups cap their loans at $5,000 and others go well above $25,000—some over $100,000. Much of this decision depends on the type of businesses you are working with and how much money they need to start or expand their business.

Many groups make *step loans*: They limit the first loan they make to a small amount, and then increase subsequent loan sizes based on business performance and need. This technique limits the risk of lending to first-time borrowers and yet supports their growth through subsequent loans. It also keeps the borrower more attentive to your ongoing advice. This technique is common with international development groups.

Consider your interest rates. Some groups set interest below market rate to help their microbusinesses get started. However, most community groups price their loans at or above prevailing bank interest rates for small business loans—typically, 2 percent to 5 percent above the prime rate. There are a number of reasons for this.

First, entrepreneurs in your community must believe they have succeeded in the real world, not with the aid of subsidies and handouts. Second, as their business grows, they will begin to borrow from banks. In the eyes of bankers, these entrepreneurs are better prepared if their credit history was developed with market-rate funds. Third, there really is no "market rate" at banks for such loans, since they are by definition loans that banks will not make. (Banks price loans based in part on risk, and these loans are too risky to make—if they did, their rates would be higher than anything they currently offer.)

Another reason is that the interest rate makes little difference on the payments of a small loan. For instance, payments on a $4,000 loan at 10 percent with a two-year term are only about nine dollars more per month than the same loan at 5 percent interest. On a $40,000 loan with the same terms, the difference in payments is nearly $91 per month. Finally, this type of lending is very time consuming to the community group, so the higher interest rate helps pay for the program.

Consider what you will finance. You're likely to encounter three basic types of small business financing requests:

1. Working capital for operating expenses such as inventory, rent, payroll, and advertising

2. Fixed-asset financing for equipment and fixtures with a life over three years

3. Real estate mortgages to buy and renovate buildings

Since the dollar amounts are small and the terms tend to be short, no level of microlending is much use for real estate lending. Most groups use their microlending fund only for working capital and fixed-asset financing. Fixed assets tend to be much better collateral than anything purchased with working capital. Yet fixed assets are also usually more expensive than the individual operating costs that working capital addresses. Being able to finance both will give you the flexibility needed to meet most of your entrepreneurs' needs.

Consider your loan application requirements. The following is a fairly standard set of requirements for a microbusiness loan:

- *A loan application.* Get samples of these from a few banks and nonprofits. Work with your attorney and board to adapt these samples to your needs.

- *A written business plan and three-year cash-flow projection.* These are important since microentrepreneurs often lack other strengths that lenders consider (business experience, credit history, collateral, and equity). Some groups will accept a less-detailed business plan—perhaps a brief version or just a thorough conversation with the borrower—particularly when borrowers are not skilled at writing in English, or at writing in any language.

- *A personal financial statement.* Get a sample from your bank and make sure you can show your borrowers how to fill it out.

- *Business financial statements* for the previous three years, if available.

- *Written permission* to check the credit report of the borrower (usually part of the loan application).

- *Tax returns*—personal, business, or both for the previous two or three years.

Consider credit history. Some potential borrowers will have a poor credit history, which you will discover when you check their credit record and review their personal financial statements. This can be due to serious difficulties in their past, such as health problems, divorce, or layoffs, or it can be due to having a lax attitude about personal debt. These factors can show up as high amounts of debt (often from credit cards) or ignoring obligations to repay debt. Some borrowers may have no credit history at all—for example, young adults and recent immigrants from countries where credit is uncommon.

Most community groups deny loans to applicants with very bad credit, but will tolerate a worse credit history than a bank will. The challenge is to define whom you *will* lend to, given that you are dealing with people who can't get a bank loan. Given equally poor credit histories, community groups will refuse loans to people who have shown a lax attitude about personal debt, but will seriously consider those whose credit has been marred by difficult life experiences.

Loan guidelines should include standards for an acceptable credit history. For instance, you could specify that you will deny any applicant with more than three reports of sixty-day payment delinquency, a bankruptcy in the past three years, or any charge-offs and judgments that they can't correct before a loan is made.

Some organizations ask people to explain the reason for their bad credit and set up a workout plan with creditors. Depending on the person's income, this may be a long schedule with modest payments, perhaps just $25 to $50 per month. This plan should be agreed to by the creditors and put into place with at least two or three months of on-time payments. Creating and acting on such a plan puts borrowers on track to eventually clean up their credit; it also emphasizes the importance of paying debt on time.

An alternative is the "peer-group-lending" technique practiced by many international development organizations that have begun microlending in the United States. With this technique, group members guarantee the timely payment of all loans made to any member of the group. While this technique is used less frequently, it could be interesting to you.[26]

Consider collateral. Lack of collateral is another common reason inner-city microentrepreneurs fail to get bank financing, and it will be a challenge for your group as well. Repossessing collateral on a nonperforming loan is unpleasant. It's also difficult, because collateral drops in value rapidly (such as office and kitchen equipment), disappears easily (such as inventory, accounts receivable, cars, and trucks), or is hard to get (such as mortgages on owners' homes). Collateral is usually sold quickly at fire-sale prices that rarely cover the amount of the loan. The challenge is to set collateral requirements at a level that recovers some loss and yet doesn't kill most deals that come to your loan fund.

Loan guidelines should include the minimum collateral requirements that you are comfortable with. That could be 100 percent coverage of the loan by the collectable value of the collateral—in other words, the collateral could be sold for the full value of the loan. Most community groups require less than 100 percent, some as low as 30 percent.

Consider that you are in a risky business, and that you will primarily be looking at loans that no bank will touch. Meet with your board and the funders of your loan program to discuss their goals for recovering defaulted loans through collateral

---

[26] Organizations with experience in peer-group lending include ACCION and FINCA.

seizure and liquidation. This could be one of the places you can take more risk, depending on the sources of your funds and the goals of your program.

Consider character. Out of the four traditional "Cs of banking"—character, credit, collateral, and capacity—character is the one your group will have to specialize in. Your borrowers are likely to be weak in some or all of the other areas. You can get a reasonable sense of borrowers' character through a loan process, by talking with them about difficult issues from their credit history, and challenging them on various aspects of their business plan. If borrowers have come through your training program, your trainer should have a good sense of their commitment to their business, their ability to follow through on each step of the start-up process, and their willingness to accept and implement advice. A borrower's reputation within the community can also be informative, especially with people whose opinion you know and trust.

Consider loan analysis and write-ups. For the microloans you are likely to work on, you do not have to learn all that goes into underwriting (analysis) of larger business loans. Microbusiness loans in the $1,000 to $25,000 range are heavily based on written business plans and projections and the management ability and character of the business owner. Besides, with microbusiness loans you seldom have three years of business financial statements to analyze.

If you take on more complex deals, you will have to learn more about underwriting from a commercial banker or through other training. One of the best training opportunities is from the National Development Council, which has trained a high percentage of loan officers in public and nonprofit organizations in the United States.

Consider your loan committee. Generally these are committees of your organization's board of directors. Occasionally you can add a few outside persons with skills in particular areas, such as banking, construction, law, and architecture. An alternative is to set up your committee with all outside professionals.

Because most loan committees include members from the board—usually local business owners—the committee has a greater personal investment in the program and knowledge of each local applicant. This can create problems of trust and confidentiality, as on occasion neighbors will be deciding on loans to other neighbors. Thus, set up your guidelines clearly, market your fund evenly, and operate it consistently.

Consider loan servicing. Once you make a loan, you have to *service* it: track the loan, send out payment notices, collect payments every month, and apply the proper amount to principal and interest in your records. This is not the fun part of microbusiness development, but it is an excellent way to keep your finger on the pulse of each borrower. You will be among the first to find out if their business has financial problems and what sort of help they need.

Some groups contract out their loan servicing and some do it in-house. Nationally, a number of firms will service loans for a fee. They can save you considerable staff time and the cost of loan-servicing software. Ask a few bankers whom they recommend. On the other hand, many community groups service loans in-house. This can be a better way to track your loans if they have a wide range of terms and conditions customized to each borrower.

One trick to collecting payments is to call borrowers immediately after a payment has been missed. If they get a friendly reminder call the day after a missed payment, you will have a better chance of getting the payment on time next month. Some community development groups send staff to collect payments at the borrower's place of business, either weekly (which is often easier for the borrower but harder on the staff) or monthly. It is quite difficult to wear both the hat of a trainer-technical assistance provider and a lender-loan collector. Many groups have different people doing these two tasks when possible—a classic good-cop, bad-cop maneuver.

Consider specialty loan funds. You can set up loan funds for almost any goal that your organization has. Facade loans, working capital loans for business expansion

Providing growth capital for Muslim business owners

Throughout the 1990s, Minneapolis and St. Paul experienced a wave of immigrants from Somalia and other Muslim countries. Neighborhood Development Center (NDC) of St. Paul and Minneapolis had a strong history of microlending and small business lending, but was unable to finance the many businesses started by new Muslim entrepreneurs, whose religious principles prohibit paying interest on loans.

Working closely with Reba Free LLC, an Islamic finance and investment consulting firm, NDC developed a program of profit-based financing as an alternative to interest-bearing loans. Patterned after models from banks in Middle Eastern countries, the financing is offered according to Islamic principles that require the provider of money to share in both the risk and reward of the business endeavor as an investor rather than as a lender. The model includes two financing forms: *Murabaha (buy-sell with deferred payment)* and *royalty investment.*

Buy-sell arrangements (called *Murabaha* or *Bai al-ajal*) involve the sale of goods on installment or deferred payments. For these, NDC purchases the equipment, goods, or other assets on behalf of the business owner, and then sells them to that owner at an agreed-upon price that includes NDC's markup (profit). The business owner makes payments by installment within a prearranged period or in a lump sum.

The royalty investment (called *limited Mudarabah*) is an agreement between an investor and an entrepreneur who wishes to expand a current business or has a special project that needs financing. The investor provides either all or a portion of the expansion capital, while the *Mudarib* (the entrepreneur) manages the project. Both parties agree in advance on the share of profit or loss from the investment. At the end of the project the investor gets the principal back plus the agreed-upon share of the profit or less the agreed-upon share of the loss.

NDC used these approaches to finance twelve Muslim businesses during the first year of the fund.

Thanks to Wafiq Fannoun, president of Reba Free LLC and board member of NDC, for contributing this information about Islamic financing.

and start-ups, microloans for start-ups, Islamic-acceptable financing for Somalian immigrants—all these can be built on the same considerations laid out above.

Support microentrepreneurs

The final piece of a comprehensive microbusiness development program involves ongoing support. Since few microentrepreneurs have formal business experience, most have a tremendous number of things to learn.

Running a business can be an overwhelming task with literally dozens of balls to keep up in the air at the same time and no one to help. Your organization can make a tremendous difference if these business owners see you as a source of trustworthy advice and assistance. By keeping a strong connection with the entrepreneurs as they come through your start-up training and lending services, you are likely to be the place they turn to when reality collides with the business plan.

When troubled, entrepreneurs sometimes dig a hole and stay in it, refusing to seek help until it is too late. Therefore, affirmative outreach is as important for your ongoing support as for initial business training. Because new business owners may overlook or ignore basic management tasks, contact each entrepreneur you train or finance every month or so.

When working with microentrepreneurs, many community groups focus on technical issues such as

- Bookkeeping and tax reporting
- Lack of sales
- Creating a new marketing strategy on a small budget
- Assistance in obtaining loans
- Cash-flow management
- Problems with landlords, contractors, suppliers, and city inspectors
- Retail store layout and design
- Reducing excessive operating expenses
- Inefficient operations
- Employee training and customer service
- Pricing of products

Your list of options for offering such assistance overlaps considerably with activities used in other pivot-point strategies. Following are some examples.

Offer one-on-one business consulting. You can provide this form of assistance to entrepreneurs *after* they open their doors for business, meeting in their place of business or in your office. Consulting can be provided by qualified staff or by experts you bring into your office on a regular basis. These can include

- Consultants from the local Small Business Development Center or Business

Information Center (nationwide networks of the SBA)
- Retired business owners and executives from the Service Corps of Retired Executives (also found at the SBA office)
- Business library personnel
- Professors or well-supervised graduate students from MBA programs
- Staff members from nonprofit partner organizations in your area

Look for the same qualities in these consultants as in your classroom trainer: knowledge of small business management, experience as owner of a small business, experience consulting or training on business management, adequate language skills, and the ability to connect quickly with microentrepreneurs from your community.

Offer professional volunteers with key specialties. You can leverage staff time—and help more entrepreneurs—by using volunteer specialists to work with your entrepreneurs. Your city probably has thousands of seasoned professionals who are experts at any business challenge: legal, accounting, tax compliance, financial planning, personnel, real estate, marketing, and many others. These potential volunteers are a great resource for the owners of small businesses and microbusinesses who need such specialized advice but can't afford to pay for it. Reach out to such professionals in your community. Local banks, business schools, churches, synagogues, and mosques are sources of a wealth of professional talent. Large corporate offices also donate expertise; many large law firms, for instance, aim to donate 5 percent of their billable hours to low-income clients.

Besides connecting such talent with your businesses, your task is to ensure that these professional relationships really help the business owners. First, locate volunteers who actually know about running a tiny business; large-scale experiences do not translate easily to microbusiness. Second, understand exactly what *part* of a business problem a volunteer can actually affect in a few hours every month or two. Make sure that everyone's expectations for the volunteer are the same. For example, legal problems often have a clear beginning point and ending point. A pro bono attorney usually knows how to go from one point to the other, and business owners can fulfill their role simply by providing the attorney with accurate information. In contrast, accounting requires the business owner to maintain complete basic books; a volunteer accountant can't do much with a pile of bills and receipts in a box. Keep these realities in mind when matching volunteers and microentrepreneurs.

Offer workshops for existing businesses in your neighborhood. Working individually with a business owner is effective—and time consuming. Therefore, many community groups provide workshops for five to thirty businesses at once. Workshops offer several advantages: They are cheaper to operate than consultation; it is easier to find volunteers to teach a two-hour workshop; you can charge a nominal fee to cover costs; and workshops enhance networking and the entrepreneurial culture. The trick is getting business owners in the door. You may find it hard to lure these folks out of their shop or office. The sidebar Personal Touch Attracts Microentrepreneurs, on page 135, shows one way of appealing to busy owners.

Promote networking. Another ingredient in business success is the network of customers, vendors, resources, and peers that most business owners live within every day. Whether networking takes place over lunch, at the chamber of commerce meeting, on the golf course, or in the evening over a drink, many small business owners network continuously.

For most inner-city microentrepreneurs, this extensive network of valuable contacts is largely missing. Your organization can help entrepreneurs build up their own network of contacts. This task plays to a strength of your group: Most likely you exist within an extensive network of area residents, leaders, funders, government agencies, nonprofits, and others.

Put this network to work for your entrepreneurs. Bring people to their stores and offices often, and encourage them to do the same with their friends. Host lunches or other gatherings where business owners can get together to share experiences and ideas or listen to a speaker on a relevant topic. Encourage your folks to join some of the traditional networks—the chamber of commerce, the Rotary, the Lions Club, and so on—and go with them the first few times.

Offer support through business incubators. Another option is to put a number of your microbusinesses under one roof, in flexible, affordable, professional space. Add a shared copier, conference room, fax, receptionist, business library, computer with high-speed Internet connections, and other useful tools for start-up businesses. Package all your training, lending, and support and put it in the building for the benefit of the tenants. In this package, you have the essential ingredients of a business incubator. Business incubators are a common and effective way to assist start-up and young businesses of all kinds—over 900 exist in the United States today.

Typically, community organizations convert an older building, often vacant, that may be a major eyesore in the community, into a business incubator. Some groups build new buildings (an expensive option) or use a number of vacant storefronts along a few blocks of a commercial district as a "scattered-site" incubator. Following the nature of the building, some incubators house office businesses. Others house light manufacturing companies or retailers. These projects sometimes aim at incubating a particular type of business, such as ethnic retailers in a marketplace setting or food product businesses in a kitchen incubator.

Incubators offer an ideal setting for many microbusinesses. They generally provide smaller spaces at a lower rental rate than these entrepreneurs can find elsewhere—an ideal step out from the home for their business. Incubators also save the entrepreneur significant costs through shared copiers, faxes, receptionists, and other typical

Personal touch attracts microentrepreneurs

Busy microentrepreneurs may be reluctant to take time for a workshop. One alternative is to combine consulting, a workshop, and a field trip. This combination provides the personal touch and relevancy of individual consulting, along with education, networking, and hands-on experience. Using trainers who are bilingual and experts in the specialty being taught, one community group uses the following format to work with Latino retailers and restaurateurs:

1. The trainer meets with participating owners in their shop.

2. The trainer gives a three-hour workshop to lay out basic principles such as merchandising, marketing, and financial management for the retailers, and food presentation, inventory, and cost controls for the restaurants.

3. Participants take a field trip to a major shopping center or restaurant to see examples of merchandising or food presentation principles in action.

4. The trainer meets with each owner in their place of business after the workshop and field trip, discussing specific ways to apply the workshop content.

Adult learners need to know their time will be well spent, and they need to observe principles in action. This combination successfully meets their needs.

office support (or kitchen equipment, in a kitchen incubator). Additionally, some retail incubators market to the general public on behalf of the tenants.

Most importantly, incubators provide valuable peer support from other entrepreneurs who are going through the same difficult process of growing a business. For more information on this topic, get in touch with the National Business Incubation Association.

Step 4: Monitor, Evaluate, and Improve

Success with any of the four pivot points calls on you to evaluate how your work is paying off. First, you are looking for *impact*: What benefits did microentrepreneurs receive, what impact have these entrepreneurs made on your community, and are there ways to improve these impacts? Second, you are looking for program *effectiveness*: Are you reaching the types of entrepreneurs you aimed at and keeping your costs within budget? Are there better ways to achieve your goals?

Start by recording all inquiries and responses that microentrepreneurs make to your outreach: contact information, business type and goals, and the specific type of assistance required. Next, make sure you track all information from the application forms that people submit to get your training. Paper-and-pencil records are better than not tracking at all, as long as records are complete. Using a computer database software program is ideal, since the software can quickly compile statistics for you.

The types of statistics to consider in your evaluation include the following:

- *Target population:* the gender, race, and age entrepreneurs you assist, the number of retailers versus service providers, and the number of immigrant entrepreneurs who don't speak English.

- *Value of your service:* what entrepreneurs received from your program, how many people actually started their business, how many made intelligent choices to drop a bad business idea, and the number of owners who are meeting their business goals.

- *Economic impact of these businesses on your community:* jobs created, who got these jobs, annual sales, annual payroll, owners' income, taxes paid, dollars recirculated within the community, and similar figures.

- *Community impact of these businesses:* community gathering places created, visible role models who emerged from your programs, goods and services brought into the community, vacant storefronts filled and renovated, and so forth.

- *Cost-effectiveness of your program:* the cost per entrepreneur trained, per business started, and per job created.

Some of these results will be easier to obtain than others. For instance, most business owners will not reveal their own income, and many are reluctant to reveal their sales figures. If you guarantee them that the data will always be used in the aggregate, never mentioning names and never using individual business figures, you will be more successful.

Using an outside consulting or research firm to conduct an independent survey of your entrepreneurs gives the entrepreneurs more comfort in revealing their personal information. It also takes a load off your staff. Most importantly, the results will have more credibility with funders and supporters than data that you generate yourself.

Using this data is the final and most important step in this aspect of your program. Look hard at what the figures tell you. While celebrating your successes, keep looking for ways to improve. Constant evaluation and improvement will help you get more of the results that your community wants.

Summary

Microbusiness development, with both domestic and international roots, has begun to take hold in inner-city development. This is an effective way to build your neighborhood economy from within. Yet tackling this pivot point presents many challenges due to the nature of microentrepreneurs. These people can be difficult to reach with training, and their businesses are typically fragile.

To overcome these challenges, use the four steps that apply to any of the pivot points discussed in this book: assess current conditions, create a vision and a strategic plan, implement your plan, and monitor the results with a constant eye toward improvement. Your planning and implementation will hinge on attracting microentrepreneurs, training them effectively, connecting them with available space, and offering them financing and support.

Using partner organizations is often the key to success with this strategy. Banks and other business loan programs are a great resource for your entrepreneurs. So are the many organizations that assist small businesses, from the local business library, to law firms and accounting firms with pro bono assistance, to the local Small Business Administration and Small Business Development Center. Your task is to bring these resources into your community in ways that local entrepreneurs trust and use, developing their businesses into a tangible asset for themselves and your community.

Chapter 6

Develop Your Community Workforce

By definition, a low-income community suffers from high numbers of unemployed and underemployed people. How much stronger would your local economy be if 20 percent or 30 percent of the *unemployed* people in your community had a decent job five years from now? What if a fourth of those currently working for very low wages were making living wages in five years? Employment goals such as these may seem out of reach for your neighborhood. Yet many communities have attacked this problem with remarkable success.

Low-income neighborhoods have something that employers want—workers. The bad news is that many residents of these neighborhoods are not getting or keeping available jobs. This may indicate that local workforce development programs are not effective, at least for some of the population. Or it could mean that more of these services are needed to really make a difference for residents and employers.

There are a variety of ways that your group can play an important role in putting more of your residents to work. There is not one "right way" to get involved. But the more you know about workforce development, the better equipped you will be to make the right choice for your group.

Overview

The basic components of a workforce program begin with *outreach* to both ends of the employment picture—workers (or those looking for work) and employers—to find out what they need to successfully come together. The next stage is either *connecting workers and employers immediately* (the "workfirst" approach) or *providing workers with skills for seeking and keeping a job*. These skills are of two broad types: "soft" job skills, such as résumé writing and punctuality, and "hard" job skills, such as machine operations or bank training. Many job seekers need additional services, such as day care, English-language instruction, transportation, housing, or counseling. These services are often provided through referrals to other organizations and

Chapter 6 at a Glance

Chapter 6 provides information about the workforce development industry in the United States. You will learn the seven basic approaches that community groups use in this strategy. After gaining this basic knowledge, you can proceed through the following core steps. Worksheets 19 through 22 are used in this process.

1. Assess current workforce conditions by examining census data. Identify groups of residents with unique employment barriers, and research regional job trends. Learn about workforce development programs and vocational training in your area, and talk with employers and other community leaders.

2. Create a vision for workforce development in your community after discussing five key questions presented in this chapter. Design a plan for your vision by identifying gaps in services and how your group could fill these gaps and by determining how you will measure results.

3. Implement your program depending on which of the seven approaches you select: partnering with other organizations, participating with a local network, participating in a national network, partnering with employers, creating an in-house program, obtaining a contract from your local Workforce Investment Board, or advocating for change in the workforce development system.

4. Monitor, evaluate, and improve. Periodically review your results. See if your workforce development program is on track with your vision and goals.

programs. *Ongoing support* to workers after they get a job is another common program element. Finally, *monitoring and evaluation of results* occurs with all good programs.

Some community groups partner with a larger nonprofit or government workforce development organization, bringing their service into the neighborhood. Others link with a large employer in the neighborhood that needs workers. Still others develop a comprehensive in-house program, serving employers and residents with a variety of services. Participating in a network of community groups is yet another model that has been successful. Finally, some groups have effectively advocated for improvements in the existing system, without providing any direct services themselves.

The strategies addressed in this chapter aim to help neighborhood residents get and keep jobs that are already available in your area. The other side of this problem may be a lack of jobs in your area that residents can get and that pay enough to keep them out of poverty. Growing better jobs at a significant rate by working with growing businesses is the focus of Chapter 7.

Understand the Workforce Development Industry

The United States has a large, well-established workforce development industry. This industry has worked for decades to help unemployed people get and keep jobs, and to help underemployed people find and keep better jobs. It involves the government, the private sector, foundations, and community-based nonprofit organizations. This section looks briefly at who the actors are, where their funding comes from, and what their basic approaches have been.

Actors

The largest workforce development actor has been the government—from the federal level to the state, county, and city levels. Early federal programs included the Manpower Development and Training Act of 1962 and the Comprehensive Employment and Training Act (CETA) of 1973. From 1982 to 1998, the overarching federal program that funded and carried out workforce development was the Job Training Partnership Act (JTPA), administered by the

U.S. Department of Labor. Under JTPA, every locality in the country had a board of citizens called a Private Industry Council (PIC) with oversight of local workforce development programs that used federal funds. Many of these programs were carried out by state, county, and city agencies, while some were contracted to nonprofits.

A wide array of programs operated in every area of the country. This maze of doors and procedures bewildered both workers and employers, who were often unable to use the system successfully. Many neighborhood groups and larger community-based organizations used funding from JTPA and their local PICs to provide services for residents. However, many of these groups became frustrated by the rigidity and complexity of the system, because it limited how they could serve their diverse populations, and because the reporting requirements became more than many could cope with.[27]

In 1998, JTPA was replaced by the Workforce Investment Act (WIA). This act required every locality to create a "One-Stop Career Center" (sometimes called "Workforce Centers"). These centers are intended to combine and coordinate the entire array of services into one user-friendly center. Each One-Stop Career Center is governed by a Workforce Investment Board (WIB), which replaced the PICs. Like the PICs, these boards are filled with local citizens. Each state also has a state-level WIB that sets standards for all local WIBs. Each local WIB must develop a comprehensive plan with public input, file it with the state board, and make it available to the public.[28]

The federal Workforce Investment Act program is administered by the Employment and Training Administration in the Department of Labor. Federal workforce development dollars now flow through this system of One-Stop Career Centers and are governed by the WIA. These dollars constitute the largest source of workforce development funding in the country; consequently, WIA programs, centers, and boards constitute the largest set of actors in the industry.[29]

The government has not been the only actor, however. Most cities have an array of organizations that focus on workforce development, including nonprofits, community action programs, community and technical colleges, public school systems, and faith-based organizations. Many major employers have approached the problem proactively with public or nonprofit partners. Some cities have networks of community-based workforce organizations that provide centralized services to member groups. National nonprofits such as the Aspen Institute, Enterprise Foundation, and Public/Private Ventures have done considerable research and dissemination of results, models, and best practices.

---

[27] For additional analysis of JTPA, contact the Enterprise Foundation, Aspen Institute, and Public/Private Ventures.

[28] You can obtain your local Workforce Investment Board plan through the Employment and Training Administration web site at www.usworkforce.org.

[29] For additional information on the Workforce Investment Act and One-Stop Career Centers, start with www.doleta.gov and www.usworkforce.org.

Funding

The funding for these programs comes from many of the same actors mentioned above. Most levels of the government provide funding, primarily through the WIA system. Some local governments have gone beyond this system and added funds through use of Community Development Block Grants or through bonding issuances or other local means.

Many foundations and corporations have provided both philanthropic funding and knowledge over the years to organizations engaged in workforce development. Finally, employers often fund local workforce programs, generally to fill a need for well-prepared workers. This trend is perhaps strongest when filling vacancies is difficult because of low unemployment rates, as it was during the last half of the 1990s. But the trend should continue even if these rates rise, because of the increasing diversity of the labor pool from which corporations draw.

Basic approaches to workforce development

Every program must answer at least three basic questions as it develops its approach. These questions will help you understand who the actors are in your area; they will also help you determine how to get involved.

1. Which types of people does the program serve? Each program must decide whether it will serve every person who walks in the door or focus on certain types of people. Examples of such a focus include immigrants from a certain country, single mothers, or youth.

2. Which types of employers does the program serve? Programs need to decide whether they will prepare people for jobs at every type of business in the area or focus on one or two types of businesses. Sector-oriented programs are increasingly common; examples include training people for bank teller, hospital aide, or machine operator positions. Aspen Institute has done considerable research on sector approaches to workforce development.

3. Preparation and training versus immediate job placement. In the past, most programs emphasized at least a basic skills training period before job placement. Increasingly, the workfirst approach is becoming common, as programs simply connect clients to available job openings without such training, sometimes providing support after clients have begun their job.

Common Elements in Workforce Development Programs

Workforce development programs provide four types of services:

1. Recruitment, assessment, and referral
2. Training
3. Job placement
4. Job retention support

Every program offers a somewhat different mix and sequence of services, and many programs offer only one or two services from this list. As mentioned, the One-Stop Career Centers administered under the WIA are intended to be comprehensive, offering the full range of services. However, even with this system, there is some difference from one center to the next in how the job seeker is routed through the various services.

1. Recruitment, assessment, and referral

This broad category of service begins with outreach to unemployed and under-employed people, conducted in their own language, in their own networks, and in other ways that make services accessible. Examples of *recruitment* techniques in a neighborhood setting include

- Flyers distributed door-to-door and at neighborhood businesses, especially those where many residents shop
- Referrals from programs throughout the neighborhood, such as at midnight basketball programs, nutrition programs, homeless shelters, recreational centers, day care centers, settlement houses, schools, and other community agencies
- Notices in the bulletins of religious congregations and in other community publications

Assessment and referral involve meeting with applicants to assess their job skills and experiences, their job preferences, and their job-seeking and retention obstacles. These barriers go beyond lack of connections or job skills and include lack of trans-portation, housing, and day care, mental illness, illiteracy, chemical dependency, remedial education needs, and lack of fluency in English. While some workforce development organizations have resources to address these barriers, most refer people to other programs in the community.

2. Training

Training can help job seekers develop *soft skills* and *hard skills*. Soft skills include effective work habits, appropriate dress, managing family crises that could inter-fere with work, maintaining motivation, and building a support system. Program participants can learn these skills in a variety of formats: group classes, individual counseling, field trips to clothing stores, and on the job.

Hard skills are job specific and as varied as the job market. Some examples include skills needed for employment as a truck driver, commercial food handler, bank teller, or hospital worker. Appropriate formats for teaching hard skills also vary widely. Classrooms and computer labs work well for some hard-skill development. Other skills call for access to a lab, an engine repair shop, a commercial kitchen, or other facilities typically found in job settings. Clients can also gain hard skills through on-the-job training—either on-site with a future employer or at a business operated by a workforce development organization.

3. Job placement

This category offers job seekers help in two areas: finding job openings and getting hired. (As mentioned, the workfirst approach skips most or all training services and moves job seekers immediately to job placement.)

Finding job openings is done in many ways. For instance, some programs

- Scan state and county job listings, newspaper want ads, and Internet sites every day
- Maintain regular contact with a network of interested employers
- Build a jobs network by speaking at business associations such as the chamber of commerce, Rotary, Lions Club, and other neighborhood business clubs
- Sponsor job fairs in which employers and job seekers can meet
- Offer useful services to employers (especially as the workforce becomes more culturally diverse), such as employee orientation, employee retention, diversity training, and customer service
- Host a job-opening web site where employers can post their openings and requirements
- Offer customized recruitment to employers for a fee

Training can help job seekers develop *soft skills* and *hard skills*. *Hard skills* are job specific and as varied as the job market. Here, graduates of the Newark-based New Community Corporation's Workforce Development Center are ready for work in the health care field as certified nurse's aides, home health aides, clinical medical assistants, or medical billers.

Photograph by Laura L. Comppen for New Community Corporation. Used with permission.

Helping job seekers *get hired* means assisting them to, for example,

- Write a résumé
- Make calls to potential employers
- Succeed in a job interview
- Dress appropriately for a job interview
- Find temporary day care while job hunting
- Get cash for tools or other supplies needed to start a job

4. Job retention support

The fourth category of services includes anything that helps clients to *keep* a job once they get hired. For instance, clients might need

- Additional job-skill training
- Transportation (bus card or car repair assistance)
- Referrals to affordable day care or housing
- Work clothes (discounts for uniforms, office attire, and so forth)
- Crisis counseling and intervention

Seven Common Approaches to Workforce Development

Community groups have successfully used seven broad approaches to workforce development. These are

1. Partnerships with other organizations
2. Participation in a local network
3. Participation in a national network
4. Partnerships with employers
5. Comprehensive in-house program
6. Workforce Investment Board contract
7. Workforce development advocacy

Many community development groups use some combination of these seven approaches. These broad approaches require varying levels of commitment and expertise from your organization. For example, outreach is fairly simple, but providing quality referrals for complex barriers to employment, such as mental illness or chemical dependency, requires more preparation. When you assess your organization's capacity to tackle this pivot point (part of Step 1), carefully consider which services your organization is qualified to provide, and which services will require you to develop in-house capacity or strong partnerships to carry out.

Before you make your final choice from the seven approaches described below, you'll need to understand the current employment picture in your community and how employment services are provided in your city. These tasks are also part of Step 1, the assessment section of this chapter. From that assessment, you will determine which key services are missing from your community, and the best way your group can help to deliver them.

1. Partnerships with other organizations

Because many organizations already specialize in workforce development, neighborhood groups often do not need to create this resource from scratch. Instead, they can attract employment resources into the community and adapt them for local residents. In this way, a neighborhood group becomes an effective local access point for these services.

Good places to look for partners include

- Local nonprofit workforce development organizations
- Community colleges
- Technical and vocational colleges
- Public school systems
- Local One-Stop Career Center (see page 141 for a description of the One-Stop Career Center)

The sidebar What to Consider When Selecting Partners, on page 164, helps your organization gauge the attributes it brings and the attributes a partner should have.

2. Participation in a local network

A second common option is to participate in a *network* of community groups doing workforce development. Through such a network, your group becomes the local door to a larger program with services that all member groups use. These services—provided by a central staff serving all members of the network—can include any or all of the services listed earlier in this chapter, such as a centralized listing of job openings, connections to larger employers, or specialized training programs. These networks often connect with other workforce development programs to expand their services.[30]

Several excellent examples of workforce development networks are worth studying, including

- Chicago Jobs Council[31]
- Minneapolis Neighborhood Employment Network (MNET)

---

[30] For further information, see *Workforce Development Networks: Community-Based Organizations and Regional Alliances* by Bennett Harrison and Marcus Weiss, pp. 50–70.

[31] Chicago Jobs Council provides training, advocacy, and information to over one hundred job training organizations.

The latter is profiled in the sidebar Network of Job Banks Serves 7,000 Annually, below.

3. Participation in a national network

Several national organizations have a strong presence in workforce development. Some of these organizations actively partner with local organizations in selected cities, bringing them a similar set of services as described above. Three of these organizations are

- Enterprise Foundation
- Goodwill Industries
- Center for Employment Training (see the sidebar Successful California Group Replicates Model, on page 148)

4. Partnerships with employers

By necessity, every workforce development program involves interactions with employers. What's unique about this fourth approach is viewing the employer as an active partner to help design and implement the program, rather than just hiring its graduates. This approach can involve groups of employers with similar workforce needs, such as clusters of small businesses needing machine operators or banks needing tellers and computer operators. It can also be done with a single large employer, such as a major hospital or factory.

Network of job banks serves 7,000 annually

Minneapolis Neighborhood Employment Network (MNET) is a network of neighborhood job banks located in fifteen community-based organizations operating in low-income neighborhoods throughout Minneapolis. About 7,000 neighborhood residents seek services each year at MNET locations; MNET is able to place about 1,000 of them. Staff members at local job banks search out job openings and act as the access point to all MNET services.

People who come to MNET for help get the following services from the neighborhood-level staff:

- Interviews to identify barriers to employment
- Referrals to appropriate sources of assistance
- Referrals to nearby job openings, based on leads generated by the local organization and by MNET staff

- Various forms of help to succeed in the workplace, from bus cards and affordable child care to training and counseling

The central MNET office supplies each local office with many of these resources, updating them regularly. Thus, by participating in MNET, the fifteen community groups can offer their residents far more employment services than they could provide acting alone.

About 60 percent of program funding comes from the Workforce Investment Act, and is raised by the central MNET office. The remaining funds are raised by each participating community group.

Successful California group replicates model

In 1967, the Center for Employment Training (CET) began working with migrant farm workers in the San Jose area who were seeking better jobs. Funded by a variety of federal and state programs and with an annual budget of $25 million, the center now operates in twenty California communities. The center is also working in ten East Coast cities to replicate its model.

CET trains at-risk youth, farm workers, welfare recipients, and adults for jobs that pay more than minimum wage. The center has trained over 75,000 low-income people since it began; about 75 percent of these people obtained jobs after the training.

This model integrates job-skills training with life-skills counseling and basic education in English, reading, and math. Center staff members offer training in twenty-five occupations, ranging from commercial food preparation to building maintenance. Students pay tuition and, on average, attend classes nearly full-time for four to five months. There is no entrance exam and students can enter and exit the training at will.

This training is employer-driven: Employers determine the skill levels required for new workers and monitor the training to ensure that standards are met. Instructors are professionals from the relevant industry. Follow-up support continues after the job placement, with counseling and additional training as needed.

Adapted from the web site for CET, www.cet2000.org.

In seeking a win-win solution to employment problems, the business partners often pay for all or part of the program costs. Businesses may also provide training facilities and expertise and assure jobs for qualified program graduates. The neighborhood organization creates the access point for local residents and may contribute funding or training ideas to the mix. This organization also acts as a clearinghouse for other employment resources, such as referrals to basic education training, English as a second language classes, or child care.

There are many good examples of such partnerships. The sidebar Cleveland Partnership Supports Workforce and Business, on page 149, describes one in depth. Other examples of program partnerships with employers include

- Project for Pride in Living, which works with Abbott Northwestern Hospital and Children's Hospitals and Clinics, two major employers in Phillips, the lowest-income neighborhood of Minneapolis. Their "Train to Work" project provides neighborhood residents with four weeks of training and eighteen months of support and mentoring on the job at local hospitals. The program has placed 487 neighborhood residents into permanent jobs. Funding comes from the hospitals, Honeywell (another local corporation), and other sources.

- Goodwill/Easter Seals of St. Paul and Minneapolis, which has a partnership with nine metro-area banks that need entry-level employees. The banks contribute the training equipment and site; they also train the program trainer and hire all qualified graduates.

Cleveland partnership supports workforce and business

Westside Industrial Retention and Expansion Network (WIRE NET), formed in 1986 by three community development corporations in Cleveland, focuses on medium-size industrial businesses that need workers.

WIRE NET conducts the outreach, screening, and training phases of workforce development and works with business members to place residents in good jobs. More specifically, WIRE NET provides specialty training in the machine trades along with a variety of other support,

such as access to child care, uniforms, and tools needed for new jobs. The businesses help design the training, contribute funding, and place the graduates. They also participate in overseeing the entire program.

WIRE NET has placed over 1,600 residents in industrial jobs close to home on the west side of Cleveland. In 1998, 180 WIRE NET applicants earned an average of $7.99 per hour, adding an estimated $3 million to the local economy.

Adapted from the web site for WIRE NET, www.wire-net.org.

5. Comprehensive in-house program

Some community development organizations take on workforce development alone. This generally takes considerably more staff time, money, connections, and expertise than other approaches. Groups usually choose this option when they have no adequate alternative *and* they are strong enough as an organization to assemble all the resources needed to succeed.

Communities Organized for Public Service (COPS) and Metro Alliance, two powerful community organizations in San Antonio, provide a good example of this approach. Motivated by the closing of a major Levi Strauss factory in 1992 (laying off 1,000 Latina women employees), these two organizations began studying the employment situation in their city. They discovered that even though many good jobs were being lost, many more good jobs were being formed in the regional economy. Unfortunately, these new jobs required training that most laid-off workers didn't have. The organizations also discovered that existing training programs were not reaching the people most in need.

Through discussions with hundreds of employers and job seekers, COPS and Metro Alliance developed an extensive training program to prepare people for new jobs in the region, and to reach across barriers of language and lack of transportation, time, or income to serve those in need. Over their first eight years, the program they formed, Project QUEST, trained more than 1,200 low-income persons, most of whom moved into good jobs.

Project QUEST has impacted how the city of San Antonio looks at workforce development, proving that making a substantial investment in training pays major dividends. It has also been innovative in obtaining funding, including convincing the city to issue bonds for some workforce development costs.[32]

---

[32] Contact information for Project QUEST is in Appendix A. Also see the Aspen Institute web site for an in-depth study of Project QUEST.

ALERT!

Common reasons for failure with workforce development

- Intense level of training and support needed for unemployed or underemployed residents with profound barriers to employment is beyond the capacity of many organizations.

- Wage expectations set too high for program, given the mismatch between skills needed for better-paying jobs and the skills of low-income job seekers.

- Lack of strong workforce development organization willing to partner with community development group.

- High amount of staffing and funding needed for comprehensive in-house program.

- Tight funding prospects, especially for the intensive training and support often necessary for residents of low-income communities.

- Groups have difficulty dealing with inflexible bureaucracy in some local One-Stop Career Centers.

- Groups have difficulty building a training program around Workforce Investment Act funds. (Because WIA-funded trainees can choose their own training site, the number of trainees is unpredictable.)

- Groups fail to keep up to date with shifting employment trends, both in terms of types of job skills required and numbers of openings.

6. Workforce Investment Board contract

As discussed earlier, the federal Workforce Investment Act programming is housed in a national network of One-Stop Career Centers, each managed by a Workforce Investment Board (WIB). Many of these boards contract with community-based service providers, provided they effectively serve an employment need.

Your organization can contact your local WIB or the management of your One-Stop Career Center to inquire about opportunities to be a provider. The WIA lays out a sequence of services that each job seeker follows:

- Core Services: initial assessment, information, and counseling
- Intensive Services: customized services to meet more profound individual barriers
- Training Services: occupational skills training, entrepreneurial training, and adult education

The local WIB determines how and when a job seeker moves from one level of services to the next. An account called an individual training account, or ITA (sometimes called a voucher), is established for people eligible for the final level of training services. Each job seeker can determine the best place to go for the training he or she needs. This can be a community organization with an appropriate program.

The problem for community groups is the unpredictability of how many ITA holders may be coming to them and when. It is very difficult to set up a solid program in the face of such uncertainty. For this reason, fewer community groups are working within the WIA system.

7. Workforce development advocacy

If your organization believes that the workforce development system could do a better job of serving people in your community, by all means let the appropriate officials know. Learn the WIA and WIB system and become an active participant in deliberations. If deeper job-skills training is needed for residents, or if lack of fluency in English is preventing access to government programs, be a voice that gets heard. Bring officials a clear picture of what is going on in your community and how they could make a better impact.

Project QUEST, mentioned earlier, has been very successful with its advocacy efforts on behalf of low-income residents. Hartford Areas Rally Together (HART) is another example.[33]

Step 1: Assess Current Conditions

As with all the pivot-point strategies explained in this book, your first step is to assess current conditions. If you are working in a low-income area, employment is obviously a major problem for you. However, you still have important questions to answer: In what form does this problem exist? Exactly whom does it affect? Who else is working on this problem, and how do they view the situation?

This assessment step does not need to become a major research project. There are plenty of experts on the topic of unemployment already. But you do need to gather enough information to understand clearly how your organization can contribute to solving the problem.

Get census data on employment and income

To begin your assessment, look at census data for your neighborhood. While census data does not capture all aspects of unemployment and underemployment, it is a good place to start. Among many other things, it will show you the rate of unemployment in your state, in your city, and in each of your neighborhood's census tracts. This data will also show the income level for neighborhood residents who are employed, their types of employment, and their education level. These factors will give you good insight into the extent of underemployment.

Find the most recent data as well as historic data going back ten years. Often the easiest place to get good data at the neighborhood level (by block or census tract) is from the local library or city government. Information from either source is usually available at no charge. You can also get data on the Internet (see the sidebar Go Online for Census Data, on page 152).

You may be able to buy additional information from a commercial service such as Demographics Now or Claritas. For example, Claritas's PRIZM™ provides up to sixty-two demographic statistics down to the block level for every neighborhood in the United States. Such services (available online) offer data by neighborhood boundaries in addition to census tract. This can be useful if you share census tracts with high-income neighborhoods and therefore get census tract data that does not truly reflect your community.

Step 1 at a Glance

- Get census data on employment and income
- Research current job openings in your community
- Listen carefully to local employers
- Look at job trends and projections
- Research local workforce development organizations
- Research vocational training in your area
- Summarize the needs and the services you found

---

[33] *The Lobbying and Advocacy Handbook for Nonprofit Organizations* by Marcia Avner provides step-by-step guidance for legislative and executive branch advocacy at state and local levels. The running case example in the book is for GREAT, a workforce development organization.

The statistics you gather are not enough; you need to look behind them. Employment problems are not spread evenly throughout all groups of people. Therefore, get as much information as you can about *which* people are most affected in your community. Common categories include

- Workers recently laid off from local industry
- Single mothers
- Young men of color
- Recent immigrants with language or other barriers
- People with a high school degree or less
- People recently released from incarceration
- Teens and young adults
- People on public assistance
- People recovering from substance abuse
- Homeless people
- Physically or mentally challenged people

Go online for census data

You can start looking online for census data with these sites:

U.S. Census Bureau—www.census.gov Click on American FactFinder and Census 2000, which break down 2000 data and historical data by census tract.

Bureau of Labor Statistics—www.bls.gov This site can give you access to a wide range of current and historical employment data by industry sector for your city and state. You can find more local data at the bureau's At a Glance Tables link.

This information will influence your program development in Steps 2 and 3. For example, some organizations specialize in providing culturally specific outreach and training for American Indian youth or Haitian refugees. Through such services, the organization adds real value to the workforce development programs serving its community.

Research current job openings in your community

For the next part of your assessment, research available jobs. Look at the want ads of your local paper and at listings posted by private and public employment agencies on the Internet. The web has become the largest posting of job openings in the country. America's Job Bank at www.ajb.dni.us is a great place to start. This federal government site breaks down over one million openings nationwide by local area, by career, by experience and education required, and by wage or salary. (The site is one of three in an award-winning suite developed by the U.S. Department of Labor and collectively called "America's Career Kit.") State or county employment agencies usually list job openings on their web sites as well.

As you scan these sites, the local paper, and other sources, compare the advertised wage levels with the average wage levels in your census tracts. Note the skills required for these job openings.

Listen carefully to local employers

Most communities have interesting job opportunities for local residents right under their nose. Some of these opportunities are located at major employers—hospitals, banks, universities, or factories. Others may be found in groups of similar businesses—small and midsize manufacturing, trucking, or food-related businesses. Search for these in and around your community. Talk to as many businesses as you can.

These businesses often have a cluster of entry-level jobs that are similar in nature—jobs that they sometimes can't fill. For this reason, businesses may be interested in your organization. Find out what their jobs are, and how a good workforce development program could fill them. You have the potential to help them solve a problem.

You will be much farther down the road if you understand how workforce development programs succeed or fail in the real world of employers. As you talk with local business owners, ask about their experience with the services of government or nonprofit employment programs. Do they have any suggestions for how such programs could meet their needs better? What types of services would they want from your organization?

Look at job trends and projections

Researching trends and projections means asking these questions:

- Which industries and professions have the most openings and the fastest rate of job growth in your area?
- What types of skills do these industries and professions look for?

These questions will help you think about services that lead people into growth careers rather than declining careers.

The web sites listed in the sidebar Go Online for Census Data, on page 152, can help you answer these questions. In addition, check the Department of Labor job market site at www.doleta.gov and America's Career InfoNet at www.acinet.org for excellent information on job trends and projections. For every state and for the country as a whole, America's Career InfoNet lists the fastest-growing and the fastest-declining occupations, occupations that have the most job openings, wage trends for different occupations, and occupations that pay the highest wages. The site breaks this information out by level of education. You can find the best-paying jobs for people with the skill levels of your neighborhood residents, and identify ideal careers to train people for, given their current level of education.

Research local workforce development organizations

Find out all you can about the workforce development organizations already active in your community. There are two reasons for doing this. First, many community groups form partnerships with existing workforce development groups rather than start from scratch. Second, you should know what is already going on in this field so you don't duplicate services, sound uninformed to potential funders, or both.

Start with your city's One-Stop Career Center. You can find your center and information on the Workforce Investment Act web site www.usworkforce.org or 1-877-US-2Jobs. Your One-Stop Career Center will have a comprehensive, current list of employment services in your community. These centers are also a potential source of partnerships.

Another web site to visit is America's Service Locator at www.servicelocator.org. This web service from the federal government has links to all major public employment agencies in the country. In turn, these agencies can refer you to nonprofit organizations in your area. Finally, talk with people at social services organizations in your community to learn about programs from their perspective.

After identifying the existing programs, you need to discover how well these programs serve the particular needs in your community, and which ones have the potential to do more. Visit local offices of these programs and ask staff members about their services. Find out

- What types of employment barriers do they address?
- What types of services do they provide?
- What types of people do they help effectively—the working poor, the homeless, or other groups?
- What is their track record—the number of clients placed in jobs and the number who keep jobs for a year or more?
- What types of jobs do they place people in? How do they know these are promising careers?
- Which employers do they have relationships with?

Also ask about their relationship to the community your organization serves:

- How many people from your neighborhood do they serve each year?
- How do they try to reach people in your neighborhood?
- Which organizations in your neighborhood do they have a relationship with, if any?
- Do staff members speak the languages of those neighborhood residents who most need workforce development services?

Talk with local social services agencies and unemployed people to learn more about employment services. Get as many opinions as you can about the quality of local services. Are the services accessible, effective, and getting enough results to matter?

Research vocational training in your area

Since training is a major part of helping people move up in the world of work, it's wise to know who does adult vocational training in your area. You may eventually form a partnership with a vocational school or community college or other organization that offers its own training. Or you may choose to create a training program of your own. Either way, find out who is doing this training locally. Visit the Department of Labor's web site America Learning eXchange at www.alx.org to find a list of such schools in your area.

Summarize the needs and the services you found

As you finish this assessment, you'll have a great deal of data and many opinions to sift through. Summarize the most important information visually on maps and graphs, to better explain your findings at meetings. Finally, begin to identify any significant gaps in the services this system provides to residents of your community who need employment services the most. These gaps will be your target. You will focus on these gaps in Step 2. Use Worksheet 19: Assess Current Workforce Conditions, on page 247, to help you summarize your findings.

Step 2: Create a Vision and Strategic Plan

As a result of the assessment you did in Step 1, you have a good sense of the employment problem and workforce development system in your community and whether there is a constructive role for your organization to play. If there is such a role, your next step is to develop a vision and plan to fill it successfully.

Step 2 at a Glance

- Share the results of your assessment and discuss five questions with your community
- Create a workforce development vision
- Design and plan your program
- Put your plan in writing

Share the results of your assessment and discuss five questions with your community

To begin the vision and planning process, make public the results of the assessment via board meetings, community newspapers, and public meetings. As you share these conclusions with people, ask for their thoughts about how to improve employment in your community and what role your group could play in that effort. Shape these discussions by asking the following questions.

1. Will we focus on certain groups of people?

You might find that the poverty in your community concentrates in particular groups, such as immigrants from Laos or Mexico or among young single mothers. If so, your vision and plan probably should focus on this group, including how you intend to customize your services to effectively assist them. This statement does not have to exclude other groups, and, in fact, many excellent programs are open to all who walk in the door. But without a strong, customized effort to reach and assist your largest groups of unemployed people, you will not change the local economy in the way you want.

2. Will we focus on certain types of jobs or businesses?

After reviewing employment data and trends, and after talking with local employers, you may decide to focus on jobs at particular types of businesses in your community, such as a bank, a large factory, or a hospital. Or you could focus on a business sector that needs workers with similar skill sets, such as a group of commercial kitchens or small machine shops.

Similar to the first question, a focus on certain jobs or businesses allows your group to develop a specialty—for training and for placement—that can have better-than-average impact. Conversely, being open to placing people in jobs anywhere gives your program more openings to pick from. As a third alternative, some groups pick three or four business sectors to focus on and add more as their capacity grows.

3. Will we focus more on job placement or on training?

As noted, there is a substantial debate about immediate job placement versus training followed by placement. Exactly how much training and what kind of training are part of the debate. There's no right side to the debate; you must choose based on local conditions, organizational vision, capacity, and community interests. If your target population has little chance to obtain the jobs that are available in your area with the skills they currently have, training is a must. Even if the major programs in your area emphasize work first, your group may need to fight for substantial training programs in order to place your target population into decent jobs.

4. How many people in our community need additional assistance?

Five years into the future, how many residents will need better employment to make a significant impact on your economy? How many do you think a new program can realistically reach?

On the one hand, even one additional resident earning more income is a gain for your community. On the other hand, your work isn't over until all residents who have the ability to work are doing so at the highest level they can. Your vision needs to intersect with reality somewhere between these two extremes.

Base your initial goals on the numbers of residents needing jobs, particularly if you selected a specific population group in question 1 above. Later you will consider the capacity of your organization and any partner organization to finalize a goal for the number of people you aim to assist.

5. What wage level and career ladder do we want for people once they get a job?

Some programs aim at placing job seekers into jobs that pay at least a few dollars over minimum wage, with advancement opportunity (versus "dead-end jobs"), so they don't remain the working poor. Other programs place people in any job available to them. Well-intentioned people can and will disagree about what constitutes reasonable goals for wages and career ladders, so be prepared for a debate.

How much do your residents need to earn in the jobs gained through your program? The easy answer is: more than they are making now. *Any* improvement is good. However, you may want to set your vision at a particular wage level, since minimum wage today does not raise a person out of poverty status.

Be realistic. Bear in mind that wages are related not only to the supply and demand for labor but also to skills, experience, education, dependability, and performance on the job. If your target group of unemployed residents has low levels of these qualities, it is not realistic to aim at jobs that pay three times the minimum wage. On the other hand, having a vision that places most program participants at minimum wage in five years is both uninspiring and insufficient.

The crucial connection is between skills and performance on the one hand and wages and career advancement on the other hand. If your vision includes higher wages and upward mobility for people with low skills, then effective training and education must be a central component of what you offer to your residents.

Even if all participants don't get good wages or advancement possibilities right away, almost any job will be better for their future than no job. In an important way, *every* job is a career ladder job. A job as a cashier or dishwasher, even at minimum wage with no obvious next step, gives a person a track record that will catch the attention of an employer in the future.

> **A reasonable wage target: self-sufficiency**
>
> An interesting and practical method of looking at appropriate wage levels, the *Self-Sufficiency Standard,* has won some national attention. Developed in the early 1990s by Diane Pearce of Wider Opportunities for Women (www.wowonline.org), this model looks at the actual living expenses in specific locations sorted by different types of family composition. Simple worksheets that draw on detailed local data have been created for a number of states and the District of Columbia. More are being developed.

A common reason that low-income people work at the bottom of the wage and career ladder is that they get frustrated, angry, or discouraged with some aspect of their job and quit, or they get fired for poor performance. Poor or inconsistent performance on the job is another major reason people are stuck at the bottom rung. These are among the issues that your initiative will have to address.

Be flexible. Rigid goals for wages and advancement opportunities—especially before you have hands-on experience with this strategy—may doom your program to failure before you begin. Don't get bogged down in a no-win community fight over this issue. Listen to what employers are telling you about wage levels. Learn from other organizations to see where they're at on these issues. Remember that you can always raise your sights over time.

Create a workforce development vision

By answering the five questions above, and by going through the assessment earlier, you have what you need to create a vision for an improved employment picture for your residents. Put this vision in writing, and remember to include your answers to the five questions. Use Worksheet 20: Write a Vision Statement for Workforce Development, on page 248, for this task.

Design and plan your program

With your vision in place, you can now plan your entry into the workforce development system. To develop your plan, you will need to

- Pinpoint gaps in services
- Identify how your group can fill these gaps
- Decide how you will measure the results of your workforce development programs

Pinpoint gaps in services. Based on your assessment results, and based on how you answered the five questions above, pinpoint one or more gaps in the existing workforce development system. (If you can't identify gaps, there is no need to get involved.)

For example, you may have learned that 30 percent of the unemployed in your community are single mothers and that several local banks are looking for bank tellers—jobs with advancement potential that pay a bit above minimum wage. However, the single mothers face employment barriers such as skill deficits and lack of affordable child care. At the present time, appropriate training and affordable child care are unavailable to them. This gap in service has significant impact on your community, given the size of the problem and the size of the opportunity.

Identify how your group can fill these gaps. During the assessment, you gained a good understanding of the workforce development groups in your city, and what businesses may have clusters of job openings appropriate for your residents. Now carefully review all of these groups and businesses as potential partners. Which come the closest to addressing the gap you have identified, and would your group be able to work with them to fill it? If you find no good prospects for a partner, what can your group do effectively on its own?

Think about the example of single mothers unable to get the bank teller jobs. How could a community program provide the services these women need? Recall the four basic types of services in workforce development programs: recruitment, assessment, and preprogram referral; training; job placement; and support. Within that framework, is there an opportunity for a new service that would help these women obtain a bank teller job?

Review the seven broad options for community groups in the workforce development industry, listed earlier—ranging from partnerships to networks to comprehensive in-house programs to advocacy. Across all these approaches, there are a few common ways that community groups fill gaps in this system:

- *Improving access to services.* Your group may have more effective means to reach target populations. For example, young single mothers might feel more comfortable coming to your office for training rather than going to some unfamiliar or distant office.

- *Customizing services to meet the unique needs of your target group of residents.* Whether your group or a partner provides these services, you can design them better than organizations that do not understand this group.

- *Increasing communication and understanding throughout the system.* Because of your networks in the community, many more people are going to be exposed to new facts, perspectives, and players involved in the local employment situation. Employers, social workers, and single mothers themselves will all converse about how to make this vision happen.

Before developing any partnership with an outside workforce development organization, be clear about the role your group wants to play (and is able to play) in providing these services in your community. The options fall on a continuum from active involvement to minimal assistance. Lay out the most practical scenarios you can think of, and start talking with potential partner organizations and employers. Let the ideas percolate until the best one rises to the top. Then move into implementation.

Decide how you will measure the results of your workforce development programs. While Step 4 in this chapter guides you to monitor and evaluate, you should decide as you plan how you will measure success. This includes deciding who will keep track of these measurements and how often you will review them.

Add numeric goals where possible. Set goals based on the number of people in your target population, the number of jobs that appear accessible, and the capacities of your organization and your partners. For instance, your goals might be to

- Help fifty single mothers from the neighborhood get jobs in the first year of the program.
- Help 75 percent of these women keep their job for a year or more.
- Ensure that 75 percent of job placements will earn $3.00 or more above minimum wage.
- Provide support so that 35 percent will have higher pay and more responsibility in one year.

Put your plan in writing

Take all the information you've collected and write up your workforce development plan. That document should include

- A summary of current employment and program conditions found in your assessment. See Worksheet 19: Assess Current Workforce Conditions, page 247.

- A vision statement that describes how you will change these conditions over five years, and how you will address issues of program focus, program approach, and target wages. See Worksheet 20: Write a Vision Statement for Workforce Development, page 248.

- Long-term goals—outcomes you can create in three years to support your vision. See Worksheet 21: Write Three-Year Goals for Workforce Development, page 249.

- Short-term goals—outcomes you can create in one year to achieve your three-year goals. See Worksheet 22: Write One-Year Goals for Workforce Development, page 250.

- A work plan that includes monthly or quarterly tasks for all partners. This can be a simple calendar listing tasks, who is responsible for each task, and deadlines for the first year of the program.

Have your board participate in all the major decisions that make up this plan. (If you plan to set up a community employment committee as described in Step 3, then these people obviously need to participate as well. See also Tips for Creating Your Vision and Strategic Plan in Chapter 3.)

Your plan does not need to be long. But it must be clear and thorough enough to avoid major misunderstandings later on. After creating a draft of your plan, review it carefully, and have any potential partner review it as well. Be particularly clear about roles, responsibilities, and timelines; attention to these is critical to implementation.

Step 3: Implement Your Plan

When you complete your assessment and planning phases, you'll have a clear sense of where your community is at in terms of workforce conditions, where you want the community to go, and how to get there. Now you can take action to make all those carefully crafted goals and your work plan come to life. Several of the most crucial actions are discussed next.

Step 3 at a Glance

- Establish a community employment committee
- Pick the best approach and get started
- Form partnerships
- Obtain funding for your partnerships

Establish a community employment committee

Set up a committee focused on your workforce development efforts— a *community employment committee* of some sort. This could be

- Your board of directors
- A committee of your board
- A new community-wide committee involving other organizations, employers, and residents within your community

If your organization does other types of work, it is probably *not* wise for your full board to be the only entity overseeing this new effort. Workforce development is a substantial effort that requires a dedicated committee.

You will have to reach many different types of people with this program—unemployed workers, funders, social services agencies, politicians, and more. As long as it does not take forever and involve endless debate over basic goals, forming a broad-based community committee brings those networks into your effort early on. If forming this committee would burn up too much time and threaten your momentum, leave the governance to a board committee (at least at first), and get community input in other ways.

Pick the best approach and get started

Now is the time to select from among the seven approaches discussed on pages 145–151. The first four of these approaches involve partnerships of some sort—with another organization already doing workforce development, with a local network of community groups doing workforce development, with a national workforce development organization, or with one or more employers. Tips for these partnership approaches are found shortly.

The other three approaches will get only a brief mention in this section, for differing reasons:

- *The comprehensive in-house approach:* Groups that choose this path generally do so because they have no good alternative to fill their workforce development gap (no strong organization or employer to partner with) and because they have the means to assemble the necessary resources.

  You will need considerably more information to succeed if you take on this challenge on your own—more than this book has space to discuss. Take the time to learn from other groups, starting with the examples cited earlier in this chapter and from your One-Stop Career Center. Also consider what you learned by examining other workforce development programs in your community—what you would do differently, and what it would take for you to be successful.

- *Contracting with your Workforce Investment Board:* Each WIB has a different approach to working with community organizations. Thus, the opportunity to fill a gap in services in your community must be determined in your own setting. Because the WIB and One-Stop Career Center operate in a public and open process, you can readily obtain these organizations' plans and talk to their staff to find out whether such an opportunity exists. Investigate what it takes to be certified as an individual training account (ITA) provider. Remember the cautionary note from earlier—under WIB, each job seeker holding an individual training account is free to go wherever he or she chooses for training, making it hard to count on a certain number of clients as you develop your program. If you are considering contracting with your WIB, the Enterprise Foundation is a good resource.

- *Advocacy:* This option takes the least amount of new planning, staffing, and funding for most community organizations. It may also be the most effective way to impact your employment situation. As just discussed, your One-Stop Career Center and WIB are open by law to community input—use your voice to advocate for changes to existing programs for the benefit of your target residents. With advocacy as with any other approach, the better prepared you are with facts, solutions, and allies, the more successful you will be.

Form partnerships

The other approaches to workforce development all involve partnerships of some form. Here are a few basic tips on succeeding with these. Also see the sidebar What to Consider When Selecting Partners, on page 164.

Photograph by Laura L. Comppen for New Community Corporation. Used with permission.

New Community Corporation Gateway to Work, the largest welfare-to-work program in New Jersey, serves more than 2,000 people annually with initiatives like the Rapid Transition to Work Program. This program provides short-term training for entry-level jobs with guaranteed employment upon completion of training.

Training for Wakefern Supermarkets, the corporate parent of ShopRite, takes place at the Partners in Training Center, a separate facility at New Community Corporation that duplicates a supermarket with stocked shelves and checkouts in addition to classroom space.

Scrutinize potential nonprofit partners. Seek to partner only with an organization with a solid track record and reputation. Such an organization is more likely to help you achieve your vision and enhance your own reputation. Therefore, do an extra level of due diligence when checking into potential partners. Your committee members may want to talk with a number of possible partners, or they may delegate this task to your staff.

Reflect on what *your* organization brings to the table. It is equally important to carefully lay out the assets that your organization brings to a potential partnership. These assets become the "carrots" by which you attract a strong partner.

You most likely bring an ability to increase the numbers of clients potential partners serve in your community. You may also bring them a new way of doing business, through your connection to the target group. You are likely to bring additional visibility to them, which every nonprofit or government agency appreciates. Further, you can perhaps offer office space in your neighborhood so that partner organizations can deliver services to your residents more easily.

You may also be willing and able to bring in some funding. Talk to your existing funders to investigate the possibilities. If your new partnership offers a clear focus, clear roles, and a strong vision for impacting your community, funders may well support the effort. While raising funds is a lot of work, it may be something you can do well, and it may be the best carrot you have to attract the best possible partner organization.

Create a written agreement. When you succeed in finding a partner, develop a written agreement with the partner. This agreement should be thorough and specific about all services, roles, expectations, timelines, and responsibilities involved in your partnership. Make sure that your committee, board, and attorney review this agreement before finalizing it.

If you're covering any of the costs of your partner organization, a "performance-based contract" is advisable. Negotiate a mutually agreeable set of results, such as the number of your residents to be placed in jobs, the types of jobs they'll get, the length of time they'll keep their job, and the timeline for all of this to happen. Also specify who does all administration work (such as the record keeping, accounting, and reporting to funders and committees) and by when. Then make your payment to your partner contingent on achieving these results.

Talk to local employers about a partnership. Most of the above considerations apply equally to partnerships with nonprofits, government organizations, and private employers. Carefully examine as much information as you can get about the reputation and stability of the employer. Be clear about what you want from your partnership with employers, what you each bring to the partnership, and how it will be coordinated, governed, and monitored.

Getting written commitments from business partners about their specific contributions to your employment program is imperative. These contributions can include program funding, training facilities, trainers, training equipment, or other program elements. In addition, your agreement must discuss the hiring commitments that your business partners are willing to make. You don't want to get a year down the road with expenditures and training, only to find that your trainees have no job possibilities.

At the same time, business partners may be concerned about your group's ability to follow through on your commitments. Partnerships between community groups and businesses are somewhat rare, and credibility issues may be more prevalent here than when you work with other nonprofits. Commit only to what you can truly accomplish.

Obtain funding for your partnerships

Where will you get funding for your new workforce development program? If you can find a partner organization with its own funding to achieve your vision, great!

What to consider when selecting partners

From any partner, you will want excellent communication and strong follow-through on promises. You will also want equal visibility and acknowledgment for your group's role in your program. Along with these general preferences, create a document that clarifies more specific preferences, such as

- The specific role your organization wants to play in the partnership
- The track record and reputation you want in a partner organization
- The list of workforce development services needed to achieve your vision
- The scale of services (the number of community residents served each year) needed to achieve your vision
- The languages you need these services delivered in
- How you want coordination and governance of the program to happen
- The ability of potential partners to serve your targeted groups (such as single mothers, Somali immigrants, or homeless persons)
- The partner's general willingness to adapt its program to your vision and goals

- The partner's willingness to locate staff and services in your community
- Whether you want the potential partner to pay for the program
- The timetable you want for your program

Also outline all the things your group can offer to a partner organization. These could include

- Your community networks and organizational reputation, which can generate new clients, new employers, and potentially new resources for your partner
- A new target group of clients that the partner has not focused on in the past
- Your ability to provide staff time for tasks that your partner would otherwise have to do
- Your willingness to raise funds for the partner to work in your community, and how much money you can raise
- Your ability to generate positive media coverage about the partnership
- An opportunity to focus on a great community with a great neighborhood organization

If not, you need funds to cover some or all of the costs. Consider sources from the following list.

Client or trainee fees. In most cases, you will not be able to raise much money from the residents you work with; they are by definition low on money. However, many programs charge a small fee for some of their services—mainly to get more buy-in from the participants. The fee needs to be small enough so that you can still include low-income or unemployed people. Consider a sliding fee feature to ensure they get your services.

Some programs do charge their clients tuition. The Center for Employment Training, profiled earlier, is one successful example. Still, most programs rely only minimally on this source of funding.

Employer fees. Even if you don't form a primary partnership with employers, you can look to them to generate some program funds. After all, you are providing them with a service that has real cost savings attached. These include costs for placing job notices, reviewing applications, interviewing candidates, checking references and credentials, and providing training. All of these activities take considerable time and would cost the business a great deal, as does leaving a job unfilled for months at a time. Bring this perspective when you talk to business owners about funding program costs.

The quality of your training and ongoing support will certainly be a factor in this discussion. But given the backgrounds of some of your residents, many employers may not jump at the chance to contribute to your program. You may get further by negotiating a fee from employers *after* the workers you place with them stay on the job for three to six months. This way employers have more certainty that they actually benefited from your service. Collecting after the fact can be a challenge, however.

Government funding. As mentioned earlier, the largest funder of workforce development in the United States is the government through its Workforce Investment Act, administered by the Employment and Training Administration at the Department of Labor. Look for contact information in Appendix A: Resources. Also contact your local One-Stop Career Center for a comprehensive listing of workforce development organizations in your area, many of which are state and local government agencies. Some of them may have funding opportunities.

Other potential sources of government funding include

- Community Development Block Grants from the Department of Housing and Urban Development
- Empowerment Zones and Enterprise Communities funding from the Department of Health and Human Services
- Local bonding authority

Use the federal web site www.firstgov.gov to start your quest.

Foundations and corporations. When seeking foundation or corporate funding, ask each funder about its grant-making priorities. See if workforce development is an appropriate request to make. Begin your search by going to the web site of the Foundation Center (www.fdncenter.org) and by requesting guidelines from individual funders online or on the phone.

If possible, talk directly to a program officer for a few minutes, on the phone or in person, before you submit a proposal. Convey in just a few sentences the uniqueness of your new partnership and the need for it in your community. Then ask if a grant request would be appropriate.

Step 4: Monitor, Evaluate, and Improve

All four pivot-point strategies discussed in this book include the step of monitoring, evaluation, and improvement. The need for these is obvious. But in the rush of daily tasks and deadline pressures, they are easy to overlook.

Build into your workforce development program the key measurements of your success, and do this from the very beginning. Decide how you intend to keep track of this data, who is responsible for doing so, and how often you intend to review it. Each month, capture the data relevant to each part of your vision statement. Your board or community employment committee and your partner organization should review this data at least quarterly. That way you can catch problems and make improvements earlier rather than later.

Besides collecting hard statistics, get general feedback from clients and employers about how your program worked for them. For instance, find out how your ways of reaching clients or listening to their employment problems differed from other programs they tried in the past. You can gather this feedback through simple evaluation forms or brief follow-up interviews. Both can be time consuming, but they offer valuable information for reaching your long-term employment vision.

Remember that measurement, evaluation, and improvement are not a one-time event. Constantly look for ways to become more effective. This can mean cycling back through the previous three steps: taking another look at current workforce conditions in your community, revising your vision and strategic plan, and implementing new elements in your plan.

Summary

Developing your community workforce begins by gaining a basic understanding of the workforce development industry in the United States and in your community, and learning the seven basic approaches that community groups use to implement this strategy. After gaining this knowledge, follow the four core steps: assess current conditions, create a vision and strategic plan, implement the plan, and continuously monitor, evaluate, and improve.

Success with this pivot point requires some important decisions. Your organization must identify the groups of people—the workforce—it will develop, and the types of businesses it will serve. It will also have to grapple with a knotty question: whether to emphasize training followed by placement, or to focus on job placement first and foremost, with subsequent support for job retention. The issues of whom you serve and how you do your work are politically charged, but your organization's strength is in its community networks and in your understanding of the needs of your local workers and employers. Remember that what works in other communities and what "leaders" say *should* work must be tempered by your organization's wisdom about what *will* work in your community and with the employers in your network. Listen to and observe other groups, and then make your best decision.

Partners can make or break you in this work. As you implement your plan, you will most certainly need to work closely with employers, other local networks, and government agencies. As the examples in this chapter have shown, wise choices and perseverance can make workforce development pay off for many residents and businesses in your community.

Chapter 7

Grow Good Neighborhood Jobs

This chapter looks at how your group can promote a core group of strong job-producing businesses in your neighborhood. You'll find out how to work with businesses that keep producing good jobs for your residents well into the future.

Overview

Across the country, community organizations work with carefully selected businesses to create a flow of good new jobs for their neighborhood residents. These groups work with businesses that have the potential to grow steadily—businesses that will hire neighborhood residents at higher wages and better benefits than most neighborhood microbusinesses or commercial district retailers can offer.

Among organizations doing community economic development, the primary approach to neighborhood job growth has been working with small- to medium-size manufacturing firms located in the neighborhood. By assisting these firms to overcome various obstacles to growth, community groups help create good jobs for neighborhood residents.

Some groups are starting to look beyond manufacturing to other neighborhood businesses with strong potential to create jobs. These groups help such businesses expand and connect them to the most dynamic sectors of their regional economy.

Community groups have always worked with scarce resources, striving to get the maximum impact from each dollar of funding and each hour of staff time. The goal is to link your neighborhood economy to carefully selected companies in specific business sectors—those that produce good jobs for your residents and can grow more jobs. By doing this, you leverage your resources in a powerful way. You help someone else—the growing companies—do much of the work of job creation, thereby magnifying your impact on the neighborhood economy.

Use the four steps of community economic development

This chapter uses the four-step process of community economic development for the purpose of growing good neighborhood jobs. These are the same basic steps you've encountered in previous chapters:

1. Assess current conditions

2. Create a vision and strategic plan

3. Implement your plan

4. Monitor, evaluate, and improve

Chapter 7 at a Glance

Growing good neighborhood jobs calls on your group to identify businesses that produce jobs, support those businesses, and attract more such businesses into your neighborhood. After defining the characteristics of a targeted job-producing business, you can move on to the four steps of community economic development.

1. Assess current conditions by defining the term *good neighborhood job*. Learn which job sectors and local businesses are likely to grow. Take inventory of resources and space that exist for job-producing businesses. Consider what your organization can add. Use Worksheets 23 through 27 for this assessment.

2. Create a vision and strategic plan. Use your vision statement to capture the essence of how your group will promote good neighborhood jobs. Then create three-year goals, one-year goals, and a work plan based on this vision. Use Worksheets 28 through 30 for this step.

3. To achieve your goals, you can adapt many of the implementation tools discussed in previous chapters. Also consider new tools such as tax incentives, opportunity scanning, and organizing groups of business owners to solve common problems.

4. Evaluate and improve. Compile data to measure progress toward your goals and review this data on a regular basis.

By doing these steps, you will *identify* neighborhood businesses that have the capacity to produce good jobs. You'll *support* these businesses as they strive to expand, thereby growing more jobs. And you'll *expand* the number of job-producing companies in your neighborhood through a campaign to attract targeted businesses.

Identify businesses that can grow good jobs

The ideal businesses must have two essential features. First, they *offer good neighborhood jobs* (a term you will define when you do Step 1). Second, these businesses will grow and *create more good neighborhood jobs*. These businesses range from very large to very small, in any type of business sector.

Businesses that have only one of these features are *not* the focus of this strategy. Some businesses grow, but they will not create jobs that your residents can access (those that require master's degrees in computer sciences, for instance). Others will create jobs, but the jobs will offer very low wages and few, if any, benefits. Other businesses offer good neighborhood jobs, but they are not creating more of them.

Identifying companies that meet both requirements listed above involves two forms of research. First, you'll *research trends* in the national and regional economy. This form of research reveals sectors and subsectors of the economy with businesses that are hiring people like your residents in good jobs and that are projected to grow more good jobs over the next five to ten years. Second, you'll also *talk with individual businesses* in your neighborhood and target a few that you want to work with more closely.

Support neighborhood businesses that produce jobs

Supporting neighborhood businesses involves many of the tools discussed in other chapters of this book, along with some new tools. These tools fall into four primary categories:

1. Providing local businesses with an access point to existing resources, such as loans and specialized technical assistance.

2. Planning and advocating for new solutions and resources to overcome common obstacles to business growth.

3. Providing direct assistance, such as loans from your own fund.

4. Facilitating networking between local and regional businesses in targeted sectors in order to increase opportunities for new customers, suppliers, partners, and other important contacts.

Expand the number of job-producing businesses in your neighborhood

If you worked on commercial district revitalization (Chapter 4), your group probably conducted a business-attraction campaign. You can use this same tool—a business-attraction campaign—to expand the number of businesses that grow good neighborhood jobs. The main ingredient you need is enough available space for these businesses to grow, and an effective marketing campaign.

You may want to go further and attract job-producing businesses that complement existing neighborhood businesses. This can create a *cluster* of firms that benefit from being next door to one another. Once you identify businesses that you want to target, you can quickly customize your property inventory and marketing campaign for that audience.

This pivot-point strategy differs from others

The strategy discussed in this chapter differs from the first three pivot-point strategies.

For one, this chapter focuses entirely on creating a significant number of good jobs that pay well for neighborhood residents. While commercial district revitalization and microbusiness development do in fact create jobs, they are not strategies that *focus* on job creation. Instead, they aim to build human capital, community confidence, and positive economic momentum. New jobs are created through these activities, but not many of them through any one business. And the jobs that *are* created tend to be lower paying.

A second difference involves organizational capacity. In order to help businesses grow faster and create more jobs for neighborhood residents, your group's capacities must correspond to what these businesses need. These needs tend to be more complex than those of most microbusinesses or small retailers in your commercial district. To be useful to these growth-oriented businesses, your organization needs to become more specialized.

Examples of Neighborhoods Growing Good Jobs

Neighborhood groups across the country are growing good jobs using this strategy. Following are two examples of successful efforts.

The Greater-North Pulaski Development Corporation

The Greater-North Pulaski Development Corporation (GNPDC) is a community-based organization in Chicago that has worked on both industrial development and commercial corridor development with impressive results.

For many years, manufacturing jobs provided the economic base of the Humboldt Park/Austin community. Then, in the 1960s, the community began to suffer from a serious decline in manufacturing jobs. Faced with large amounts of vacant, blighted, and often polluted industrial land, GNPDC took on a variety of initiatives to rejuvenate these parcels and boost its neighborhood economy.

A major strategy has been to promote government programs for industrial development. GNPDC used city of Chicago programs to get several major projects done. These projects improved industrial facades and modernized infrastructures, which involved removing low viaducts, relocating sewer and water lines, and widening streets. As a result, GNPDC helped clean up the neighborhood as well as expand the workforce.

GNPDC has also become expert at helping local business owners access federal, state, and county tax credits for hiring new workers. The group organized 150 business owners along one industrial corridor to plan industrial redevelopment of a 62-acre railroad yard that was abandoned. This plan, adopted by the Chicago Economic Development Commission in 1990, blocked a competing plan for upscale housing that would have gentrified the community rather than add manufacturing jobs.

GNPDC received city contracts to do strategic planning and consensus building along another industrial corridor. The organization involved dozens of businesses and neighborhood groups in identifying problems plaguing manufacturing businesses and their commercial and residential neighbors. GNPDC helped these parties develop plans to solve those problems. For example, the organization pushed the city to demolish long-vacant and severely blighted buildings—over the objections of inactive owners—that opened up sites for industrial redevelopment.

Beyond planning and advocacy, GNPDC has helped business owners to access public and private loan dollars. Over the past twenty years, this involved packaging over $35 million in loans from the Small Business Administration and other federal agencies, the state, the city, and banks. GNPDC also staffed a job bank referring residents into neighborhood jobs.

The organization receives funding from a variety of sources, including from the SBA. GNPDC is now a designated Small Business Development Center, reaching businesses not served by other such centers. (The Small Business Administration operates a national network of small business development centers [SBDCs]. Often co-located with a community college or university, SBDCs offer a menu of small business training, counseling, and materials at low cost.)

ICIC-Boston

ICIC-Boston, a nonprofit affiliate of the Initiative for a Competitive Inner City (ICIC), has worked since 1995 with growing businesses in the inner-city neighborhoods of Boston. Though not a community-based organization itself, ICIC-Boston works in partnership with groups doing community economic development.

ICIC-Boston developed a variety of ways to work with the fastest-growing and largest businesses within a neighborhood either to maintain current jobs or help those businesses create more jobs. ICIC-Boston's strategy begins with two interesting economic evaluations—one of the regional economy and one of a neighborhood's economy. (As explained below, the community portfolio methodology is one that your community group can also use.)

In the mid-1990s, ICIC-Boston identified eight clusters of business growth in the Boston metro area. One of these clusters was tourism and entertainment, leading ICIC-Boston to work with Franklin Zoo, which is located in a low-income neighborhood. ICIC-Boston studied what it would take for the zoo to grow as a tourist attraction and thereby catalyze the economy of the surrounding neighborhood. Using the results of this 1997 study, the zoo doubled its visitor count and tripled its sales over the next few years. This increase in visitors has improved public perceptions of the community and provided an opportunity for adjacent businesses to pull in new customers.

With help from Anderson Consulting, ICIC-Boston also developed a *community portfolio methodology*. Using information gathered from door-to-door visits with business owners, this methodology includes five measurements to identify the highest-impact businesses in the neighborhood. The loss of a high-impact business significantly hurts a low-income neighborhood, yet community development groups often give little attention to such businesses.

ICIC-Boston funnels specialized assistance to these high-impact businesses, much of it provided by teams of MBA candidates from area business schools. ICIC-Boston also provides highly specialized assistance from volunteer professionals in areas such as strategic planning, financial management, and human resources.

As of 2001, ICIC-Boston has worked with fifteen businesses chosen specifically for growth potential and neighborhood hiring practices, including a nonprofit health clinic and a midsize independent grocery store. These companies have created 167 jobs, adding $2.9 million in wages to the neighborhood economy.

ICIC-Boston is now launching an expanded tool for analyzing neighborhood business mix, identifying businesses with the most growth potential, and creating a solid strategy for connecting those businesses to the regional economy. The tool can be found at www.neighborhoodconnections.org.

Pre-assessment: Define the Features of a Job-Producing Business

Before you take the four key steps explained in this chapter, do a pre-assessment. Consider these perspectives on what makes for a job-producing business in your neighborhood:

- Growth characteristics of an individual business
- Growth characteristics of business sectors
- Business reasons that a firm locates in your neighborhood
- Advantages of business clusters in your neighborhood

The companies you choose to work with may or may not shine in each of these categories. Even so, your approach will be fundamentally the same for all businesses—identify them, support them, and expand their numbers. Most importantly, focus on businesses with growth potential.

Growth characteristics of an individual business

A business needs a variety of ingredients to grow. Many books are devoted to this subject. But, at minimum, those ingredients include

- A strong management team
- Access to expert, specialized advice (and a willingness to use it)
- Products or services that meet customer requirements
- An ability to build customer demand via effective marketing
- An ability to read market trends and respond effectively
- A solid growth plan

- Adequate space and access for customers, employees, and shipping
- Access to a competent workforce
- Access to capital and financing
- A position in a growing sector of the economy (preferable but not mandatory)

What this means for your organization: Do not expect to find many neighborhood businesses with all these ingredients in place. Instead, most of your prospects will be businesses that have many of these ingredients but lack others. These may be the businesses that your group can help.

Growth characteristics of business sectors

Besides considering the minimum factors needed for an individual business to grow, you'll want to look at business and employment trends both nationally and regionally. The reason is simple: A business with growth ingredients that is *also* positioned in a growing sector of the economy will have an easier time creating new jobs than an equally well-run business in a declining sector.

Consider national trends, but look more carefully at regional trends and projections. Further, don't limit your investigation of growth sectors of the economy to the largest categories like "manufacturing" or "service." Look at subsectors for the real opportunities.

At this point, a brief look at the manufacturing and service sectors is useful.

The manufacturing sector. For the past several decades, the manufacturing sector has not grown many jobs. Even so, manufacturing firms offer an excellent economic opportunity: Many economically distressed neighborhoods have a history of hosting local manufacturers, providing employees for such businesses, and providing proper manufacturing zoning regulations. Manufacturing is still an excellent source of good jobs for people without a college education. Manufacturers often train workers on-site, and manufacturing usually pays well above minimum wage.

While the sector as a whole has not grown new jobs, it is still a very significant portion of the U.S. economy, and numerous subsectors are increasing employment. Further, an industry that is declining in jobs nationally could be growing in your region or neighborhood. Finally, large numbers of manufacturing jobs are available through turnover and new business creation. Often these jobs are a great fit with entry-level workers.

The service sector. This sector includes subsectors such as health care, finance, insurance, and real estate services. Companies in these subsectors could be anything from a strong catering business to an expanding building maintenance firm, from a home health care company to a growing nonprofit medical clinic.

Many service sector businesses do not create jobs that pay well or that neighborhood residents can access. The challenge is to find service sector businesses that create accessible, well-paying jobs and develop effective ways to work with them.

What this means for your organization: To create good neighborhood jobs, community groups most often work with the following sectors:

- Small and medium-size manufacturing businesses
- Service sector businesses in subsectors such as health care, financial, insurance, and real estate services that offer good local jobs

The sidebar Selected National Business Sectors, on page 178, provides a snapshot of major business categories. Whether you work with businesses in one of these subsectors or more than one, you will approach them in generally the same manner. You'll identify subsectors that offer good neighborhood jobs and job growth. For businesses in these subsectors, you'll offer resources to support their growth. You'll also consider bringing in more such businesses to your neighborhood.

A note of caution: Early on, determine the type of space that's available in your neighborhood. This impacts the size and type of businesses that you can attract.

Business reasons that a firm locates in your neighborhood

In the opinion of Michael Porter of the Harvard Business School, the only way inner-city neighborhoods will ever be revitalized economically is to apply the principles of "competitive advantage" to redevelopment efforts. In a 1995 article in the *Harvard Business Review,*[34] Porter outlined three areas in which inner-city businesses have a competitive advantage over businesses in the suburbs:

- An available workforce in an era of worker shortages
- Proximity to a high concentration of customers—both businesses and consumers
- The fact that inner cities are significantly under-retailed

Porter argues that assisting companies that *lack* a strong business reason for being in your neighborhood is not a sustainable strategy. This is true even if businesses initially respond in a positive way to assistance and subsidies from your group or other sources. This point is missed by cities and states as they battle to lure businesses into their area. Neighborhood development groups, which seldom operate with incentives large enough to swing a business decision one way or the other, grasp this business truth more readily.

What this means for your organization: Assess—and use—your competitive business advantages when attracting businesses to your community. Don't rely on incentives alone. You need businesses that have good reason to be strongly rooted in your local economy.

---

[34] Michael E. Porter, "The Competitive Advantage of the Inner City," *Harvard Business Review* (May–June 1995): 55–71.

Advantages of business clusters in your neighborhood

The term *business cluster* refers to companies operating in related industries that benefit from being located close to each other. These benefits come in various forms—the presence of a specialized workforce, specialized suppliers and distributors, and specialized professionals such as attorneys and technical consultants. Clusters can also enhance competition among rival businesses, thereby promoting higher standards of excellence.

What this means for your organization: Consider whether your job growth strategy can include business clusters. Is there already a concentration of related companies in your neighborhood with this potential—for instance, commercial printers, health clinics, or machine shops? Do these companies work together in any fashion to train employees? Do they happen to use the same distributors who specialize in their niche?

Perhaps these businesses already benefit from being in a cluster. You could enhance this cluster through a variety of tools, such as

- Organizing them for joint planning
- Helping them advocate jointly for new resources
- Helping these firms with ongoing market research (*opportunity scanning*)
- Connecting businesses to one another so that they can take on larger contracts than they could individually

Such tools are discussed later in this chapter under Step 3.

ALERT!
Common reasons for failure with neighborhood job growth

- Your organization lacks a sharp, clear focus on which types of businesses you will work with, what you will provide to them, or what they will provide in turn to the community.
- Your community lacks usable land for business growth.
- Residents and growing businesses have conflicts about land use.
- Your organization lacks staff capacity to apply to this strategy.
- Your organization (or the community you serve) can't offer anything of real value to targeted businesses.
- Problems that are expensive to solve, such as cleaning up badly contaminated land or replacing obsolete buildings and infrastructure, prevent business growth.

Step 1: Assess Current Conditions

If you have been working on any of the pivot-point strategies described in previous chapters, you have a great base to start your work on job growth. And if you've thought through the pre-assessment issues described above, you're even better prepared. Now you're ready for Step 1 in growing good neighborhood jobs.

This step will widen your understanding of your local economy. In particular, you'll discover the most dynamic players from a neighborhood job creation perspective and the best way to harness their energy to meet your neighborhood's job creation goals. Step 1 has seven parts.

- Part A involves a board discussion about what constitutes a *good neighborhood job.*

Selected national business sectors

What will you find when you research business sectors? Following is a picture based on data available as of the publication of this book. As you look at the picture, note the size of various sectors and the various growth rates. Remember: Local and regional information is far more important to your planning than national data.

Size of selected business sectors in 1997:*

Business Sectors	Establishments	Employees	Sales
Manufacturing	377,800	17.5 million	$4 trillion
Service industries (taxable)	2,100,000	25.3 million	$1.8 trillion
Construction	639,500	5.6 million	$835 billion
Retail trade	1,600,000	21.2 million	$2.5 trillion
Wholesale trade	521,000	6.5 million	$4.2 trillion
Financial, insurance, and real estate services	661,400	7.3 million	$1.8 trillion

Five-year trends, 1992 to 1997:*

Business Sectors	Establishments	Employees	Sales
Manufacturing	+ 2%	+ 4%	+ 32%
Service industries (taxable)	+ 14%	+ 31%	+ 53%
Construction	+ 12%	+ 19%	+ 55%
Retail trade	+ 2%	+ 15%	+ 34%
Wholesale trade	+ 5%	+ 12.4%	+ 31%
Financial, insurance, and real estate services	+ 13%	+ 12%	+ 35%

Ten-year projections, 1998 to 2008:**

The largest and fastest-growing sector of the U.S. economy is the service sector. Within this sector, the most new jobs will be found in

- Business-to-business services (for example, personnel and data processing): 4.6 million jobs.
- Health care (home health care, nursing, nurses aides, personal care facilities): 2.8 million jobs.
- Professional and miscellaneous services (management, public relations, research and testing services): 1.1 million.

Some of the job categories with the most openings fore-

cast over the next decade *for people with no post-high-school education* are

- Health care jobs such as nurses aides, orderlies, and attendants.
- Cooks.
- Bank tellers.
- Laborers and groundskeepers.

* 1997 Economic Census, Comparative Statistics for United States, U.S. Census Bureau. Rounded numbers.

** America's Career InfoNet, U.S. Department of Labor.

- Part B looks at which businesses have the capability to grow more good neighborhood jobs.
- Part C takes you into the job-producing businesses in your neighborhood to learn about their growth plans and the resources they need.
- Part D takes an inventory of space available in your neighborhood that these businesses can use to grow.
- Part E looks at what resources currently exist to assist your job-producing businesses.
- Part F considers what resources your group can add.
- Part G summarizes your entire assessment.

> **Step 1 at a Glance**
>
> There are seven parts to this step:
>
> Part A: Define a *good neighborhood job*
>
> Part B: Identify job-producing businesses
>
> Part C: Find businesses that can grow good neighborhood jobs
>
> Part D: Do a property inventory
>
> Part E: Find existing resources for business expansion
>
> Part F: Determine what resources you can add
>
> Part G: Summarize your assessment

Part A: Define a *good neighborhood job*

Be clear about the types of jobs you are interested in growing. You may have already had this discussion if you did workforce development (Chapter 6). And your board may want to spend more time discussing this issue later, as part of the planning process in Step 2. In either case, take time now to get a sense of what types of jobs you want. To find businesses that grow *good neighborhood jobs,* you must define what you mean by that term.

Keep your definition simple and attainable, and allow it to evolve as you get more experience. For example, you could define *good neighborhood jobs* as those that

- Your residents can get with training provided in your community or on the job
- Pay two or three dollars more than minimum wage
- Offer benefits—at minimum, paid holidays, vacation, and partial health insurance
- Provide a chance for promotion

Your goal in this strategy is to help create jobs that have *the best mix* of these characteristics as possible.

A good neighborhood job is simply the best job you can realistically get your unemployed and underemployed residents into. Your board can get as specific and ambitious as you think is realistic.

Also remember to look at your goals from the perspective of business owners—the people you are counting on to create these jobs. Setting your sights too high could damage your chances of engaging these owners; setting them too low may make your efforts seem pointless.

Use Worksheet 23: Assess Current Conditions—Part A, on page 252, to record your definition of a good neighborhood job.

Part B: Identify job-producing businesses

Now zero in on businesses that are the best source for the type of new jobs you want. This information is available at national, state, county, and metropolitan levels. Most of this information is broken down first by business sector and then into three or four layers of specific subsectors. At all these levels, you'll find company statistics such as

- Number of employees
- Size of payroll
- Number of businesses (establishments)
- Amount of annual sales revenues

Your research can aid you in several ways. First, this information will help you identify businesses already in your neighborhood that are in a growth sector of your metropolitan economy. Second, you can use this information to identify opportunities for your neighborhood businesses to connect to rapidly growing parts of your metropolitan economy—in particular, to find new customers and suppliers. Third, this information will identify metropolitan business sectors that you may want to target in a business-attraction campaign.

Conduct your research to answer three questions:

1. What are the largest business sectors and subsectors in your metropolitan economy today?
2. Which sectors and subsectors have been growing the most over the past five years?
3. Which sectors and subsectors are expected to grow the most over the next five years—and grow the most good neighborhood jobs?

Collect detailed answers to these questions, because this information will help you decide which businesses to target as you seek to grow good neighborhood jobs. Speak with business school professors, commercial bankers, business writers, and economic development officials in government offices. Also contact the staff of regional workforce development organizations, who usually know which subsectors are hiring. Finally, you can do a great deal of research on the Internet. Appendix B provides directions for collecting this information via Internet resources.

The sidebar A Partial Profile of the Chicago Metropolitan Economy in 1997, on page 182, shows the kinds of information you can gather. A truly useful profile would supplement this information with more local data gathered from other sources.

Use Worksheet 24: Assess Current Conditions—Part B, on page 253, to sum up your research on business sectors and subsectors.

Part C: Find businesses that can grow good neighborhood jobs

Armed with a better understanding of which types of businesses can create good jobs, you can now go out and find them in your neighborhood. Look for individual businesses with the growth characteristics described in the pre-assessment section of this chapter.

Many inner-city businesses exhibit little growth in sales or employment. Their owners are often content with this situation and have no desire to manage twenty more employees or take on the other headaches and pressure that come with growth. Often the profits that the owner lives on are just fine at their current level, and the owner has no interest in growing for the sake of growth. This attitude is common for older owners but also is typical of younger business owners who have already achieved their vocational goal.

Other business owners in your neighborhood may be stuck in a low- or no-growth situation even if they want to get larger. They may be in a declining industry, helplessly watching a shrinking market. They may not have the money or management skills to grow their business. These owners strive to pay their stack of bills each month, and most are not realistically positioned to grow.

However, nearly every neighborhood also has some business owners who want to grow and have much of what it takes to do so—especially if they get a little help. You know better than anyone how to find these owners. Go out and pound the pavement. Drive every street in your community. Go to the business club meet- ings. Talk to bankers. Talk to business owners about other business owners they know and to residents about where they work. Check the rosters of the local business club. Use the reverse directory to find names of businesses or business property owners. If people are in business, they should not be hard to find.

Talk to the owners of the businesses you have discovered. Beyond assessing their reputation and the appearance of their business, the only way you can discover what they need to grow is to ask them.

See Worksheet 25: Assess Current Conditions—Part C, on page 254, for a list of questions to ask when you talk to owners of the businesses you've targeted. In addition, plot out business locations on a neighborhood map.

Part D: Do a property inventory

If you worked on commercial district revitalization as described in Chapter 4, you should have an inventory of the space in that part of your neighborhood.

A partial profile of the Chicago metropolitan economy in 1997

Following is an abbreviated economic profile assembled from online 1997 data. (The next data from the 2002 Economic Census will not be available until 2004.) A finished profile would contain detailed information on many more subsectors and data beyond the number of employees. This sample, however, gives a sense of what a profile looks like.

Current size*

The following major business sectors had the most employees in Chicago in 1997:

Manufacturing 594,764

Retail trade 398,282

Health care and social assistance
    (taxable and exempt) 390,617

Administrative, support, waste management,
    and remediation services 286,557

Accommodation and food services....................................264,904

Wholesale trade 258,217

The following manufacturing subsectors had the most employees:

Fabricated metal products 91,645

Computer and electronic products 68,085

Machinery manufacturing 64,758

Food..57,111

Plastics and rubber products 46,728

Printing and related support activities...............................42,441

The following fabricated metal products subsectors had the most employees:

Machine shops, turned product, screw, nut,
    bolt manufacturing 23,165

Forging and stamping 17,557

The following machine shops and turned product, screw, nut, and bolt manufacturing subsectors had the most employees:

Machine shops..11,746

Turned product, screw, nut, and
    bolt manufacturing 11,419

Statewide trends**

Employment trends in two sample business sectors in Illinois between 1992 and 1997 were

Manufacturing..+ 4.6 percent

Service sector (taxable) ....+ 27.5 percent

Profile continued...

The manufacturing subsectors with the fastest-employment growth were

Transportation equipment...............................+ 17.4 percent

Instruments and related products.................+ 17.4 percent

Rubber and miscellaneous
   plastic products ....+ 12.9 percent

Fabricated metal products ....+ 12.8 percent

The service subsectors with the fastest-employment growth were

Social services ....+ 51.3 percent

Business services...+ 50.9 percent

Educational services ....+ 49.3 percent

County trends*

Sample employment growth trends between 1993 and 1997 in Chicago.

Sample manufacturing subsectors:

Household furniture .... − 37.3 percent

Office furniture ....+ 27.2 percent

Sample service subsectors:

Health services... + 4.3 percent

Personal services.. + 1.5 percent

Business services...+ 24.7 percent

Sample business service subsectors:

Mailing, copying, stenographic......................+ 23.2 percent

Building maintenance... + 2.8 percent

Projection of job growth between 1998 and 2008 in Illinois***

Fastest-growing occupations that require work experience only or on-the-job training:

Electronic pagination system operators ....+ 74 percent

Electronic semiconductor processors............ + 51 percent

Medical assistants.. + 49 percent

Human service workers....................................... + 43 percent

Bill and account collectors .... + 35 percent

---

   * 1997 Economic Census: Summary Statistics for Chicago, IL, U.S. Census Bureau at www.census.gov.
  ** 1997 Economic Census: Comparative Statistics for Illinois.
 *** County Business Patterns, U.S. Census Bureau.
**** America's Career InfoNet, U.S. Department of Labor.

Now expand that inventory to include all of the commercial and industrial space throughout your community. Know where you have room for a business to grow.

Start with the basics: ownership, size, condition, availability, and price. Also take a hard look at what prevents space from being available in your neighborhood for growing businesses. Some common space constraints include

- Ownership by someone not interested in selling or using the property (typical behavior of speculators waiting for values to rise)
- Contamination inside or outside buildings
- Obsolete or severely deteriorated buildings
- Poor access for trucks
- Resident opposition to use by industry because of factors such as noise, dust, and smell
- Poor utilities
- Inadequate size
- Inadequate parking or truck maneuvering space
- Uninviting or dangerous surroundings that frighten customers and employees
- Zoning restrictions

Working with property owners or city government, your group can take on the challenges posed by these constraints. Talk to people experienced in redeveloping such spaces: private developers, contractors, architects, and city officials. Get a sense of what it will take to make the properties in your neighborhood useful for a growing business.

Prioritize your inventory, ranking each space according to availability and what's needed to make it useable. With luck, your property inventory includes some spaces that are already available for reuse.

Use Worksheet 26: Assess Current Conditions—Part D, on page 256, to record the results of your property inventory.

Part E: Find existing resources for business expansion

Before you consider whether new resources are needed to help businesses grow, be sure you know about all existing resources that can help business owners. Look for resources such as

- Favorable loan programs
- Tax incentive programs
- Specialized technical assistance
- Networking opportunities within various industries
- Good sources of trained workers
- Assistance to clean up contaminated property

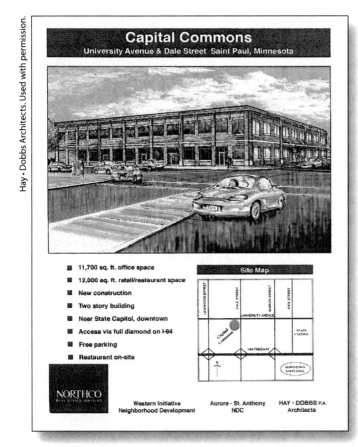

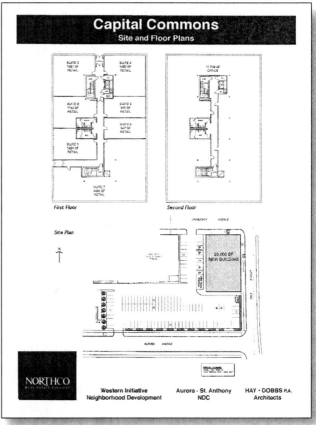

You can get high-impact results in commercial district revitalization when you fill an empty building with a new business. Site maps and floor plans of commercial buildings can help attract prospective businesses.

Review what your business owners need to help with their growth plans, and then look farther afield for more resources. Contact business associations, technical schools, business schools, and government agencies and programs at every level. Seek associations, schools, and agencies that have resources these businesses need.

Part F: Determine what resources you can add

The next step of the assessment is to think about what your organization can contribute to your targeted neighborhood businesses. Compare the needs of business owners with your list of existing resources. Then consider three different directions your group can go.

One is to act as an access point to existing resources. You may find that everything your businesses need to grow is available already. Your role can be to effectively connect businesses to these resources.

Second, you may find that some resources are missing and that your organization can provide them directly. For example, you could offer loans that bridge a financing gap for a good expansion project by providing below-market interest, deferred payments, or a subordinated position on collateral to a bank loan. Perhaps you can help a business acquire an abandoned property and clean it up, making room for the business to expand.

Third, you could advocate to create new resources. This is an option when you find that necessary resources do not exist in a useful form, and that the complexity or scale required makes these resources difficult for your organization to provide directly. Faced with this situation, some neighborhood groups work with local business owners and other community members to discuss common problems and plan solutions. Then as a group they advocate for other larger entities, typically public bodies, to accept and implement their plans. The resulting new resources—such as a cleanup of polluted land, a new loan program, new road access, or better telecommunication infrastructure—can then lead to business and job growth. For more details about this option, see Step 3 later in this chapter.

Part G: Summarize your assessment

In light of all the assessment you've done so far, what are the best job-producing businesses in your community? What do these businesses need to grow more jobs, and how can your group help them? Use Worksheet 27: Assess Current Conditions—Part E, on page 257, to summarize the main points of your assessment.

Step 2: Create a Vision and Strategic Plan

The hard part of this pivot-point strategy is done. You've identified the best job-producing businesses in your community. You've considered how you can support these businesses to grow more jobs and expand the number of job-producing businesses.

Begin this step by presenting the assessment information you gathered in Step 1 to your board and your community. Using this information, the board can discuss the questions laid out below. Make sure that the board participates in all the major decisions that make up this vision and work plan.

Write a vision statement that answers four key questions

The vision statement *briefly* explains the core impact you want to make on neighborhood jobs. Use Worksheet 28: Write a Vision Statement for Growing Good Neighborhood Jobs, on page 259. As preparation for using this worksheet, answer the following questions. Review the worksheets you've filled in as well as the information you gathered during the pre-assessment (pages 174–178).

1. **What type of jobs do you want in your neighborhood?**
What is your group's definition of a *good neighborhood job?*
What skill levels are required for such jobs? What wage levels
and benefits do you want them to offer? Review Chapter 6 for
more background on these topics.

2. **What types of businesses will you target to help create such jobs?**

3. **What problems currently prevent your existing targeted businesses
from growing?**

4. **What resources or actions are needed to help these businesses
grow, and which can your organization effect?**

Step 2 at a Glance

- Write a vision statement that
answers four key questions
- Write a strategic plan that
answers six key questions
- Review your vision statement and
strategic plan

Write a strategic plan that answers six key questions

Now translate your vision statement into specific goals that you can achieve. Your
plan should answer the following questions:

1. **What specific businesses in the neighborhood will you work with?** Given
available space, how many existing neighborhood job-producing businesses
have room to expand, and how many more can you bring into the community?
Based on your analysis of sectors and subsectors, what types of businesses do
you want to attract? From Worksheet 27: Assess Current Conditions, pick the
businesses with the most positive job growth characteristics and the obstacles
that your group can help to remove.

2. **How many new jobs can you help to create?** Look at your answers to the
previous questions and at Worksheet 27. How many neighborhood businesses
are ready to create more jobs with your assistance? How much space do you
have for these businesses to grow and for new businesses? What obstacles do
each of these businesses face, and how long will it take to overcome these obstacles? Given all this, what is your best estimate for the number of new good
neighborhood jobs you hope to grow in three years? In one year?

3. **What kind of program makes sense?** Choose one of (or a mix of) the three
primary ways that your group can grow good neighborhood jobs: identify businesses that have the capacity to produce good jobs, support these businesses
as they strive to expand, and expand the number of job-producing companies
in your neighborhood by attracting targeted businesses. Review what your
targeted businesses need, and decide what type of service you could provide
that would make an impact on their ability to grow.

4. **Do you have the organization capacity to carry out your plan?** Your plan
must consider the amount of funding and staff time you will devote to this
strategy, the skills your staff will need, how much of your board time will be
needed, and whether you will form a committee to work on this strategy.
This analysis depends largely on the types of resources you intend to bring

to the targeted businesses. Some resources involve organizing, some involve comprehensive planning, some involve lending, and others involve real estate development. Each will make its own demands on your group's time, knowledge, and budget.

5. **How will you connect neighborhood residents to new jobs?** Don't overlook this question. If you succeed at helping a business grow good neighborhood jobs, then ensure that your neighborhood residents get most of them. Consider getting a commitment from the business in advance. These are sometimes known as "first-source agreements," whereby your group becomes the business's first source for job candidates. Also consider how to prepare your residents for these jobs by connecting them to good workforce development programs, as explained in Chapter 6.

6. **How will you track progress?** Choose key measurements of your success in growing good neighborhood jobs—outcomes such as the number of new jobs created and the number of new businesses attracted to your neighborhood. Also track how much time and money your organization devotes to this pivot point and compare these figures to your outcomes. Decide how to keep track of this data, who is responsible for doing so, and how often you intend to review it, right from the start. (This decision is the key to Step 4: Monitor, evaluate, and improve.)

Now put your answers in writing. Prepare a strategic plan by completing the following worksheets:

- Worksheet 29: Write Three-Year Goals for Growing Good Neighborhood Jobs, on page 260.
- Worksheet 30: Write One-Year Goals for Growing Good Neighborhood Jobs, on page 261.

Review your vision statement and strategic plan

After creating first drafts of your vision and plan, review them carefully. Make sure you answer all the questions listed above. The vision statement, three-year goals, and one-year goals constitute a strategic plan. This plan gives board members and staff a clear road map to follow as they implement your program. Later, the plan will provide the basis for monitoring and evaluating your program.

Also see Tips for Creating Your Vision and Strategic Plan in Chapter 3.

Step 3: Implement Your Plan

To implement this pivot-point strategy, you need to support the growth of existing job-producing businesses and attract more of these businesses. The tools explained in this section help achieve both goals.

Many of these tools are closely related to those used in implementing other pivot-point strategies. For example, you can

- Act as an access point that connects businesses to existing resources, such as bank and government loans (see Chapters 4 and 5)
- Create workforce development programs that provide businesses with potential employees—neighborhood residents who are trained and supported (see Chapter 6)
- Do direct lending with your own specialized loan fund (see Chapters 4 and 5)
- Develop obsolete space (see Chapter 4)
- Develop, own, and operate business incubators (see Chapter 5)

Step 3 at a Glance

- Create networks and partnerships
- Offer specialized technical assistance
- Find tax incentives
- Organize business owners and residents to work on common problems
- Create a specialized loan fund
- Scan for opportunities
- Connect businesses to opportunities
- Attract more neighborhood job-producing businesses

The majority of such tools will be familiar to most organizations that do community economic development. Following are ways you can adapt them to job-producing businesses, along with some new tools.

Create networks and partnerships

Networks and partnerships are fundamental to all pivot-point strategies. In growing good neighborhood jobs, you will benefit from expanding these networks and partnerships. You are dealing with a new set of businesses and business needs. Finding businesses within and beyond your neighborhood and bringing them the resources needed to grow good neighborhood jobs will take new allies. These can include experts and organizations—citywide or industry-specific business associations, professors from business schools, public agencies such as port authorities, and other resources you identified in Step 1, Part E. (For more tips on partnerships and networks, see Chapter 6.)

Offer specialized technical assistance

Chapter 5 described ways that volunteer professionals can assist microentrepreneurs with a variety of business issues. However, businesses that you target to grow good neighborhood jobs often need more complex assistance on issues ranging from a specific manufacturing process to a legal, human resources, or sales issue. Use your networking and partnership skills to bring in the best possible experts for the specific needs of targeted companies. Some experts may be available free; others cost money. For the latter, your group can raise funds, bargain for reduced rates, arrange for businesses to pay all or part of their own way, or use all these options. The key is to get truly expert and timely advice—not just free advice.

Find tax incentives

Look at all levels of government for tax incentives that reduce payroll taxes, property taxes, and corporate income taxes for your targeted businesses. Particularly look for incentives that kick in when businesses move into your neighborhood, when new jobs are created, or when polluted lands are cleaned up. Examples include Empowerment Zones and Enterprise Communities incentives and the New Markets Tax Credit Program. Contact the U.S. Department of Health and Human Services and the Treasury Department, respectively, for more information on these tax incentives.

Organize business owners and residents to work on common problems

Many owners of growing businesses are so busy that they have no connection with owners of similar businesses nearby. These owners miss out on important opportunities to benefit from each other's knowledge and experience. Additionally, these business owners may be isolated from the rest of the community and find themselves in conflict with residents or community groups.

Instead, owners can band together to remove obstacles to growth. A group can often successfully address problems that are too big for individual businesses. This group can also work with neighborhood residents and organizations to address problems that affect the entire community.

As the Greater-North Pulaski Development Corporation demonstrated, organizations that do community economic development can help to form and staff such a group. (See pages 172–173.) This effort takes time. It also takes skill at organizing, running focused meetings, gathering information, and making unified proposals to the powers-that-be for resources to solve common problems. Your organization can provide these skills.

Following are sample issues that a group of business owners and residents can address.

Business networking. Business owners can find out about other local firms, learn from one another, and form beneficial new relationships. See the sidebar A Leader in Networking—the Chicago Association of Neighborhood Development Organizations, on page 192.

Crime and negative community image. Group members can address crime and image problems: graffiti; poor lighting; high crime rates; lack of police and security presence; and negative perceptions that inhibit owners' efforts to hire employees, attract customers, and control costs. Police officers should join the discussion along with other local officials and neighborhood residents.

Workforce issues. Owners can address hiring and training problems with guests from various workforce development programs and technical colleges active in the area. Human resource professionals can share tips on recruiting, training, and retaining a good base of employees from the local community. (See Chapter 6 for more tips on workforce issues.)

Land use planning. Owners can work with residents to plan adequate space for business growth while reducing conflicts with residential uses. With these plans in hand, the group can advocate for new city policies and resources that stimulate business and job growth. See the sidebar Land Use Planning Preserves Neighborhood Industrial Base, on the right.

Public policies and investments. The group can advocate and lobby at city hall and other places where decisions are made on issues that could help business growth. Such issues include

- Necessary zoning changes
- Infrastructure investments (such as new truck access roads, new utilities, broadband access, and removal of low overpasses)
- Plans for new industrial parks
- New loan and tax incentive programs useful to the growth of your targeted businesses
- Cleanup of contaminated land in the neighborhood
- Clearance of abandoned and deteriorated industrial properties
- Resale of city- or county-owned properties to your targeted businesses

To succeed with such efforts, the group needs early involvement from your city council representative, county commissioner, mayor, or other city officials. Equally important is early involvement from area residents and community organizations (if they are not already part of this group). Requests for policy and investment decisions should consider their impact on your entire neighborhood—not just business owners. For this you need the support of your entire community, which may be greatly affected in both positive and negative ways by business growth.

Land-use planning preserves neighborhood industrial base

An excellent example of land-use planning to ensure long-term survival of a neighborhood's industrial base is the Local Economic and Employment Development Council (LEED Council) of Chicago. In 1992 a new wave of retail and housing development threatened to displace industrial businesses in the Clybourn corridor. The LEED Council was formed to fight to keep the strong job base that these industries represented.

The council's efforts led to the passage of Chicago's first planned manufacturing district (PMD) in 1998, preserving the Clybourn corridor for industrial businesses and jobs. Together with two subsequent PMDs, the LEED Council's efforts have resulted in $150 million in public infrastructure investment and $200 million in private industrial investment.

Create a specialized loan fund

A loan fund aimed at growing businesses will differ from one aimed at microbusinesses or retail businesses—for instance, higher maximum loan amounts and more use of lines of credit based on accounts receivable. This fund will also require more sophisticated underwriting, since these deals are more complex. Your staff may require additional training. Or your group may need to contract with an experienced commercial lender or partner with a bank.

See Chapters 4 and 5 to gain a starting knowledge of operating loan funds, and for suggestions on where to get good training. Also get help from experienced commercial lenders and attorneys before you get into this new line of lending.

Scan for opportunities

Many owners of growing companies could use a hand in identifying opportunities to grow their business, such as sources of new customers and suppliers. Owners can also benefit from staying up-to-date on trends in their industry and in the regional and national economy. Their ability to plan for the future and react effectively to market changes would be enhanced if they could get this type of information sooner rather than later. Your neighborhood benefits when this information leads to new jobs for residents.

A number of community organizations in Europe and South America supply their targeted businesses with such information. Sometimes known as *market observatories*, these organizations keep up-to-date on market information and look for specific emerging business opportunities. While this concept—called *opportunity scanning*—has not received much attention in the United States, it is a simple idea that could have a powerful impact.

Starting with the resources you used in Step 1, Part B, your group can do the same for your targeted businesses. You can track sector and subsector growth patterns and projections along with projections for customer spending in specific markets. The key is to efficiently distribute useful, timely, and accurate information.

Connect businesses to opportunities

Your group could go beyond opportunity scanning to directly connect targeted businesses with opportunities: new customers, suppliers, investors, industry experts, and networks, especially in rapidly growing sectors of the economy. This could be done business by business or in a group format such as a trade show or a breakfast meeting. You could also assemble a group of your targeted businesses to jointly pursue and carry out contracts that would be too large for any of them to pursue individually. These contracts could even be used for export, with help from your state's economic development or world trade office.

Attract more neighborhood job-producing businesses

If you have been doing a business-attraction campaign to revitalize your commercial district, simply adapt your business attraction techniques to growing good neighborhood jobs. In Steps 1 and 2 of this chapter, you defined what types of businesses to target and where you have space to put them. You may want to build up a business cluster for benefits discussed earlier in this chapter. As explained in Chapter 4, any business attraction effort will require well-crafted marketing materials, mailings, and follow-up calls to successfully land each business, along with a cooperating property owner.

Step 4: Monitor, Evaluate, and Improve

In order to be effective, you need to know whether your efforts to grow good neighborhood jobs are paying off. Your strategic plan should list the outcomes that indicate success, such as the number of new jobs created and the number of new businesses attracted to your neighborhood. You also want to compare such outcomes with the number of hours your staff devotes to this strategy and the number of dollars that you're spending on it.

Photograph provided by CANDO. Used with permission.

Attracting neighborhood job-producing businesses takes a well-crafted plan. Here, members of DevCorp North celebrate the groundbreaking for a new supermarket. They worked for over a decade to bring the plaza to Chicago's Rogers Park Community.

Besides collecting hard statistics, obtain more global impressions. Conduct brief follow-up interviews with residents and businesses involved in your programs to grow good jobs, or ask these people to fill out simple questionnaires.

Your board should review this data at least quarterly. Catch small problems before they turn into big ones. Constantly look for ways to improve. Celebrate your successes and see what lessons you can learn from your mistakes.

Summary

The pivot-point strategy discussed in this chapter calls on your group to identify businesses that produce jobs, support those businesses, and attract more such businesses into your neighborhood. To do this, you first define the characteristics of a targeted job-producing business. At a minimum, these businesses must create good neighborhood jobs and have the ingredients needed to grow. Ideally, these businesses will be part of an expanding sector in the economy, have a competitive reason to locate in your neighborhood, and join a cluster of related businesses. With this definition, you can move on to the four steps of community economic development: assess current conditions, create a vision and strategic plan, implement the plan, and evaluate and improve your work.

Careful research and networking will prepare your group for success. Your community must agree on what constitutes a good neighborhood job, which will influence later decisions about what businesses to attract and grow. Other research involves finding out which businesses and job types are likely to grow in the near term and longer term, and the assets your community can use to attract businesses—its workforce, its space availability, and other incentives.

Payoffs for this pivot point can be large scale, but they do require careful juggling, the right opportunities, and dogged determination. However, this pivot point can fall together neatly when you can match community aspirations and resources to regional business trends and your organization's business and political contacts.

Conclusion

The work of revitalizing an economically distressed community is not mysterious and not impossible, but success requires strong beliefs, thoughtful principles, and vigorous dedication.

To be successful, you will need a deep understanding and appreciation of the abilities local people—your friends and neighbors—bring to this challenge. You will need an exceptional eye for partnerships, networks, and communications that can make an impact within a difficult environment. Finally, you will need to engage in continuous learning as you apply (and invent) an astounding variety of tools to your community development opportunities—from the tools required to manage your own organization to small business assistance, microlending, real estate development, and community organizing. These and more are required to turn a community economic development vision into reality, neighbor by neighbor, business by business, block by block.

With this set of attributes, your organization *will* improve economic conditions for the people and families within your neighborhood, and for your community as a whole. It takes extraordinary persistence, but time after time, the courage and dedication of people who ultimately rely on their own resilience have yielded remarkable results.

Appendices

Appendix A

Resources

Community economic development is a dynamic field with tremendous amounts of information, models, best practices, and emerging developments. To keep current—and to find out how specific community groups succeed in this field—contact the following organizations and agencies. They offer a variety of programs and publications related to community economic development.

The following list of resources has been broken into four categories and the specific topics or pivot-point strategies they relate to have been noted. The categories are

1. Community economic development resources

2. Federal government resources

3. Examples cited in the book

4. Publications

Please note that web site addresses change frequently (as do organization and government agency names). The web sites and organizations listed in this resource section were current upon publication, but may change over time.

1. Community Economic Development Resources

Aspen Institute
One Dupont Circle, NW, Suite 700
Washington, DC 20036-1133
Phone: (202) 736-5800
Web site: www.aspeninstitute.org
Focus: microenterprise, workforce development

Asset-Based Community Development Institute (ABCD)
Institute for Policy Research
Northwestern University
2040 Sheridan Road
Evanston, IL 60208-4100
Phone: (847) 491-8712
Web site: www.nwu.edu/IPR/abcd.html
Focus: organizational development and microenterprise

Association for Enterprise Opportunity (AEO)
1601 N. Kent Street, Suite 1101
Arlington, VA 22209
Phone: (703) 841-7760
Web site: www.microenterpriseworks.org
Focus: microenterprise

CharretteCenter.com
3137 Hennepin Avenue
Minneapolis, MN 55408
Phone: (612) 823-1966
Web site: www.charrettecenter.com
Focus: commercial district revitalization, community planning and design

Claritas
5375 Mira Sorrento Place, Suite 400
San Diego, CA 92121
Toll-free phone: (800) 866-6520
Web site: www.claritas.com
Focus: market analysis and demographics for all pivot-point strategies

Congress for New Urbanism
Hearst Building
5 Third Street, Suite 725
San Francisco, CA 94103
Phone: (415) 495-2255
Web site: www.cnu.org
Focus: neighborhood planning and design

Corporation for Enterprise Development (CFED)
777 N. Capital Street, NE, Suite 800
Washington, DC 20002
Phone: (202) 408-9788
Web site: www.cfed.org
Focus: microenterprise, public policy

Council on Foundations
1828 L Street, NW
Washington, DC 20036
Phone: (202) 466-6512
Web site: www.cof.org
Focus: organization development

Demographics Now
c/o SRC
131 N. Glassell Street, Suite 200
Orange, CA 92866
Phone: (714) 516-2400
Web site: www.demographicsnow.com
Focus: market analysis and demographics for all pivot-point strategies

Development Training Institute
2510 St. Paul Street
Baltimore, MD 21218
Phone: (410) 338-2512
Web site: www.dtinational.org
Focus: real estate development for all pivot-point strategies

Enterprise Foundation
10227 Wincopoin Circle, Suite 500
Columbia, MD 21044
Phone: (410) 964-1230
Web site: www.enterprisefoundation.org
Focus: workforce development

Fannie Mae Foundation
4000 Wisconsin Avenue, NW
North Tower, Suite 1
Washington, DC 20016-2804
Phone: (202) 274-8000
Web site: www.fanniemaefoundation.org
(see especially this site's KnowledgePlex,
which offers online community development
information)
*Focus: community development information and
resources, primarily focused on housing*

FINCA International, Inc.
1101 14th Street, NW, 11th Floor
Washington, DC 20005
Phone: (202) 682-1510
Web site: www.villagebanking.org
Focus: international microlending

Foundation Center
79 Fifth Avenue
New York, NY 10003
Phone: (212) 620-4230
Web site: www.fdncenter.org
Focus: fundraising, organization development

Initiative for a Competitive Inner City
727 Atlantic Avenue, Suite 600
Boston, MA 02111
Phone: (617) 292-2363
Web site: www.icic.org; see also www.neighborhood-
connections.org
Focus: neighborhood business and economic analysis

International Council of Shopping Centers
1221 Avenue of the Americas
New York, NY 10020-1099
Phone: (646) 728-3800
Web site: www.icsc.org
Focus: commercial district revitalization

**International CPTED Association (Crime
Protection Through Environmental Design)**
439 Queen Alexandra Way, SE
Calgary, Alberta, Canada T2J3P2
Phone: International + 1 (403) 225-3595
Web site: www.cpted.net
Focus: commercial district revitalization

Kauffman Center for Entreprenurial Leadership
c/o Ewing Marion Kauffman Foundation
4801 Rockhill Road
Kansas City, MO 64110-2046
Phone: (816) 932-1000
Web site: www.emkf.org
Focus: entrepreneurial development

Landscape Forms
431 Lawndale Avenue
Kalamazoo, MI 49048
Toll-free phone: (800) 430-6209
Web site: www.landscapeforms.com
*Focus: products and resources for streetscape
improvements*

Local Initiatives Support Corporation (LISC)
733 Third Avenue, 8th Floor
New York, NY 10017
Phone: (212) 455-9800
Web site: www.liscnet.org
Focus: commercial district revitalization

National Business Incubation Association

20 E. Circle Drive, Suite 190

Athens, OH 45701-3571

Phone: (740) 593-4331

Web site: www.nbia.org

*Focus: business incubators for all
pivot-point strategies*

**National Community Capital Association
(NCCA)**

Public Ledger Building

620 Chestnut Street, Suite 572

Philadelphia, PA 19106

Phone: (215) 923-4754

Web site: www.communitycapital.org

*Focus: lending for all pivot-point strategies and
the Woodstock Institute*

National Community Reinvestment Coalition

733 15th Street, NW, Suite 540

Washington, DC 20005

Phone: (202) 628-8866

Web site: www.ncrc.org

*Focus: commercial district revitalization,
microenterprise*

**National Congress for Community Economic
Development (NCCED)**

1030 15th Street, NW, Suite 325

Washington, DC 20005

Phone: (202) 289-9020

Web site: www.ncced.org

Focus: all strategies

National Development Council (NDC)

51 E. 42nd Street, Suite 300

New York, NY 10017

Phone: (212) 682-1106

Web site: www.nationaldevelopmentcouncil.org

*Focus: lending and real estate development for all
pivot-point strategies*

**National Federation for Community
Development Credit Unions**

120 Wall Street, 10th Floor

New York, NY 10005

Phone: (212) 809-1850

Web site: www.natfed.org

Focus: finance related to all strategies

National Trust Main Street Center

National Trust for Historic Preservation

1785 Massachusetts Avenue, NW

Washington, DC 20036

Phone: (202) 588-6219

Web site: www.mainst.org

Focus: commercial district revitalization

Neighborhood Reinvestment Corporation

1325 G Street, NW, Suite 800

Washington, DC 20005-3100

Phone: (202) 220-2300

Web site: www.nw.org

Focus: all strategies

PolicyLink

101 Broadway

Oakland, CA 94607

Phone: (510) 663-2333

Web site: www.policylink.org

*Focus: nonprofit research; offers information on
gentrification*

Public/Private Ventures

2000 Market Street, Suite 600

Philadelphia, PA 19103

Phone: (215) 557-4400

Web site: www.ppv.org

Focus: workforce development

Seedco and Non-Profit Assistance Corporation
915 Broadway, 17th Floor
New York, NY 10010
Phone: (212) 473-0255
Web site: www.seedco.org
Focus: community partnerships with larger institutions, particularly with universities

Social Compact
7201 Wisconsin Avenue, Suite 650
Bethesda, MD 20814
Phone: (301) 961-4982
Web site: www.socialcompact.org
Focus: regional and neighborhood economic analysis

Sweet's Product Marketplace
22 W. Pennsylvania Avenue
PO Box 365
Stewartstown, PA 17363
Web site: www.sweets.construction.com
Focus: catalog and reference source for architects and contractors; useful for commercial district revitalization

Urban Land Institute
1025 Thomas Jefferson Street, NW, Suite 500 W.
Washington, DC 20007
Phone: (202) 624-7000
Toll-free phone: (800) 321-5011
Web site: www.uli.org/indexJS.htm
Focus: real estate development

Wilder Publishing Center
919 Lafond Avenue
St. Paul, MN 55104
Phone: (651) 659-6024
Toll-free phone: (800) 274-6024
Web site: www.wilder.org/pubs
Focus: publications on nonprofit organization development and community building

Woodstock Institute
407 S. Dearborn, Suite 550
Chicago, IL 60605
Phone: (312) 427-8070
Web site: www.woodstockinst.org
Focus: community reinvestment and economic development

2. Federal Government Resources

The web addresses for these resources are listed in "drill-down" form. Web sites indented farther to the right on the page are nested within the site to the left. For more personal contact, most of these resources have offices in each state.

Department of Commerce
1401 Constitution Avenue, NW
Washington, DC 20230
Phone: (202) 482-2000
Web site: www.doc.gov

Home of:
   Economic Development Administration (EDA)
   Minority Business Development Agency
   U.S. Census Department

Department of Health and Human Services
200 Independence Avenue, SW
Washington, DC 20201
Phone: (877) 696-6775
Web site: www.hhs.gov

Home of:

Administration for Children and Families (ACF)
Temporary Assistance to Needy Families (TANF)
Center for Faith-Based and Community Initiatives
Office of Community Services (OCS)
Community Services Block Grants (CSBG)
Empowerment Zones and Enterprise Communities
Individual Development Accounts (IDAs)
Job Opportunities for Low-Income Individuals (JOLI)

Department of Housing and Urban Development
451 Seventh Street, SW
Washington, DC 20410
Phone: (202) 708-1112
Web site: www.hud.gov

Home of:

Community planning and development
Community Development Block Grants (CDBG)
Affordable housing programs
Economic development (various programs)

Department of Labor
200 Constitution Avenue, NW
Washington, DC 20210
Phone: (866) 4-USA-DOL
Web site: www.dol.gov

Home of:

Employment and Training Administration (ETA)
Workforce Investment ACT (WIA)
Bureau of Labor Statistics (BLS)

General Services Administration (GSA)
750 17th Street, NW, Suite 200
Washington, DC 20006-4634
Phone: (800) 333-4636
Web site: www.firstgov.gov
(Note: Firstgov is web site of the U. S. government.)

Small Business Administration
409 Third Street, SW
Washington, DC 20416
Phone: (800) U-ASK-SBA
Web site: www.sba.gov

Home of:
Small Business Development Centers (SBDC)
Service Corps of Retired Executives (SCORE)
Women's Business Centers
Tribal Business Information Centers
Business Information Centers (BICs)

Treasury Department
1500 Pennsylvania Avenue, NW
Washington, DC 20220
Phone: (202) 622-1260
Web site: www.ustreas.gov

Home of:
New Markets Tax Credit Program

3. Examples Cited in the Book

ACCION
120 Beacon Street
Somerville, MA 02143
Phone: (617) 492-4930
Web site: www.accion.org
Focus: microenterprise

Center for Employment Training (CET)
701 Vine Street
San Jose, CA 95110
Phone: (408) 287-7924 or (800) 533-2519
(affiliated centers in other states)
Web site: www.cet2000.org
Focus: workforce development

Chicago Association of Neighborhood Development Organizations (CANDO)
123 W. Madison Street, Suite 1100
Chicago, IL 60602-4589
Phone: (312) 372-2636
Web site: www.candochicago.org
Focus: all pivot-point strategies

Chicago Jobs Council
29 E. Madison Street, Suite 1700
Chicago, IL 60602-4415
Phone: (312) 252-0460
Web site: www.cjc.net
Focus: workforce development

**Church Avenue Merchants Block
Association, Inc. (CAMBA)**
1720 Church Avenue, 2nd Floor
Brooklyn, NY 11226
Phone: (718) 287-2600
Web site: www.camba.org
Focus: commercial district revitalization

**Community Development Corporation
of Kansas City**
2420 E. Linwood, Suite 110
Kansas City, MO 64109
Phone: (816) 924-5800
*Focus: microenterprise, workforce development,
growing neighborhood jobs*

Dudley Street Neighborhood Initiative (DSNI)
504 Dudley Street
Roxbury, MA 02119
Phone: (617) 442-9670
Web site: www.dsni.org
Focus: community planning and organizing

**Goodwill Industries, Inc./
Easter Seals Minnesota**
2543 Como Avenue
St. Paul, MN 55108
Phone: (651) 646-2591
Web site: www.goodwilleasterseals.org
Focus: workforce development

Goodwill Industries International
9200 Rockville Pike
Bethesda, MD 20814
Phone: (240) 333-5200
Web site: www.goodwill.org
Focus: workforce development

**Greater North-Pulaski Development
Corporation (GNPDC)**
4054 W. North Avenue
Chicago, IL 60639-5220
Phone: (773) 384-7074
Web site: www.gnpdc.org
Focus: all strategies

Greater Southwest Development Corporation
2601 W. 63rd Street
Chicago, IL 60629
Phone: (773) 436-1000
Focus: all four pivot-point strategies

Hartford Areas Rally Together
227 Lawrence Street
Hartford, CT 06106
Phone: (860) 525-3449
Web site: www.hartnet.org
Focus: workforce development

ICIC-Boston
Initiative for a Competitive Inner City
727 Atlantic Avenue, Suite 600
Boston, MA 02111
Phone: (617) 292-2363
Web site: www.icic.org/programs/boston_advisors.
html
Focus: growing good neighborhood jobs

**Local Economic and Employment
Development Council (LEED)**
1909 N. Clifton
Chicago, IL 60614
Phone: (773) 868-3493
E-mail: tedwysocki@prodigy.net
Focus: growing neighborhood jobs

Minneapolis Neighborhood Employment Network (MNET)
Room 331 City Hall
350 S. Fifth Street
Minneapolis, MN 55415
Phone: (612) 673-2110
Web site: www.mtn.org/~netmpls
Focus: workforce development

Neighborhood Development Center, Inc. (NDC)
651 1/2 University Avenue
St. Paul, MN 55104
Phone: (651) 291-2480
Web site: www.windndc.org
Focus: commercial district revitalization, microenterprise, growing good neighborhood jobs

New Community Corporation
233 W. Market Street
Newark, NJ 07103
Phone: (973) 623-2800
Web site: www.newcommunity.org
Focus: all pivot-point strategies

Northeast Entrepreneur Fund, Inc.
200 Olcott Plaza
820 N. Ninth Street
Virginia, MN 55792
Phone: (218) 749-4191
Web site: www.neefund.org
Focus: microenterprise

Project for Pride in Living
2516 Chicago Avenue S.
Minneapolis, MN 55404
Phone: (612) 874-8511
Web site: www.ppl-inc.org
Focus: workforce development

Project QUEST
301 S. Frio, Suite 400
San Antonio, TX 78207-4446
Phone: (210) 270-4690
Web site: www.questsa.com
Focus: workforce development

Reba Free LLC
Islamic Financial, Investment &
Consulting Services
Contact: Wafiq Fannoun, President
325 Cedar Avenue, Suite 7
Minneapolis, MN 55454
Phone: (612) 677-1464
Web site: www.rebafree.com
Focus: alternative Islamic finance and investment

Westside Industrial Retention and Expansion Network (WIRE NET)
6516 Detroit Avenue, Suite 3
Cleveland, OH 44102
Phone: (216) 631-7330
Web site: www.wire-net.org
Focus: workforce development

Wider Opportunities for Women
815 15th Street, NW, Suite 916
Washington, DC 20005
Phone: (202) 638-3143
Web site: www.wowonline.org
Focus: workforce development

4. Publications

American Demographics magazine. Stamford, CT: Cowles Business Media, Inc. www.demographics.com.

The American Marketplace: Demographics and Spending Patterns. Ithaca, NY: New Strategist Publications, 1997.

Angelica, Emil. *The Wilder Nonprofit Field Guide to Crafting Effective Mission and Vision Statements*. St. Paul: Amherst H. Wilder Foundation, 2001.

Angelica, Marion Peters. *Resolving Conflict in Nonprofit Organizations: The Leader's Guide to Finding Constructive Solutions*. St. Paul: Amherst H. Wilder Foundation, 1999.

Avner, Marcia. *The Lobbying and Advocacy Handbook for Nonprofit Organizations: Shaping Public Policy at the State and Local Levels*. St. Paul: Amherst H. Wilder Foundation, 2002.

Barry, Bryan W. *Strategic Planning Workbook for Nonprofit Organizations*. Revised and Updated. St. Paul: Amherst H. Wilder Foundation, 1997.

Gerl, Ellen. *Bricks and Mortar: Renovating or Building a Business Incubation Facility*. Athens, OH: National Business Incubation Association Publications, 2000.

Harrison, Bennett, and Marcus Weiss. *Workforce Development Networks: Community-Based Organizations and Regional Alliances*. Thousand Oaks, CA: Sage Publications, 1998.

Hayhow, Sally. *A Comprehensive Guide to Business Incubation*. Athens, OH: National Business Incubation Association Publications, 1996.

Hummel, Joan M. *Starting and Running a Nonprofit Organization*. 2nd ed. Minneapolis: University of Minnesota Press, 1996.

Kretzmann, John P., and John L. McKnight. *Building Communities from the Inside Out*. Chicago: ACTA Publications, 1993.

Mancuso, Anthony. *How to Form a Nonprofit Corporation*. 4th ed. Berkeley, CA: Nolo Press, 2000.

Mattessich, Paul, and Barbara Monsey. *Community Building: What Makes It Work*. St. Paul: Amherst H. Wilder Foundation, 1997.

Miles, Mike E., Gayle Berens, and Marc A. Weiss. *Real Estate Development: Principles and Process*. 3rd ed. Washington, DC: Urban Land Institute, 2000.

Oliver, Melvin L., and Thomas M. Shapiro. *Black Wealth/White Wealth: A New Perspective on Racial Inequality*. New York: Routledge, 1995.

Russell, Cheryl. *Racial and Ethnic Diversity: Asians, Blacks, Hispanics, Native Americans, and Whites*. 2nd ed. Ithaca, NY: New Strategist Publications, 1998.

Shelterforce magazine. Orange, NJ: The National Housing Institute.

Struhl, Steven. *Market Segmentation: An Introduction and Review*. Chicago: American Marketing Association, 1992.

Thompson, George, and Jerry Jenkins. *Verbal Judo: The Gentle Art of Persuasion*. New York: Morrow, 1993.

Appendix B

Internet Research on Your Metropolitan Economy

Appendix B is a supplement to Chapter 7. It guides you to the Internet to explore economic growth in your metropolitan area. But don't rely on the Internet alone; ask experts such as business school professors, commercial bankers, business writers, economic development officials, and regional workforce development organizations about which local sectors are growing and declining.

Internet sites change, so they may work differently than described as of this writing. If you know what information to look for, you'll still be able to navigate the sites described here or related sites.

Your research should answer three key questions:

1. What are the largest business sectors and subsectors in your metropolitan economy today?
2. Which sectors and subsectors have been growing the most over the past five years?
3. Which sectors and subsectors are expected to grow the most over the next five years—and grow the most good neighborhood jobs?

In your research, start with the large sector classifications such as *manufacturing* and *service*. Analyzing sectors at this level tells you which specific niches are growing the most. You can get information by subsectors (two-digit classifications) and even by components of each subsector (three- and four-digit classifications).

Until 1997, these classifications were known as *Standard Industrial Classifications (SICs)*. The SIC system was replaced in 1997 by one that is now shared by Mexico, Canada, and the United States—the *North American Industry Classification System*, or *NAICS*. In your research, you will need to look at historical trends. Some of this information will be classified in SIC form, and some in NAICS form.

Question 1. What are the largest business sectors and subsectors in your metropolitan economy today?

Start by looking at the size of different business sectors in your city. Information on the current size of each of these sectors and subsectors is available on the Internet from the U.S. Census Bureau. Go to the home page for the U.S. Census Bureau—www.census.gov—and look at the main menu under the category Business. Click on Economic Census. (The Economic Census is conducted by the Census Bureau every five years, including 1997 and 2002.)

On the home page for Economic Census, find the link to the most recent North American Industry Classification System (NAICS) data by U.S., state, county, and metro areas. This site gives the current size of all business sectors by metropolitan area, number of business establishments, value of shipments (essentially their sales levels), annual payroll, and number of employees.

Scan through as many subsectors as you can by clicking on More Data. Look for subsectors that hold potential for growing good jobs in your neighborhood. Remember that it isn't only the subsectors with the most jobs that are of interest. Even a subsector with only a few thousand jobs in your city could present opportunities for your neighborhood, if that subsector has the right kind of jobs. In the next step you can find out how fast various subsectors are growing these jobs.

Question 2. Which sectors and subsectors have been growing the most over the past five years?

Information from the *previous* economic survey done by the Census Bureau is just another click away, allowing you to track the growth in each sector and subsector. With this information you can focus on sectors and subsectors that are increasing their jobs the most.

The Economic Census site described in question 1 has a link on its home page that compares the two latest economic census statistics. It will quickly give you current industry data and compare it to data from five years earlier. This information is available only at the national and state level, but it gives a comprehensive view of those levels of the economy.

Trend information is also available at the county level—often the most useful level for understanding your metropolitan economy. At the U.S. Census Bureau home page, go to Search and type in "County Business Patterns." This site gives economic profiles of every county in the nation over a five-year period, providing you with a quick and powerful way to look at changes in business sectors in your metropolitan area. Since most large cities occupy either an entire county or major parts of several counties, this level of data is excellent for understanding what business sectors are the strongest and the fastest growing near your neighborhood.

Look in every business sector for subsectors that show strong job growth over the last five years and that appear to have good neighborhood jobs as your organization has defined them.

Question 3. Which sectors and subsectors are expected to grow the most over the next five years—and grow the most good neighborhood jobs?

Here you will kill two birds with one stone: You'll get projections on business sector growth *and* job growth from the same source, one that offers data on employment. Employment is one of the major ways that business sectors are measured and projected into the future. This is fortunate, since jobs are exactly what you're most interested in.

Find America's Career InfoNet from the U.S. Department of Labor at www.acinet. org. This is the same site mentioned in Chapter 6, and you're essentially looking for the same information mentioned there. (You can also call the department at 877-348-0502.) This site provides employment information on a state level that you can use to find out which sector of your regional economy is projected to grow jobs that you are interested in over the next decade. For your state, look at the

- Fastest-growing and fastest-declining occupations
- Occupations that will have the most job openings
- Wage trends of different occupations
- Occupations that pay the highest wages, by education level

That last category of information is especially helpful if the people you want to place in good jobs have a high school degree or less.

The America's Career InfoNet site also has a Career Resources library on its home page. By clicking on this link, you can find local, state, and national career and labor market information sites, which have links to statistics and career trends for every state. Many of these sites will give you statewide data and data for the major metropolitan statistical areas (MSAs) as well. For instance, the Illinois Department of Employment Security, found via this link, has labor market information for MSAs in Illinois.

If web crawling is not your favorite form of research, you can also collect good information about metropolitan economic growth sectors in various publications at the library.

Appendix C

Worksheets

Electronic versions of these worksheets may be downloaded from the publisher's web site. Use the following URL to obtain the worksheets

http://www.wilder.org/pubs/workshts/pubs_worksheets1.html?369ced

These online worksheets are intended for use in the same way as photocopies of the worksheets, but they are in a form that allows you to type in your responses and reformat the worksheets to fit your community economic development work. Please do not download the worksheets unless you or your organization has purchased this workbook.

To assess the condition of your commercial district, ask residents and business owners in your community the following questions. Make a copy of this worksheet for each person you interview and briefly summarize his or her answers.

1. What is your general impression of the current health of our commercial district?

2. What specific factors lead you to that impression? (Consider factors such as the number of vacant buildings, the presence of boarded-up buildings or buildings otherwise in need of renovation, and the number of stores that can attract customers to our neighborhood.)

3. What types of stores and services are missing from our neighborhood?

(continued)

Published by the Amherst H. Wilder Foundation   Copyright © 2002 Mihailo Temali

4. Compared to what it was like five years ago, is our commercial district worse, better, or about the same?

5. What do you think our commercial district will be like in three years assuming that current trends continue?

6. If you own or operate a business here, what plans do you have for your business over the next three years?

Part One—The need for a steady supply of new locally owned businesses in your community

For Part One of this worksheet, read each criterion and mark if it is true, partially true, or not true of your neighborhood. Then comment on your answer.

Criterion	Rating	Examples and comments
1. Commercial properties typically stay vacant for more than three or four months.	❏ True ❏ Partially true ❏ Not true	
2. Many commercial properties are used in ways that add little value to our community. (Think of value in terms of jobs, goods and services, or the attractiveness of the properties.)	❏ True ❏ Partially true ❏ Not true	
3. Important types of businesses have been missing from our community for a while.	❏ True ❏ Partially true ❏ Not true	
4. Our community has a culture of entrepreneurship that is visible and inspirational, especially to our young people.	❏ True ❏ Partially true ❏ Not true	

(continued)

Published by the Amherst H. Wilder Foundation   Copyright © 2002 Mihailo Temali

Part Two—The potential supply of residents who want to start microbusinesses

To fill out Part Two of this worksheet, locate and survey local residents who operate businesses from their homes. Find out what work they do and what it might take for them to start a microbusiness in your community.

5. How many residents currently operate a business out of their home, either "underground" (avoiding tax and zoning officials) or legitimately?

6. What types of businesses did you include in your answer to the previous question? (For example, cleaning services, auto repair, day care, and so on.)

7. What businesses could benefit the community if they grew larger by adding jobs, expanding goods and services, or fixing up a building?

Part Three—Obstacles to success cited by potential local entrepreneurs

List the conditions in your neighborhood that create barriers to microbusiness. Possible examples include lack of accessible business assistance, inability to get money to start a business, and lack of commercial space to start a business.

Part One

To assess the condition of your community workforce, answer the following questions.

1. What is the unemployment rate in your community for

   All residents? _____

   Single mothers? _____

   Persons of color? _____

   Young adults? _____

   Other particular group in your community? _____

2. Are these unemployment rates increasing, decreasing, or staying about the same?

   All residents: _____

   Single mothers: _____

   Persons of color: _____

   Young adults: _____

   Other group: _____

3. What group of people in your community has the most severe problems with unemployment? What is their rate of unemployment? Would they be a good target population to focus on?

4. What employment training and job placement services exist for people in your community?

(continued)

Published by the Amherst H. Wilder Foundation   Copyright © 2002 Mihailo Temali

5. How effective are those employment training and job placement services, especially for your target groups?

6. Which business sectors and subsectors offer the most jobs to people with skills similar to those of your neighborhood residents?

Part Two

To assess the potential for growing good neighborhood jobs in your community, answer the following questions.

7. Which of the subsectors you listed for the previous question are growing? Which are stagnant or declining?

8. How many small and midsize manufacturing firms are located in your neighborhood? What sector of industry are they in? Are these businesses and these sectors growing or declining?

9. Does your community include firms that could form into a dynamic cluster of related businesses? If so, does you community have available land that these businesses could use to grow?

Part One—Your organization's core resources

Fill in information about the resources your organization currently has for each pivot point.

Resource	Revitalize your commercial district	Develop micro-business	Develop your community workforce	Grow good neighborhood jobs
Amount of staff time your organization can devote to this pivot point. (For example, if one person can work full-time on this pivot point, the amount of staff time is 1.0.)				
Types of skills your staff members can devote to this pivot point				
Amount of money you can devote to this pivot point over the next three years				
Amount of office space and types of office equipment you can devote to working on this pivot point over the next three years				

(continued)

Published by the Amherst H. Wilder Foundation   Copyright © 2002 Mihailo Temali

Part Two—Other resources

Consider all the other resources—both tangible and intangible—available to your organization, such as your

- *Board and committee members*
- *Supporters at foundations and in government agencies*
- *Network of contacts with key people in community development—local, regional, and national*
- *Ability to partner with other organizations and coordinate them*
- *Reputation and visibility*

Now revise the chart you used in Part One, changing your answers in light of these added resources.

Resource	Revitalize your commercial district	Develop micro-business	Develop your community workforce	Grow good neighborhood jobs
Amount of staff time your organization can devote to this pivot point				
Types of skills your staff members can devote to this pivot point				
Amount of money you can devote to this pivot point over the next three years				
Amount of office space and types of office equipment you can devote to working on this pivot point over the next three years				

Part Three—Threats and opportunities

In the space below, list any external forces that could have a major impact on the ability of your organization to succeed with the pivot points. These forces could include

- *Local government initiatives*
- *Preferences of local foundations and corporate donors*
- *Major events about to happen in your local economy, such as closing your main street for recon- struction for six months, or a closing of a large factory that will lay off many residents*

(continued)

Published by the Amherst H. Wilder Foundation   Copyright © 2002 Mihailo Temali

Read each criterion and mark if it is true, partially true, or not true of your neighborhood. Then comment on your answer.

Criterion	Rating	Examples and comments
1. As a whole, our commercial district looks vibrant and shows an overall trend toward improvement.	☐ True ☐ Partially true ☐ Not true	
2. The commercial district attracts private sector investments (customers and new businesses).	☐ True ☐ Partially true ☐ Not true	
3. Most businesses are in sound physical and financial condition.	☐ True ☐ Partially true ☐ Not true	
4. Vacant storefronts fill up quickly.	☐ True ☐ Partially true ☐ Not true	
5. The district is unified in design.	☐ True ☐ Partially true ☐ Not true	
6. Local residents patronize businesses in the commercial district.	☐ True ☐ Partially true ☐ Not true	
7. Residents use some businesses as places to congregate as well as to shop.	☐ True ☐ Partially true ☐ Not true	

Fill in the table below for each local commercial and industrial space. (Make additional copies of this page as necessary.)

Name and Type of Business	Status	Square Feet	Cost	Parking	Special Features*	Physical Condition	Contact Information
	☐ occupied ☐ vacant ☐ possible change in occupancy		☐ rental ☐ for sale $____				
	☐ occupied ☐ vacant ☐ possible change in occupancy		☐ rental ☐ for sale $____				
	☐ occupied ☐ vacant ☐ possible change in occupancy		☐ rental ☐ for sale $____				
	☐ occupied ☐ vacant ☐ possible change in occupancy		☐ rental ☐ for sale $____				
	☐ occupied ☐ vacant ☐ possible change in occupancy		☐ rental ☐ for sale $____				

*Special Features can include truck access, loading dock, status of soil and building contamination, heavy-duty electrical service, zoning, utilities, elevator, etc.

On separate paper, make a simple map of your commercial district. Include the main street in this district and any adjoining alleys. Then complete the following steps.

Use color coding to indicate existing business clusters.

Often these clusters are groupings of businesses that seek the same customers, such as a group of stores that sell home furnishings, hardware, paint, carpet, tile, or antiques. In other cases, clusters attract people who make related buying decisions. This type of cluster could include a video store, take-out restaurant, and grocery store that customers would patronize during a single stop on their way home from work. Also indicate businesses around which you could build such a cluster.

Label each property on your map with the following terms, as appropriate:

- Convenience retailer (residents shop here on their routine driving route)
- Destination retailer (residents make a special trip here to shop)
- Anchor locations—places that people go to most often, such as grocery stores, banks, libraries, hospitals, large manufacturers, or business clusters that attract many customers
- Restaurant
- Office
- Wholesale business
- Manufacturing business
- Residential
- Historic site (include brief summary of history)
- Community gathering place (or potential for such use)
- Potential location for new office or business (describe type of business)
- High-traffic property (indicate how many people visit this location daily)

Using arrows, indicate the direction of traffic in your district.

Use thicker arrows to indicate heavier traffic. Label each arrow with the time(s) of day that traffic is heaviest in this direction.

Copy this worksheet for each business you contact. Talk with every business owner in your district and answer the questions below. This may be too much information to gather in one visit. Let business owners know you'll stop by again soon to get their general impression of the district.

1. Business name, address, phone number, and owner's name?

2. Owner's list of pros and cons of doing business in this location?

3. Owner's plans for the business and types of assistance needed?

4. Owner's overall impression of the commercial district and its prospects for the future? (Ask about the costs of buying, renting, and renovating a building; customer traffic; the adequacy of parking; beliefs about how customers view the area; and the presence of other viable businesses in the immediate area.)

5. Owner's suggestions for new businesses in the district? (Ask the business owners what types of businesses they think could work in your district. Also ask owners if they have any contacts with such businesses.)

Published by the Amherst H. Wilder Foundation   Copyright © 2002 Mihailo Temali

Use this worksheet to summarize the results of your market research.

1. Categorize your community residents by racial group, age group, occupation, housing status (renters and homeowners), and income levels.

2. List the amounts of money that community residents will spend annually on clothing, groceries, pharmacy items, restaurant visits, and other types of consumer goods.

3. List the number of stores that your community could support with its retail buying power. Classify the stores according to the type of goods they sell. Estimate the size (in square feet) of each store.

4. List the number of stores in each category that already exist in your community. List the size (in square feet) of each store.

5. List stores in each category that already exist outside your community. (In other words, name your competition—places outside the community where your residents go to shop.) List the size (in square feet) of each store.

6. List stores in each category that your community could support—businesses that do not currently exist in the community.

7. List businesses in your commercial district that currently do well.

8. List buildings that are currently vacant or filled with undesirable businesses.

9. Which types of businesses can fit into the storefronts and office space that are vacant in your district, as identified in your property inventory?

10. Which types of businesses add the most to your community well-being, by serving as a community gathering place, giving people new role models to look up to, or providing goods and services your neighborhood needs the most?

11. Based on your responses to the above items, list the new businesses that you would like to attract to your commercial district.

Review the results you obtained when you assessed conditions in your commercial district. (See the previous worksheets in this chapter.) Then, in the space below, write a one-paragraph vision statement for revitalizing your commercial district. Keep this paragraph short—one to three sentences to sum up the essence of your organization's intended impact on this pivot point.

Write a list of three-year goals for your commercial district in the categories listed below. Make sure that these goals are consistent with the vision statement for your commercial district. When writing goals, be specific and use as many numbers as you can.

Category 1: Impact goals

In the space below, describe exactly how your commercial district will be different in three years if your organization succeeds (for example, the number of storefronts renovated or new businesses started).

Category 2: Program goals

In the space below, describe what programs will be operating in three years to revitalize your commercial district (for example, the number of loans made or grants awarded).

(continued)

Category 3: Goals for your organization

In the space below, describe in detail how your organization will operate three years from now (for example, the number of volunteers and staff members, the annual budget and financial controls, and the number of board members and their duties).

Category 4: Other goals

In the space below, describe any other goals beyond impact goals, program goals, or organizational goals.

Highest-priority goals

Label one or two goals from each of the above categories as high-priority goals—those your organization will definitely commit to achieve in three years.

Step 1: Write one-year goals

In the appropriate spaces below, list each of the high-priority goals you identified for Worksheet 11: Write Three-Year Goals for Your Commercial District. Then write one-year goals that you will meet in order to achieve each three-year goal. Be specific and use numbers where possible. (Make extra copies of this worksheet as needed.)

Three-year goal:

One-year goals to support this three-year goal:

Three-year goal:

One-year goals to support this three-year goal:

(continued)

Step 2: Rank and implement your one-year goals

From each list of one-year goals, choose one or two as your highest priorities. Write them in the space below. These are goals that your organization will definitely commit to achieve in one year. On separate paper, create a detailed, month-by-month work plan that describes exactly what your organization will do in the coming year to achieve each high-priority goal.

Study your community. Talk to residents, seek out microbusiness owners, and speak with storefront owners to answer the following questions.

Criterion	Rating	Examples and comments
1. Small storefronts and offices in our community stay vacant for less than three months.	☐ True ☐ Partially true ☐ Not true	
2. Residents can buy most essential products and services from businesses in our own community.	☐ True ☐ Partially true ☐ Not true	
3. Attempts to attract new business into our community usually succeed.	☐ True ☐ Partially true ☐ Not true	
4. Our community has several gathering places where people meet on a regular basis to eat, shop, or mingle.	☐ True ☐ Partially true ☐ Not true	
5. Most people who own businesses in our community also live in our community.	☐ True ☐ Partially true ☐ Not true	
6. People who own businesses in our community represent the same ethnic groups and races who live in our community.	☐ True ☐ Partially true ☐ Not true	
7. Businesses in our community regularly hire neighborhood residents.	☐ True ☐ Partially true ☐ Not true	

Survey your community residents to find people who could start or expand a microbusiness. To summarize the key findings of your survey, complete the following statements.

Number of residents who want to start or expand a small business:

Number of residents who already operate a home-based business.
(Also describe the types of businesses they operate.)

Number of residents who are interested in using commercial or office space in the community. (Also describe the kinds of spaces that these residents want.)

Number of residents who need help to obtain commercial or office space in the community. (Describe the kinds of help that these residents want.)

Number of residents who want business training before they start or expand a microbusiness. (Describe the kinds of training that these residents want.)

Assess your organization's ability to operate an effective program to assist microentrepreneurs.

Criterion	Rating	Examples and comments
1. We have the networks and credibility necessary to reach the underground entrepreneurs throughout our community.	❑ True ❑ Partially true ❑ Not true	
2. We have enough staff time to develop the outreach materials, application forms, and other materials needed to reach entrepreneurs throughout our community.	❑ True ❑ Partially true ❑ Not true	
3. We have staff members with a strong background in small business management who can work effectively with entrepreneurs in our community.	❑ True ❑ Partially true ❑ Not true	
4. Organizations in our community will provide any on-site business expertise that our staff lacks.	❑ True ❑ Partially true ❑ Not true	

Criterion	Rating	Examples and comments
5. We can contract with enough skilled people to train the micro-entrepreneurs in our community.	☐ True ☐ Partially true ☐ Not true	
6. We can get funding to contract with an adequate number of business trainers.	☐ True ☐ Partially true ☐ Not true	
7. We have the expertise to package small business loans offered by other organizations (loan packaging.)	☐ True ☐ Partially true ☐ Not true	
8. We have the time and skills to develop our own loan program, including the necessary forms and systems to underwrite, close, and service those loans.	☐ True ☐ Partially true ☐ Not true	
9. We have the resources to work with all micro-entrepreneurs in our neighborhood.	☐ True ☐ Partially true ☐ Not true	

Review the results you obtained when you assessed conditions for microbusiness in your commercial district. (See the previous worksheets in this chapter.) Then, in the space below, write a one-paragraph vision statement for developing microbusiness in your community. Keep this paragraph short—one to three sentences to sum up the essence of your organization's intended impact on this pivot point.

Write a list of three-year goals for microbusiness in the categories listed below. Make sure that these goals are consistent with your vision statement for developing microbusiness. Be specific and use as many numbers as you can.

Category 1: Types of entrepreneurs you will reach

Write goals to describe the entrepreneurs that your organization will support. Choose from among the following categories:

- Entrepreneurs who will fill empty storefronts in your commercial district
- Entrepreneurs who will develop a particular type of retail business that would help your neighborhood most (for example, a cluster of Latino retailers, or antique dealers, or restaurants)
- Entrepreneurs who will create jobs for local residents in manufacturing trades
- Specific kinds of neighborhood residents (for example, low-income single mothers who want to find work)
- Entrepreneurs from a certain racial, ethnic, or immigrant group
- Other kinds of entrepreneurs (describe)

Category 2: Goals for business training programs

Describe the content of your programs to train entrepreneurs in business planning and management.

(continued)

Published by the Amherst H. Wilder Foundation   Copyright © 2002 Mihailo Temali

Category 3: Goals for connecting entrepreneurs to commercial space

Describe how you will connect entrepreneurs to available commercial space.

Category 4: Goals for financing programs

Describe the content of your loan programs to help entrepreneurs start or expand their microbusiness.

Category 5: Goals for support programs

Describe the content of ongoing programs to support entrepreneurs.

Highest-priority goals

Label one or two goals from each of the above categories as high-priority goals—those your organization will definitely commit to achieve in three years.

Step 1: Write one-year goals

In the appropriate spaces below, list each of the high-priority goals you identified for Worksheet 17: Write Three-Year Goals for Microbusiness. Then write one-year goals that you will meet in order to achieve each three-year goal. Be specific and use numbers where possible. (Make copies of this worksheet as needed.)

Three-year goal:

One-year goals to support this three-year goal:

Three-year goal:

One-year goals to support this three-year goal:

(continued)

Step 2: Rank and implement your one-year goals

From each list of one-year goals, choose one or two as your highest priorities. Write them in the space below. These are goals that your organization will definitely commit to achieve in one year. On separate paper, create a detailed, month-by-month work plan that describes exactly what your organization will do in the coming year to achieve each high-priority goal.

Review all the data you gathered about current workforce conditions in your community (Step 1 of Chapter 6): facts about income levels, current job openings, job trends, workforce development organizations (including your One-Stop Career Center), and vocational training. Also consider the opinions of the people you interviewed about workforce conditions. Then produce your preliminary conclusions about workforce conditions by answering the following questions. In addition to answering yes or no to each question, support your answer with the most compelling statistics you found during your assessment.

1. Are there particular groups of people in your community with unique barriers to employment that you want to focus your efforts on?

2. Are there any existing programs that could serve these groups? Would they be willing to partner with you?

3. Are there particular employers in your community that have a high need for new workers? Would they be willing to partner with you?

4. Will you need to provide significant training, or will a workfirst approach work for your target group?

5. Which of the seven basic approaches to workforce development fits your need and your capacity the best?

   - ❏ Partnerships with other organizations
   - ❏ Participation in a local network
   - ❏ Participation in a national network
   - ❏ Partnerships with employers
   - ❏ Comprehensive in-house program
   - ❏ Workforce Investment Board contract
   - ❏ Workforce development advocacy

Review your preliminary conclusions about workforce conditions in your community. (See Worksheet 19: Assess Current Workforce Conditions, page 247.) Then, in the space below, write a one-paragraph vision statement for developing your community workforce. Keep this paragraph short—one to three sentences to sum up the essence of your organization's intended impact on this pivot point.

In the space below, write a list of long-term goals for workforce development in your community—specific new outcomes that your organization commits to create in three years. Make sure that these goals are consistent with your vision statement for workforce development (Worksheet 20: Write a Vision Statement for Workforce Development, page 248). Be specific and use as many numbers as you can.

Step 1: Write one-year goals

In the appropriate spaces below, list each of your long-term goals for workforce development. (See Worksheet 21: Write Three-Year Goals for Workforce Development.) Then write one-year goals that you will meet in order to achieve each three-year goal. Be specific and use numbers where possible.

Three-year goal:

One-year goals to support this three-year goal:

Three-year goal:

One-year goals to support this three-year goal:

Step 2: Write a work plan from your one-year goals

From each list of one-year goals, choose one or two as your highest priorities. Write them in the space below. These are goals that your organization will definitely commit to achieve in one year. On separate paper, create a detailed, month-by-month work plan that describes exactly what your organization and any partner organizations will do in the coming year to achieve each high-priority goal.

In the space below, write your definition of the term good neighborhood job. *In your definition, include criteria to use when evaluating jobs created by local businesses. Keep your definition simple and allow it to evolve as you complete the remaining assessment worksheets.*

Refer to Appendix B: Internet Research on Your Metropolitan Economy before completing this worksheet. Use this worksheet to record your answers to three questions:

1. *What are the largest business sectors and subsectors in your metropolitan economy today?*
2. *Which sectors and subsectors have been growing the most over the past five years?*
3. *Which sectors and subsectors are expected to grow the most over the next five years— and grow the most good neighborhood jobs?*

	1-digit SIC (or 2-digit NAICS sector)	**2-digit SIC** (or 3-digit NAICS subsector)	**3- and 4-digit SIC** (or 4-plus-digit NAICS subsector)
Largest sectors			
Sectors with most growth in past five years			
Sectors expected to grow most in next five years			

Published by the Amherst H. Wilder Foundation

Talk to business owners in your neighborhood. Summarize their answers to the following questions. (Make a copy of this worksheet to use for each person you interview.)

1. Have you added any jobs in the past two years? If so, what type of jobs were they? (Include details about skill level and wages.)

2. Do you have plans to grow jobs in the next two years? If so, how many and what type of jobs? (Include details about skill level and wages.)

3. What is your timetable for this plan?

4. What ingredients will it take to succeed with those plans?
   - ☐ Changes in your company's products or services
   - ☐ More space
   - ☐ Better space (such as loading docks and high-speed Internet access)
   - ☐ Better access for customers or trucks
   - ☐ New employees
   - ☐ More customers
   - ☐ More money
   - ☐ More management training or assistance
   - ☐ Other:

5. Which of these growth ingredients could you use help with?

6. Exactly what sort of help will you need?

7. Where do you plan to get this help?

8. If you have no growth plans, are there any types of assistance that could change your thinking on this topic?

9. Is your business subsector growing?

10. What business advantages do you gain by locating in this neighborhood?

11. Are businesses similar to yours located nearby?

Fill in the table below for each local commercial and industrial space. (Make additional copies of this page as necessary.)

Name and Type of Business	Status	Square Feet	Cost	Parking	Special Features*	Physical Condition	Contact Information
	☐ occupied ☐ vacant ☐ possible change in occupancy		☐ rental ☐ for sale $ _____				
	☐ occupied ☐ vacant ☐ possible change in occupancy		☐ rental ☐ for sale $ _____				
	☐ occupied ☐ vacant ☐ possible change in occupancy		☐ rental ☐ for sale $ _____				
	☐ occupied ☐ vacant ☐ possible change in occupancy		☐ rental ☐ for sale $ _____				
	☐ occupied ☐ vacant ☐ possible change in occupancy		☐ rental ☐ for sale $ _____				

*Special Features can include truck access, loading dock, status of soil and building contamination, heavy-duty electrical service, zoning, utilities, elevator, etc.

Use this worksheet to summarize the results of your previous assessments. Use Table 1 to summarize your research on business subsectors in your metropolitan economy. Use Table 2 to summarize your research about individual businesses in your neighborhood. Circle the names of your target businesses—those that your group can work with to grow good neighborhood jobs.

Table 1

Subsector	Potential to grow good jobs?	Number of jobs grown over past five years	Number of jobs projected to grow in next five years	Part of neighborhood business cluster?	Business advantages for neighborhood

(continued)

Table 2

Name of business	Plans for growth	Existing resources for growth (including available space)	Resources that your group could add

Write a one-paragraph vision statement for growing good jobs in your neighborhood. Keep this paragraph short—one to three sentences to sum up the essence of your organization's intended impact on this pivot point.

Write a list of long-term goals for growing good jobs in your neighborhood—specific new outcomes that your organization commits to create in three years. Make sure that these goals are consistent with your vision statement. Be specific and use as many numbers as you can.

Step 1: Write one-year goals

In the appropriate spaces below, list each of your three-year goals for growing good neighborhood jobs. Then write one-year goals that you will meet in order to achieve each three-year goal. Be specific and use numbers where possible. (Make copies of this worksheet as needed.)

Three-year goal:

One-year goals to support this three-year goal:

Three-year goal:

One-year goals to support this three-year goal:

(continued)

Step 2: Write a work plan from your one-year goals

From each list of one-year goals, choose one or two as your highest priorities. Write them in the space below. These are goals that your organization will definitely commit to achieve in one year. On separate paper, create a detailed, month-by-month work plan that describes exactly what your organization and any partner organizations will do in the coming year to achieve each high-priority goal.

Published by the Amherst H. Wilder Foundation   Copyright © 2002 Mihailo Temali

Index

Notes
    b indicates information in gray boxes
    n indicates information in footnotes. For example, "16n5" means that the information will be found on page 16 in footnote 5.
    p indicates photographs or illustrations

Notes
    b indicates information in gray boxes
    n indicates information in footnotes. For example, "16n5" means that the information will be found on page 16 in footnote 5.
    p indicates photographs or illustrations

Notes
  b indicates information in gray boxes
  n indicates information in footnotes. For example, "16n5" means that the information will be found on page 16 in footnote 5.
  p indicates photographs or illustrations

Notes
    b indicates information in gray boxes
    n indicates information in footnotes. For example, "16n5" means that the information will be found on page 16 in footnote 5.
    p indicates photographs or illustrations

Notes
  b indicates information in gray boxes
  n indicates information in footnotes. For example, "16n5" means that the information will be found on page 16 in footnote 5.
  p indicates photographs or illustrations

Notes
    b indicates information in gray boxes
    n indicates information in footnotes. For example, "16n5" means that the information will be found on page 16 in footnote 5.
    p indicates photographs or illustrations

Notes
b indicates information in gray boxes
n indicates information in footnotes. For example, "16n5" means that the information will be found on page 16 in footnote 5.
p indicates photographs or illustrations

W

Notes
  b indicates information in gray boxes
  n indicates information in footnotes. For example, "16n5" means that the information will be found on page 16 in footnote 5.
  p indicates photographs or illustrations

More results-oriented books from the Amherst H. Wilder Foundation

Community Building

Community Building: What Makes It Work
by Wilder Research Center

Reveals twenty-eight keys to help you build community more effectively. Includes detailed descriptions of each factor, case examples of how they play out, and practical questions to assess your work.

112 pages, softcover   Item # 069121

Community Economic Development Handbook
by Mihailo Temali

A concrete, practical handbook to turning any neighborhood around. It explains how to start a community economic development organization, and then lays out the steps of four proven and powerful strategies for revitalizing inner-city neighborhoods.

288 pages, softcover   Item # 069369

The Wilder Nonprofit Field Guide to
Conducting Community Forums
by Carol Lukas and Linda Hoskins

Provides step-by-step instruction to plan and carry out exciting, successful community forums that will educate the public, build consensus, focus action, or influence policy.

128 pages, softcover   Item # 069318

Collaboration

Collaboration Handbook
Creating, Sustaining, and Enjoying the Journey
by Michael Winer and Karen Ray

Shows you how to get a collaboration going, set goals, determine everyone's roles, create an action plan, and evaluate the results. Includes a case study of one collaboration from start to finish, helpful tips on how to avoid pitfalls, and worksheets to keep everyone on track.

192 pages, softcover   Item # 069032

Collaboration: What Makes It Work, 2nd Ed.
by Paul Mattessich, PhD, Marta Murray-Close, BA, and Barbara Monsey, MPH

An in-depth review of current collaboration research. Major findings are summarized, critical conclusions are drawn, and twenty key factors influencing successful collaborations are identified. Includes The Wilder Collaboration Factors Inventory, which groups can use to assess their collaboration.

104 pages, softcover   Item # 069326

The Nimble Collaboration
Fine-Tuning Your Collaboration for Lasting Success
by Karen Ray

Shows you ways to make your existing collaboration more responsive, flexible, and productive. Provides three key strategies to help your collaboration respond quickly to changing environments and participants.

136 pages, softcover   Item # 069288

Lobbying & Advocacy

The Lobbying and Advocacy Handbook for Nonprofit Organizations
Shaping Public Policy at the State and Local Level
by Marcia Avner

The Lobbying and Advocacy Handbook is a planning guide and resource for nonprofit organizations that want to influence issues that matter to them. This book will help you decide whether to lobby and then put plans in place to make it work.

240 pages, softcover   Item # 069261

The Nonprofit Board Member's Guide to Lobbying and Advocacy
by Marcia Avner

Written specifically for board members, this guide helps organizations increase their impact on policy decisions. It reveals how board members can be involved in planning for and implementing successful lobbying efforts.

96 pages, softcover   Item # 069393

Finance

Bookkeeping Basics
What Every Nonprofit Bookkeeper Needs to Know
by Debra L. Ruegg and Lisa M. Venkatrathnam

Complete with step-by-step instructions, a glossary of accounting terms, detailed examples, and handy reproducible forms, this book will enable you to successfully meet the basic bookkeeping requirements of your nonprofit organization—even if you have little or no formal accounting training.

128 pages, softcover   Item # 069296

Coping with Cutbacks
The Nonprofit Guide to Success When Times Are Tight
by Emil Angelica and Vincent Hyman

Shows you practical ways to involve business, government, and other nonprofits to solve problems together. Also includes 185 cutback strategies you can put to use right away.

128 pages, softcover   Item # 069091

For current prices, a catalog, or to order call 800-274-6024

Venture Forth! The Essential Guide to Starting a Moneymaking Business in Your Nonprofit Organization
by Rolfe Larson

The most complete guide on nonprofit business development. Building on the experience of dozens of organizations, this handbook gives you a time-tested approach for finding, testing, and launching a successful nonprofit business venture.

272 pages, softcover   Item # 069245

Management & Leadership

Benchmarking for Nonprofits
How to Measure, Manage, and Improve Results
by Jason Saul

Benchmarking—the onging process of measuring your organization against leaders—can help stimulate innovation, increase your impact, decrease your costs, raise money, inspire your staff, impress your funders, engage your board, and sharpen your mission. This book defines a formal, systematic, and reliable way to benchmark, from preparing your organization to measuring performance and implementing best practices.

128 pages, softcover   Item #069431

Consulting with Nonprofits: A Practitioner's Guide
by Carol A. Lukas

A step-by-step, comprehensive guide for consultants. Addresses the art of consulting, how to run your business, and much more. Also includes tips and anecdotes from thirty skilled consultants.

240 pages, softcover   Item # 069172

The Wilder Nonprofit Field Guide to
Crafting Effective Mission and Vision Statements
by Emil Angelica

Guides you through two six-step processes that result in a mission statement, vision statement, or both. Shows how a clarified mission and vision lead to more effective leadership, decisions, fundraising, and management. Includes tips, sample statements, and worksheets.

88 pages, softcover   Item # 06927X

The Wilder Nonprofit Field Guide to
Developing Effective Teams
by Beth Gilbertsen and Vijit Ramchandani

Helps you understand, start, and maintain a team. Provides tools and techniques for writing a mission statement, setting goals, conducting effective meetings, creating ground rules to manage team dynamics, making decisions in teams, creating project plans, and developing team spirit.

80 pages, softcover   Item # 069202

The Five Life Stages of Nonprofit Organizations
Where You Are, Where You're Going, and What to Expect When You Get There
by Judith Sharken Simon with J. Terence Donovan

Shows you what's "normal" for each development stage which helps you plan for transitions, stay on track, and avoid unnecessary struggles. This guide also includes The Wilder Nonprofit Life Stage Assessment to plot and understand your organization's progress in seven arenas of organization development.

128 pages, softcover   Item # 069229

The Manager's Guide to Program Evaluation:
Planning, Contracting, and Managing for Useful Results
by Paul W. Mattessich, PhD

Explains how to plan and manage an evaluation that will help identify your organization's successes, share information with key audiences, and improve services.

96 pages, softcover   Item # 069385

The Nonprofit Mergers Workbook
The Leader's Guide to Considering, Negotiating, and Executing a Merger
by David La Piana

A merger can be a daunting and complex process. Save time, money, and untold frustration with this highly practical guide that makes the process manageable and controllable. Includes case studies, decision trees, twenty-two worksheets, checklists, tips, and complete step-by-step guidance from seeking partners to writing the merger agreement, and more.

240 pages, softcover   Item # 069210

The Nonprofit Mergers Workbook Part II
Unifying the Organization after a Merger
by La Piana Associates

Once the merger agreement is signed, the question becomes: How do we make this merger work? *Part II* helps you create a comprehensive plan to achieve *integration*—bringing together people, programs, processes, and systems from two (or more) organizations into a single, unified whole.

248 pages, includes CD-ROM   Item # 069415

Nonprofit Stewardship
A Better Way to Lead Your Mission-Based Organization
by Peter C. Brinckerhoff

You may lead a not-for-profit organization, but it's not your organization. It belongs to the community it serves. You are the steward—the manager of resources that belong to someone else. The stewardship model of leadership can help your organization improve its mission capability by forcing you to keep your organization's mission foremost. It helps you make decisions that are best for the people your organization serves. In other words, stewardship helps you do more good for more people.

272 pages, softcover   Item #069423

For current prices or to order visit us online at www.wilder.org/pubs

Resolving Conflict in Nonprofit Organizations
The Leader's Guide to Finding Constructive Solutions
by Marion Peters Angelica

Helps you identify conflict, decide whether to intervene, uncover and deal with the true issues, and design and conduct a conflict resolution process. Includes exercises to learn and practice conflict resolution skills, guidance on handling unique conflicts such as harassment and discrimination, and when (and where) to seek outside help with litigation, arbitration, and mediation.

192 pages, softcover   Item # 069164

Strategic Planning Workbook for Nonprofit Organizations, Revised and Updated
by Bryan Barry

Chart a wise course for your nonprofit's future. This time-tested workbook gives you practical step-by-step guidance, real-life examples, one nonprofit's complete strategic plan, and easy-to-use worksheets.

144 pages, softcover   Item # 069075

Marketing & Fundraising

The Wilder Nonprofit Field Guide to
Conducting Successful Focus Groups
by Judith Sharken Simon

Shows how to collect valuable information without a lot of money or special expertise. Using this proven technique, you'll get essential opinions and feedback to help you check out your assumptions, do better strategic planning, improve services or products, and more.

80 pages, softcover   Item # 069199

The Wilder Nonprofit Field Guide to
Fundraising on the Internet
by Gary M. Grobman, Gary B. Grant, and Steve Roller

Your quick road map to using the Internet for fundraising. Shows you how to attract new donors, troll for grants, get listed on sites that assist donors, and learn more about the art of fundraising. Includes detailed reviews of 77 web sites useful to fundraisers, including foundations, charities, prospect research sites, and sites that assist donors.

64 pages, softcover   Item # 069180

Marketing Workbook for Nonprofit Organizations Volume I: Develop the Plan
by Gary J. Stern

Don't just wish for results—get them! Here's how to create a straightforward, usable marketing plan. Includes the six Ps of Marketing, how to use them effectively, a sample marketing plan, tips on using the Internet, and worksheets.

208 pages, softcover   Item # 069253

Marketing Workbook for Nonprofit Organizations Volume II: Mobilize People for Marketing Success
by Gary J. Stern

Put together a successful promotional campaign based on the most persuasive tool of all: personal contact. Learn how to mobilize your entire organization, its staff, volunteers, and supporters in a focused, one-to-one marketing campaign. Comes with *Pocket Guide for Marketing Representatives*. In it, your marketing representatives can record key campaign messages and find motivational reminders.

192 pages, softcover   Item # 069105

Board Tools

The Best of the Board Café
Hands-on Solutions for Nonprofit Boards
by Jan Masaoka, CompassPoint Nonprofit Services

Gathers the most requested articles from the e-newsletter, *Board Café*. You'll find a lively menu of ideas, information, opinions, news, and resources to help board members give and get the most out of their board service.

232 pages, softcover   Item # 069407

The Nonprofit Board Member's Guide to Lobbying and Advocacy
by Marcia Avner

96 pages, softcover   Item # 069393

Keeping the Peace
by Marion Angelica

Written especially for board members and chief executives, this book is a step-by-step guide to ensure that everyone is treated fairly adn a feasible solution is reached.

48 pages, softcover   Item # 860127

Funder's Guides

Community Visions, Community Solutions
Grantmaking for Comprehensive Impact
by Joseph A. Connor and Stephanie Kadel-Taras

Helps foundations, community funds, government agencies, and other grantmakers uncover a community's highest aspiration for itself, and support and sustain strategic efforts to get to workable solutions.

128 pages, softcover   Item # 06930X

Strengthening Nonprofit Performance
A Funder's Guide to Capacity Building
by Paul Connolly and Carol Lukas

This practical guide synthesizes the most recent capacity building practice and research into a collection of strategies, steps, and examples that you can use to get started on or improve funding to strengthen nonprofit organizations.

176 pages, softcover   Item # 069377

For current prices, a catalog, or to order call 800-274-6024

Violence Prevention & Intervention

The Little Book of Peace
Designed and illustrated by Kelly O. Finnerty

A pocket-size guide to help people think about violence and talk about it with their families and friends. You may download a free copy of *The Little Book of Peace* from our web site at www.wilder.org/pubs.

24 pages (minimum order 10 copies)   Item # 069083
*Also available in **Spanish** and **Hmong** language editions.*

Journey Beyond Abuse: A Step-by-Step Guide to Facilitating Women's Domestic Abuse Groups
by Kay-Laurel Fischer, MA, LP, and Michael F. McGrane, LICSW

Create a program where women increase their understanding of the dynamics of abuse, feel less alone and isolated, and have a greater awareness of channels to safety. Includes twenty-one group activities that you can combine to create groups of differing length and focus.

208 pages, softcover   Item # 069148

Moving Beyond Abuse: Stories and Questions for Women Who Have Lived with Abuse
(Companion guided journal to *Journey Beyond Abuse*)

A series of stories and questions that can be used in coordination with the sessions provided in the facilitator's guide or with the guidance of a counselor in other forms of support.

88 pages, softcover   Item # 069156

Foundations for Violence-Free Living:
A Step-by-Step Guide to Facilitating Men's Domestic Abuse Groups
by David J. Mathews, MA, LICSW

A complete guide to facilitating a men's domestic abuse program. Includes twenty-nine activities, detailed guidelines for presenting each activity, and a discussion of psychological issues that may arise out of each activity.

240 pages, softcover   Item # 069059

On the Level
(Participant's workbook to *Foundations for Violence-Free Living*)
Contains forty-nine worksheets including midterm and final evaluations. Men can record their progress.

160 pages, softcover   Item # 069067

What Works in Preventing Rural Violence
by Wilder Research Center

An in-depth review of eighty-eight effective strategies you can use to prevent and intervene in violent behaviors, improve services for victims, and reduce repeat offenses. This report also includes a Community Report Card with step-by-step directions on how you can collect, record, and use information about violence in your community.

94 pages, softcover   Item # 069040

ORDERING INFORMATION

Order online, or by phone or fax

Online: www.wilder.org/pubs
E-mail: books@wilder.org

Call toll-free: 800-274-6024
Internationally: 651-659-6024

Fax: 651-642-2061

Mail: Amherst H. Wilder Foundation
Publishing Center
919 Lafond Avenue
St. Paul, MN 55104

Our NO-RISK guarantee

If you aren't completely satisfied with any book for any reason, simply send it back within 30 days for a full refund.

Pricing and discounts

For current prices and discounts, please visit our web site at www.wilder.org/pubs or call toll free at 800-274-6024.

Do you have a book idea?

Wilder Publishing Center seeks manuscripts and proposals for books in the fields of nonprofit management and community development. To get a copy of our author guidelines, please call us at 800-274-6024. You can also download them from our web site at www.wilder.org/pubs/author_guide.html.

Visit us online

You'll find information about the Wilder Foundation and more details on our books, such as table of contents, pricing, discounts, endorsements, and more, at www.wilder.org/pubs.

Quality assurance

We strive to make sure that all the books we publish are helpful and easy to use. Our major workbooks are tested and critiqued by experts before being published. Their comments help shape the final book and—we trust—make it more useful to you.